Kevin Perkins is regarded as one of Australia's best journalists, writers and biographers.

He was introduced to crime as a police cadet at Sydney's CIB, where he worked with the leading detectives of the day, including the famous Ray Kelly. Being a policeman was not Perkins' *milieu*. But investigative journalism was.

He "covered the waterfront" for almost 40 years on Sydney's tabloids, including The *Daily Mirror, Truth, Daily Telegraph, Sunday Telegraph, Sun-Herald* and *The Sun*. A hard-hitting columnist whose *On the Inside* column on the backpage of the *Sun-Herald* was the best read in Australia, he was also a news executive for 20 years. His two daughters are journalists.

Perkins, who has travelled widely, is the author of several best-selling books, including *The Gambling Man,* the extraordinary saga of the Waterhouses.

He has written this revealing life story of famous private eye Tim Bristow from the inside. Having associated with Bristow for 40 years, he knew him better than most.

Kevin Perkins

BRISTOW
LAST OF THE HARD MEN

First published in Australia by Bonmoat Pty Limitd
296 Liverpool Road, Ashfield NSW 2131
November 2003

Copyright © Bonmoat Pty Limited

National Library of Australia
Cataloguing-in-Publication Data

Bristow - Last of the hard men

ISBN 0-9751197-0-2

Distributed by Gary Allen Pty Ltd, 9 Cooper Street, Smithfield
NSW
Telephone 02-9725 2933

Cover Design: Darian Causby
Typeset: J.A. Crouch

Printed in Australia by Griffin Press Ltd

TABLE OF CONTENTS

INTRODUCTION

WHEN Howard Hughes bribed President Nixon and tried to install his own man in the Oval Office in the last few years of his bizarre life, it had a sequel in Australia. The drug-addicted, paranoid billionaire, instead of "buying" the US Government, helped bring it down by triggering Watergate in 1972 and destroying Nixon.

The Hughes aide most responsible for causing Watergate was John Herbert Meier, scientific adviser and general courtier to Hughes from 1966 to 1970. In the shadowy intrigue of Washington politics, Meier made enemies, especially within the CIA and the Secret Service.

He was involved in paying substantial secret cash bribes into Nixon's slush fund. The bribes were to persuade the President to stop the underground nuclear tests in Nevada.

After leaving the Hughes empire, Meier continued to meddle in the big league of politics. He boasted he would tell all about Nixon and claimed the CIA had tried to take over the Hughes organisation. The CIA targeted him and the Hughes Tool Company sued him for allegedly swindling it of $8 million in mining leases.

President Nixon, worried about what explosive information on the Hughes pay-offs and other Meier allegations might be in the files of the chairman of the Democratic National Committee, secretly ordered the break-ins of the chairman's Watergate office. Exposed as a crook, Nixon was forced to resign and Meier began a running fight with various US authorities over the mining leases, his knowledge of Nixon's corruption and his relationship with Hughes.

In the wake of all that, Meier turned up in Sydney in 1977 flaunting a diplomatic passport from Tonga. CIA operatives came to town to arrest him as a fugitive from justice. Australian Federal Police jumped the gun, but had to release him because his diplomatic passport was still intact. Before they could get their documents in order, Meier went on the run, wanting to get back to Canada where he had citizenship rights.

Desperate, with Federal Police and the CIA searching for him and hotels and airports being checked, he sought help. Who could he turn to?

Tim Bristow, the legendary Sydney private eye. Big Tim, Bruiser Bristow. Earthquake. The Enforcer. The Underdog's Friend.

Bristow was probably the only man in Australia prepared to put himself on the line against such powerful forces. To the tough private investigator, it was just another job, Meier just another fellow in trouble. Bristow had helped thousands, many at odds with the law. He'd never backed off a situation in his life, no matter how dangerous or confronting.

When John Meier rang him, trying to explain his dilemma in a torrent of words, Bristow cut him short with "come and see me." Meier made his way to Bristow's home at Newport on Sydney's northern beaches where Bristow wanted to look him in the eye, make sure he wasn't being set up in some way. The shrewd investigator could read a man in seconds.

Tim listened to his story, decided Meier had no doubt done the wrong thing along the way but knew instinctively the bureaucratic bodies pursuing him probably had cheated too. "All right, I'll get you out of the country," he said.

Tim reached out a huge hand that had knocked hundreds of men cold, gripping Meier's limp hand with such force that the tall, pasty-faced deposed diplomat winced. Bristow's action was a man-to-man thing. He carried his authority in his fists. But once he shook hands, looked a man in the eye and agreed on a deal, that was it. Old-fashioned honour would be observed.

In their subsequent six or eight meetings, some at Tim's home, others at rendezvous spots around the city, Meier talked of what went on behind the scenes in Washington, his days with Hughes, Nixon in the White House, the CIA plot to murder Fidel Castro and JFK's assassination. The JFK shooting interested Bristow most. He knew only the obvious truth that there had been a massive cover-up of Kennedy's killing.

Meier's opinion, that FBI director J. Edgar Hoover had arranged the killing, encouraged Bristow to make his own inquiries. One of his strengths as a private eye was an infallible memory to link people and events stored up over the years. He produced evidence to support the theory there were *two* gunmen that day in Dallas on 22 November 1963, not one as the Warren Commission, the CIA and FBI claimed.

Bristow helped Meier leave Australia safely.

I first met Tim Bristow in 1964 when a reporter on Sydney's *Daily Telegraph*. As I typed an exposé of a shifty retailer who advertised with the paper, a big impeccably-dressed man suddenly appeared at my desk in the newspaper office and said in a booming voice: "Tim Bristow. I don't want you to publish that story." I told him my boss Frank Packer and not his client paid my wages, took him by an arm and put him out of the office. But oddly the story never appeared. Later I learned Bristow had it pulled by giving the newspaper's advertising manager a case of whisky to argue a reprieve for the advertiser.

After that he began giving me stories on crime, corruption and injustice and we became friends. Our paths crossed often. The city that he knew so intimately with its characters, nightclubs, crooks, criminals, cops, celebrities, politicians, the good and the bad, the honourable dishonest men and dishonourable honest men of power, was my beat too. His life reflected a kind of social history of post-war Sydney, especially its more colourful underbelly, touching also on the lifestyle of the so-called beautiful, respectable people.

Bristow's work as a private eye was so outlandish, so unreal, that without our long association it would have been impossible to trace his life and the events he figured in. Even then it was difficult at times to know where the reality and fiction overlapped. I knew this much, though. Not even Hollywood's most imaginative writers had dared to create a fictional gumshoe as audacious as Bristow. Even in that celluloid world of murder, corruption and deceit he would have been considered way out. Yet, he was for real. And unique, for toughness and humour.

Like Raymond Chandler's *Philip Marlowe* and Dashiell Hammett's *Sam Spade* - both played by Humphrey Bogart - Bristow came out of the hard-boiled school. Hammett saw it for himself in real life, working initially as a sleuth for Pinkerton's, America's first private detective agency which was established in 1850. The Pinkerton Agency trademark, an all-seeing eye with the motto, "We never sleep," originated the term *private eye*.

The hard-boiled fictional private detective first emerged as a hero in the cheap pulp magazines of the 1920s, particularly *Black Mask*. Writers who joined the trend included Hammett, James M. Cain and Chandler, who portrayed his characters on paper as they thought and talked in real life. The character of fictional detectives changed in the 1930s due to the rising crime and gangster activity of Prohibition and the Great Depression. In the 1940s, that was translated into radio drama and *film noir* or dark cinema.

These detectives were called hard-boiled because they needed to develop a shell like a six-minute egg to protect their feelings from the cruel, violent criminal types and risky situations they met along the way. Hammett, in his classic novel *The Maltese Falcon*, established the prototype of a tough, cynical and sometimes cruel character in *Sam Spade* who kept his code of honour in a world dominated by deception and betrayal in all levels of society.

Cain (*Double Indemnity*), portrayed his characters in a more brutal way, often drawing on tabloid front page news stories of sensational crimes for inspiration. He offered few psychological insights. Chandler cared more for characterisation than violent death. His *Marlowe* was more humane, though still a lone wolf with a sense of honour, a mixture of cynicism and idealism. Tough like *Spade*, but usually fair.

Here's the point. All the classical gumshoes of pulp fiction and the movies have common or similar qualities based on real life. They work on the seamier side, bending or breaking the law to bring criminals to justice or merely to get results for their clients. But always against their desire to uphold the law and assist justice, they have to balance their need to survive. They can be brutal as well as lovable and don't normally stoop to bribery, although they appear low enough to take a bribe. However, a bit of forbidden "bread" on the side can often be quite okay.

Those tough private eyes of fiction display a cynical sense of humour masking a battered romantic underneath. They have a love/hate relationship with the cops and criminals, they're disillusioned with the corruption that exists in all levels of society, and they operate in a world of evil where really nobody is on the side of good. At the end of the day when they finish a case, the city is still essentially lawless.

These heroes remain tarnished at best, feeling victims like their clients, because they know they can defeat evil only on a minor scale. There's so much evil in their world - as there is in real life - that they cannot win a complete victory. They just mop it up in patches.

But it's not all hard work. Much of their time is spent dallying with man-hungry females.

All that was Tim Bristow, only more so.

He was just as cunning as *Marlowe* in *The Big Sleep* and *Spade* in *Maltese Falcon* but much more confrontational and less worried by danger. He was fearless and would do almost anything. He was loved, hated, feared, a hero to many, a villain to others, he bribed cops and boasted about it, he was notorious, egotistical, he shamelessly sought publicity, he repeatedly fell for beautiful clients and seduced them. He was a hard man right through to a saint, and everything in between.

Bristow was tough all right, but he wasn't a tough guy all the time. He bragged of belting people from all walks of life, yet he had a soft heart. Although he made no moral claims, he wasn't without scruples and even if brutal and ruthless at times, he could be kind and compassionate. He was seen by many as being a bit like Ned Kelly in his gameness, but essentially as a man prepared to help others where the law failed them.

He was so much larger than life that he went far beyond the normal private eye's world. If born in earlier times he would have been a rollicking buccaneer or a resourceful bounty hunter. Before that, a gladiator.

Yet, unlike most of those seedy fictional detectives, he came from a morally upright background, a top private school and was born to be a gentleman. Bristow lightened the dark side of his work by being a Sydney-style larrikin, with a dry sense of knockabout humour that enabled him to laugh at himself and life's little stings. Often he crumpled the starched shirts of hypocrites and poseurs with witty one liners.

But Big Tim was the last of his line. Nobody like him exists out there any more. The tough confrontational gumshoes of the old movie days, whom he personified in real life, no longer prowl the world's mean streets. They've all gone soft, corporate and technological.

It's said that those who know don't tell, and those who tell don't know.

Well, see for yourself.

1

A Racket in Everything

PROBATIONARY Constable Tim Bristow was pounding his beat near Sydney's Circular Quay waterfront area, alert for anything unusual. Although only 19, he was big and powerful for his age. In his new blue serge uniform, cap, neat blue shirt and tie, the boxer, model, surfer and footballer weighing in at more than 15 stone and standing six feet three inches, looked like a recruiting advertisement for the NSW police force.

There was an easy athleticism about him in spite of bulges under his tunic from gun, handcuffs and truncheon. And although his manner was friendly, he moved with an air of authority. Obviously a man to be taken seriously.

On this night in 1949, carrying a big torch, he was working with a senior cop, "Possum" Courtney. Passing Macquarie Place they suddenly heard a mighty crash from a jeweller's shop across the square. They ran over. Tim stood in front of the smashed door while Possum went for support from Phillip Street station - no mobiles or walkie-talkies then.

Another crash sounded and a shadowy figure came in the back door. Gun in hand, Tim shouted "stop or I'll shoot" in a voice that could be heard several blocks away. The shadowy figure collapsed. He turned out to be the nightwatchman and had to be taken to hospital because of a heart attack. The smash and grab thieves had gone out a side laneway door.

Back at Phillip Street Station, headquarters of the inner city's No 4 Division where Tim worked, he was "put on paper" for threatening to shoot the watchman but the boss, Inspector Harry Boswell, smoothed things over in a fatherly way. Almost at once Tim redeemed himself on the beat by catching thieves doing a series of break-ins.

One evening while training for boxing at nearby Langridge's gym over the top of Grimes' garage, he learned that two street sweepers were borrowing cars left parked in the garage at night by members of the public. They would do a robbery and return the car. Tim reported it and detectives set a successful trap.

Because Tim could handle himself, Inspector Boswell gave him a beat at Millers Point, the tough waterfront area around the southern end of the Harbour Bridge where seamen and desperates hung out. "Bunger" Sykes, notorious as one of the toughest union men on the waterfront, cheeked Tim one day while he was patrolling the wharf at 9 Walsh Bay. Bristow beat Bunger up, humiliating him further by frog-marching him all the way back to Phillip Street Station where he charged him with offensive behaviour. Drunkenness was then an offence in a public place and Tim was asked to clean up the unsightly drunks around Circular Quay and Millers Point. He brought them in three and four at a time. Any who resisted were given a quick jab in the ribs.

Noting his enthusiasm, Inspector Boswell began taking an interest in the keen, ambitious young constable. He was conscientious, capable, presentable, intelligent and could be relied on to do the hard tasks. Boswell was no slouch himself, having formed 21 Division, the crack police group that went around as a kind of flying squad cleaning up troublemakers in popular places like Bondi, spreading fear among the hoodlums. He was considered an untouchable on corruption. As an officer with pips he was saluted by cops and called Mister or Sir.

An unusual thing happened. Normally a young constable would not be trusted beyond routine matters but Boswell took Tim into his confidence and gave him a special job - to arrest the fruit barrowmen who operated on city streets without licences.

Only those who had City Council licences were left unhindered, although they still had to "sling" regularly for protection while those without licences were harassed. Tim was given lists by Boswell of unlicensed barrowmen who were to be arrested and charged under the *Summary Offences Act*. A privileged few without licences also could operate if they slung generously.

Ernie O'Dea, the Labor Lord Mayor, ran the racket with the cops. Ernie was copping a handsome bribe for issuing the licence as well as sharing the regular slings with senior police like Boswell for keeping out interlopers. As well as making the pinches, Tim collected the protection payoffs from barrowmen in brown paper bags, called "the rent." He handed them to Boswell. Tim was offered a share but declined with thanks.

While on that job Tim had a running battle with the itinerant barrowmen, who traded from horse-drawn carts. When they saw Tim coming, they'd move off smartly. "Cheeky Charlie" was a particularly hard man to catch. One day, returning to the station, Inspector Boswell said to Bristow: "Cheeky Charlie is operating in Rowe Street near the Hotel Australia. He has a nice load of peaches. Arrest him and bring the peaches back here."

Tim caught a tram up Pitt Street, got off at the GPO and moved in on Charlie. But when he went to grab Charlie's horse, the nag bit a piece out of his tunic. Tim jumped up on the cart but the horse bolted and Tim couldn't stop the nag, doing a merry clip through several of the inner city's main streets against traffic cops' hand signals, peaches rolling off as pedestrians scattered. He was lucky to miss two trams.

After tying up his depleted load outside the station, Tim waited in Mr Boswell's office while he made a good fellow of himself on the phone, telling the matron at Sydney Hospital he'd send the peaches around in a few minutes. But when Boswell went down to inspect the booty there wasn't a peach left. Light-fingered station cops had knocked the lot off.

Boswell strode into the roster room, opened lockers and gladstone bags, then marched into the station office and declared belligerently: "All right you men. I want to see every peach put back in the cart. Get to it." Tim had to walk around behind the inspector like his lap dog, making him look an informer and creating animosity with the men. Then he had to deliver the peaches.

Some time after that incident Cheeky Charlie saw Tim coming a block away and moved off, driving his horse and cart across the King Street boundary of No 4 Division and into No 1 Division, thinking he'd set up there with impunity. But Tim being Tim, although not supposed to go outside his area, pursued the barrowman almost all the way to Central Railway before arresting him. Charlie had to walk back more than a mile through the city to be charged in the station dock while Tim rode on the cart.

To give Tim more experience as a reward for his keenness, Inspector Boswell lent him out to the Vice Squad and 21 Division when they were short of men for a mission. For some of these jobs, Tim changed into plain clothes.

Once he went out on the harbour to help arrest punters betting illegally on the 18-footer races. Another time he helped keep order at the Manly Mardi Gras with a young Detective Merv Beck, an honest cop who would later become famous as head of Beck's Raiders, breaking down doors with sledge-hammers to arrest illegal Sydney casino operators. The only person Tim arrested at the Mardi Gras was a young lout who thrust an exploding firecracker up a girl's dress. In time, Tim arrested all types of common offenders, from pickpockets to violent assailants.

In his occasional role outside normal duty at Phillip Street Station, Tim also went on the beat in Kings Cross with famous cop and Newtown footballer Frank "Bumper" Farrell, becoming good friends at once. The Cross was then an outwardly friendly place, a little bohemian and naughty perhaps, its residents made up of artists, writers, painters, poets, journalists. People generally felt safe there, often not locking their car doors and leaving their keys in the ignition. Drugs were not part of the scene then, except in Chinatown where opium was smoked.

On his first night, on Bumper's instructions, Tim arrested the eccentric Shakespeare-quoting Bea Miles, wearing her Army great coat and tennis shade, having a pee on the footpath outside the Hampden Court Hotel. Bea gave him a bit of trouble and a free character reading while he eased her into a police motorcycle sidecar.

In those days Bumper was the cop who looked after the Cross and Tim saw how in effect he ran the place. If someone caused minor trouble, Bumper would call them over and ask their name. He'd write it down and say"Right. You're barred. I don't want to see you here in the Cross for the next two months. If I do, I'll give you three months for consorting."

And he would. Anyone booked three times for meeting criminals went inside for three months under the *Consorting Act*. If necessary, to teach a criminal a lesson, they were "loaded up" with the charge and magistrates in the police courts usually supported the cops. To beat consorting rules, some crims and smarties used a signalling system among themselves like holding out the bottom of their coat or rubbing their mouth to warn others that Bumper was approaching.

At other times Bumper might ask undesirable characters where they lived, if they had a job and what money they had in their pockets. Unless they could produce at least five shillings, he'd charge them with vagrancy and into the cells they went. Tough, but the system worked and kept the streets mostly clear of crims and undesirables - generally there was order, respect for the law and trouble was often stopped before it began.

But there was plenty going on in the Cross, gambling, sly grogging and prostitution, all of which Tim would soon get to know about.

Having joined the force thinking that policemen were all honest and above board and policing was a clear case of bobbies and bushies or cops and robbers, Tim could not believe the corruption that went on all around him. He was no boy scout but he'd led a protected life away from the seamy side, and wasn't prepared for the shock.

Even when he went to the City Morgue to arrange a body identification, he was reminded of it. Many cops kept their free ducks, poultry, turkeys and grog in the freezers where bodies were stored. To add to his queasiness, a cadaverous morgue employee with a withered arm and an odd sense of humour made him ill when he poked a body's stomach with his finger and it went arrrrrgh from escaping air.

A rort also existed in fruit from the City Markets, including supplies sold by some barrowmen. City Council officers often reported gluts of certain fruits, and supplies not sold in normal market trading were supposed to be auctioned, dumped or given to hospitals. Instead, they were sold cheaply to unlicensed barrowmen and the money pocketed by officials, while growers got nothing. The Lord Mayor controlled the markets.

[*I was aware of the same market rackets as Bristow In this period I obtained my first big newspaper scoop as a cadet reporter on November 2, 1951, filling pages one and two of the Daily Mirror about City Market racketeers artificially forcing up prices, in spite of the fact that Lord Mayor Ernie O'Dea surreptitiously warned them to leave the markets because the Mirror was coming with a photographer*].

Police attending break-ins at night were also involved in the common practice of stolen goods. If they got there first before the owner or manager after an alarm went off, many cops would load up their paddy wagon with goods. The attitude was, 'oh well, it's covered by insurance.'

While Tim was noting all this, two cops were sacked for stealing expensive furs after attending a burglary in an upmarket city shop at the corner of King and Castlereagh Streets. The owners found the furs in their paddy wagon. Same with pillaging on the wharves - cops and wharfies helped themselves from "breakages" of crates, deliberately dropped.

This larceny extended even to the simple matter of lost property which, if unclaimed six months after being handed in to police stations, was auctioned with proceeds going to State consolidated revenue. Tim looked on in disbelief to see the CIB's best-known detectives happily sifting through the pile in the CIB yard and helping themselves to cameras and other costly items. It was the accepted thing. He knew a cop who exchanged the squad car's new tyres for those old ones on his own car.

Yet, the rules governing police in those days were so strict. They had to swear allegiance to the then commissioner, Jim Scott, a pisspot spending a lot of time dining and wining free at exclusive Romano's and Prince's restaurants. Policemen's private lives also needed to be exemplary. They could be dismissed if getting divorced.

It was illegal for police to have any other form of income or own a business. But many did, even senior officers, with fruit shops, *Monte de Pietes* or pawn shops and various other side arrangements. Bristow knew a lot of honest cops who just tolerated the rest, minding their own business and pressing on with the job. They were in the majority, the backbone of the force. But the dishonest ones had the power and the strength to get things done. Dobbing in was strictly against the culture, and offenders risked being ostracised by their workmates.

The corruption and dishonesty he saw was not blatantly out in the open. The crooks picked their marks and it was fairly subtle, more sensed than obvious when it came to showing their hands with those working alongside them. Bristow was surprised that the money from rorts was not looked upon as corruption, just income. In fact, the stealing side of dishonest police practices was just the tip of the iceberg. The real hub of crookedry in the force where the big money changed hands was in gambling, sly grog, SP betting, abortions and prostitution, centred on cosmopolitan Kings Cross.

By keeping his eyes and ears open as he met more police and gained more experience, Tim Bristow gradually realised that protection rackets were rife in the community, that you could do just about anything you wanted if you played by the unwritten rules and paid your dues. He came to the conclusion that people with money and the right connections could even get away with murder. Court cases could be fixed, charges pulled out or amended, drivers' licences adjusted, records mislaid, evidence subverted, witnesses suborned.

This sub-structure of power aimed at overturning the normal system of justice to benefit the rich or privileged, extended right up through the most senior sections of the force to politics at the highest level. Politicians dictated many of these situations. The Premier and some of his Ministers were in league with the Police Commissioner and the word came down when something was to be fixed.

On a wider scale, Bristow understood that the main man in Parliament House to fix things was the Chief Secretary, Gus Kelly, who administered licences, an area of potentially lucrative graft. It was a standing joke among cops that Gus would say: "I don't handle money - leave it in the drawer." One Minister had the reputation when approached of saying nothing but holding up a piece of paper with a sum of money written on it. Tim was too young and inexperienced at that stage to know that this was not unique to cops and politicians in NSW. It was simply the way of the world, just the way things worked.

Sydney was recovering from the grimness of the Second World War when Bristow was a young cop, jobs were easy to get, people were out for a good time as life returned to normal, but rationing still existed with liquor, especially beer. The shortage was a hangover from the war when the NSW Government imposed a quota on sales in order to service the troops. The Federal Government drastically cut imports of Scotch whisky and as expected, a thriving blackmarket in sly grog sprang up. The situation for ordinary drinkers was curtailed even more because 6 p.m. closing was still in force in hotels.

New suppliers had emerged to cater for the wartime demand as tens of thousands of American servicemen whooped it up in Sydney from 1942, with a boom in SP betting, other forms of gambling and the oldest profession. A new form of gambling, baccarat, was introduced, with most of this sudden increase in entertainment taking place in or around the Cross. A small army of hostesses, escorts and working girls grew up overnight to meet the new demands, followed by an increase in pimps and crooks. A blackmarket operated with anything that was rationed or in short supply. One of Sydney's biggest sly grog merchants blatantly operated opposite the police boys club at inner-city Woolloomooloo.

Just after the war, several new nightclubs and theatre restaurants featuring chorus girls and artists had opened up, heralding the most glamorous era of Sydney night life ever. The most colourful and popular of these at the time was the Roosevelt in Orwell Street, Kings Cross, under the old 2KY radio station where famous announcer John Harper sat at the mike in his underpants.

Sammy Lee, a Canadian band drummer who settled in Sydney in 1940, opened the Roosevelt then and sold it to his partner Reg Boom in 1946, opening another called Sammy Lee's in Oxford Street, Woollahra. One of his partners was Perce Galea, big punter and operator of illegal casinos.

A young Abe Saffron took over the Roosevelt in 1948, beginning his climb to fame as an entrepreneur of girlie houses, turning it into a kind of fantasy palace with soft lights, flowers and large mirrors. It soon became a rendezvous for the rich and famous, cops, criminals, bookmakers, politicians, good-time girls, newspaper columnists and assorted questionable characters.

While Tim was doing the rounds of the Cross with Bumper, he met Abe Saffron there, also neck-or-nothing punter Hollywood George Edser. And guarding the Roosevelt's big red leather doors was Richard Gabriel (Dick) Reilly, even then gaining notoriety as a feared standover man. Many of those characters he met on the beat would become important contacts in Bristow's later career. Also going full swing as a mecca of city entertainment where you could get a drink was the Celebrity Club in York Street, run by death-or-glory punter Joe Taylor, whom Bristow also knew as the proprietor of Thommo's floating two-up school - of which two police commissioners would humorously say they'd never heard.

Outside the city proper there were other sly-grog clubs like the Colony Club, one of several near Tom Ugly's in southern Sydney. In the CBD the first upmarket Chequers of Shanghai migrants Denis and Keith Wong was about to open in Pitt Street. The famous strip shows and other breezy Kings Cross shows of the '50s were just about to emerge.

But many folk, dressed to kill for a special night out, still preferred the exclusive city restaurants of Romano's in Castlereagh Street and Prince's in Martin Place, where the waiters added to an aura of elegance by wearing tails. Neither restaurant had a liquor licence but like the new clubs they easily got around the archaic liquor laws by breaking the law, as all patrons and everyone else in town knew. It provided a little spice of illegality to the occasion.

First the clubs got over the shortage of liquor by simply having supplies from hotels diverted to their use. Then they skirted the problem of not having a licence by having customers ring up and book a table for the night and supposedly order beer, wine or spirits which the clubs would "buy" for them. When you sat down in the nightclub you'd find several bottles of beer placed on your table in the names of Smith, Jones, Brown, Greene and so on.

Abe Saffron beat the problem by transferring liquor from the nearby Gladstone Hotel which he owned and others he owned through dummies and selling it in the Roosevelt at blackmarket rates. He and others ran into a bit of trouble over that in the Liquor Royal Commission, which would run from 1951 to 1954 aimed at reforming the liquor industry. But Abe donated generously to police boys clubs and the cops didn't worry about it. Nobody did. The laws were unpopular anyway and conducive to being broken. The situation was ready made for crooked cops and crooked operators.

Even if restaurants were licensed - and few were - you had to order a meal before they could serve you liquor. The main brewery, Tooth and Co. had a monopoly on hotels through a tied house system and the hotels they owned could buy only from them. Other regulations made it tough on the public such as a two-gallon licence, which meant you could buy spirits only by the dozen bottles.

Tooth and Co. had reinforced the system by supplying the ruling Labor Party with most of its funds, but its power would soon be broken by the Liquor Commission after Mr Justice Maxwell freed up the system by licensing clubs and restaurants. Even so, six o'clock closing of hotels, introduced temporarily in 1919, would not be changed due to wowsers until 1955 and not fully reformed until the 1970s.

That was the licensing background when Tim Bristow pounded the beat at the Cross. Arrests were few and far between then for sly grogging because the Vice Squad cops were paid by the illegal nightclubs. The queens of the underworld in the inner eastern suburbs, Kate Leigh and Tilly Devine, whom Tim met with Bumper, were sly groggers, although both were into prostitution as well. Kate staged generous Christmas parties for the kids of the Surry Hills slum area.

At the time, as a residue from the boom war years when money was thrown about with abandon, illegal baccarat and other gambling games were prevalent around the Cross, Elizabeth Bay and Double Bay. That was before the rise of the big casinos beginning in the '50s. Most of the pre-casino gambling in Tim's experience as a policeman was associated with the nightclubs, the games regarded as upmarket social occasions in nicely decorated premises. Prominent characters such as Perce Galea and Reg Boom were among the operators.

From an illicit police income point of view, payoffs from SP bookmakers were just as lucrative, better overall in fact because SP existed not only at the Cross but also in suburbs and towns and cities all over Australia. The system was the same as in all other illegal forms of enterprise - you paid for the privilege to operate and were protected from others infiltrating your area. Even a prostitute had to pay, or face arrest. As Tim told his friends: "I joined the police force but I think I've joined the crooks. There's a racket in everything in the city."

That view was even enhanced when Tim met the legendary tough cop Ray Kelly through Freddie Baddrum, a Lebanese friend who owned Paramount Shirts, which Tim modelled before joining the force. Kelly wore silk shirts, monogrammed with his initials, provided by Freddie on the house. Kelly, assisted by another senior detective, Don Fergusson, ran the abortion racket operated by Dr Reginald

Stuart-Jones, a Macquarie Street surgeon and sly grogger with a notorious reputation. They were partners with Roosevelt doorman Dick Reilly, who was bagman and strongarm protector.

Bristow met Kelly at Stuart-Jones's office in Elizabeth Bay where Kelly worked when not at the CIB. Tim thought him the hardest man imaginable. Kelly justified his role by offering the explanation that it was better to have the then illegal abortions performed by a skilled doctor in proper clinical conditions than have pregnant girls forced to go to risky unhygienic backyard operators.

Soon after their friendly meeting Tim took part with Kelly and others in the dramatic capture of notorious escapees Darcy Dugan and Billy Meares on Sydney's northern beaches, at dawn on 14 February 1950 - "loaned" out once again from routine beat work for a special job. Described as Public Enemy Number One and the subject of blazing tabloid headlines, Dugan had escaped with Meares yet again by breaking out of Central Court cells and went on the run for two months, writing cheeky letters to the Press and wanted for shooting a bank manager, Leslie Nalder, in an attempted holdup.

Kelly received a tip that the State's most wanted pair were hiding out in a house at 44 Alexander Street, Collaroy, wearing disguises and even surfing at popular Collaroy beach. Thick bushland covered the area at the back of the house, making it a good spot for a quick getaway.

A team of more than 20 heavily-armed detectives and uniformed cops including Tim, were secretly mustered. They crept into position from the bush just before dawn. Tim was scared he'd be shot by friendly fire because each time a possum jumped in the trees or a bird flapped, nervous cops would swing tommy guns or shotguns past him as they looked about. They expected shooting from Dugan.

Although the intended pinch technically belonged to the senior man, Det-Sgt Jack Aldridge, Kelly took over. In Tim's words later, the gutsy Kelly drove up to near the front of the house at the last minute like Lord Rockcake visiting Buckingham Palace. The sleeping escapees were taken by surprise as cops with tear gas burst in through smashed doors and windows shouting "Police - hands up or we'll blast you."

The dicks put the criminals in separate rooms and Kelly and his team worked on Meares first. Kelly was a master of the verbal. From outside Tim could hear the beating. Meares signed a confession which Kelly then flourished at Dugan, but he wouldn't sign even when Kelly held a gun to his head, counted and pulled the trigger which clicked on an empty chamber.

Kelly had leaked to his newspaper contacts and the *Daily Mirror's* picture headlines that day screamed "Dugan, Meares arrested!"

Both got the death sentence, later commuted to life imprisonment.

Later Tim learned the truth. Kelly obtained the tip from his fizz gig, the heavy criminal Lennie McPherson, who had arranged the accommodation for Dugan and Meares at Collaroy and had visited them, driving members of the Meares family there in an ostensibly kind gesture. That treachery was always understood to be the truth by the Meares family. That's how Big Lennie survived - "fizzing" to Kelly in return for protection.

While on the run Dugan and Meares had held up the Mort's dock offices at Balmain, shooting one man and pistol whipping another. McPherson planned that robbery for them for a share in the takings. He'd done the same thing previously, even helping them escape from prison so they could commit the crimes.

Despite all the excitement that being a young policeman engendered, Bristow began to feel disillusioned. He didn't mind being used as a battering ram because of his strength and aggression, but he felt uncomfortable in the role of bagman. And he started complaining. He talked about what he was doing and expressed his dislike of corruption to a friend, Vice Squad Sgt Ron "Rocky" Walden, with whom he had an affinity through boxing. Walden, a straight cop and later Chief of the CIB, was amateur heavyweight champion of Australia. His advice to Tim was: "Don't worry about it. There has to be some bile and guile in the community."

Asked what that meant, Walden said: "To lubricate the economy." That didn't assuage Tim. He complained directly to Inspector Boswell who listened stony-faced and took him off bagman duties and arresting barrowmen at once.

But two incidents occurred which brought Tim to the brink. He had his watch stolen while teaching boxing in the North Sydney Police Boys' Club and bought another from a pawnbroker in his police division near Circular Quay. The watch was a dud and Tim returned it and gave the fellow a grilling, going through his books and finding stolen property on display. He didn't realise the shop was part-owned by a police superintendent who had another shop at Wynyard. Boswell paraded Tim and warned him off any further action on the pawnbroker.

On wharf duty soon after, at No 9 Walsh Bay where the big ships came in, Tim was keeping the crowd back as some early post-war migrants arrived on an Italian ship. Italian friends and relatives meeting them tended to be excited and Tim was holding them back in line as the newcomers surged down the gangway.

One man, dressed in suit and hat, stood out of the line and took no notice when Tim ordered him back. Thinking he was a member of the public, Tim stamped on his left foot, causing him to double up in pain. "Sorry," said Tim sarcastically, before the man hobbled away, "if I'd seen your foot I'd have sent you a telegram." He thrived on direct action.

An hour or so later a paddy wagon arrived at the wharf, the driver bringing instructions to take him back to Phillip Street station at once. He went up to see Inspector Boswell wondering what it was about and there sitting in his office was the man from Walsh Bay with his left foot in a warm bowl of water, nursing a broken toe. "I'd like you to meet Det-Sgt Fred Hanson," said Boswell. Tim had never heard of him but he would later become renowned as "Slippery Fred," the Police Commissioner.

Before Tim had a chance to apologise or say anything, Boswell came right to the point. "You've torn it this time," he said dryly. "I'm transferring you to the bush. Broken Hill."

2

THE BOY FROM SHORE

Tim Bristow had joined the police force because he wanted to be a boxer. Indeed, his ambition was to be world heavyweight champion, but his father refused to sign the papers for him to turn professional at a time when the age of consent was 21.

So Tim defiantly joined the force to teach boxing in the boys' clubs and box as an amateur with inter-collegiate opponents until he could turn pro. It broke his mother Josie's heart and bitterly disappointed his father, Charles, when he started wearing a suit of blue.

Charles Bristow, who had studied law at Sydney University with future judge Garfield Barwick but not gone on with it, wanted him to be a professional man, a barrister, and to play classical piano like him and Tim's German grandmother. That's why he sent him to Sydney's best private school, hoping he'd make the right connections and be a gentleman.

But all Tim wanted to do was fight. And fight he did. At Shore, the Sydney Church of England Grammar School at North Sydney, he was the school bully, thrashing anyone who wanted to take him on, even far bigger and older boys. But he always stood up for the underdog too.

Tim was a bundle of trouble almost from the time he was born, on August 26, 1930. Christened a catholic as Charles

John but called Tim by his mother, he was hyperactive and aggressive. In many ways it seemed a burden to have been born so big and strong. A natural sportsman, he excelled at every sport without apparent effort or training, with the big heart to go with it. As a result, he was inclined to be a showoff who attracted trouble and caused embarrassment.

Charles Bristow, whose idol was Max Schmeling after the German heavyweight stopped Brown Bomber Joe Louis in an epic non-title battle in 1936, passed on his sporting prowess and interests to Tim. Charles was a good boxer and swimmer and had Tim taught boxing from an early age, also sending him to the best swimming coach of the day, Harry Hay, at Manly pool. He wanted Tim and his younger son, Max, to be the best at everything and to have every opportunity in life.

Tim's father was awarded the Royal Humane Society's Bronze Medal for pluckily rescuing a drowning woman at Collaroy on 18 January 1919. He swam out to a man and woman in difficulties off the rock pool, agreeing with the man that he should take the woman in first and return for him. But before reaching the shore, Bristow heard the man scream and saw him pulled under in a pool of blood - the first shark attack on Sydney's northern beaches.

Charles Bristow was the first trustee of Collaroy surf club and the vice president. He was a proud man who instilled strong family and personal values in Tim and his second son Max. There was right and wrong, no in-betweens. His interest in boxing arose from the need to defend himself when, as a youth in Sydney's Hunters Hill area during the First World War, he was called a "dirty German" and picked on because of his Germanic background on his mother's side. Young Tim inherited some of that insecurity from his father and drew flak in the

Second World War for what were seen as his Germanic attitudes. Tim the Hun, they called him.

Tim's grandmother, Maggie Bristow, was a strong, resourceful character. Her maiden name was Leudesdorf, but she was born in Manchester to a German-Jewish father and an English mother. Her mother was married a second time, to a wealthy silk merchant and had maids to do all the chores. One of Maggie's brothers was a don at Oxford University.

Maggie was sent to a finishing school in Leipzig to study music and art. She later met her future English middle-class husband, the original Charles Bristow, in Manchester through music. He played cello and violin and his family helped to found the Trinity School of Music in London. Against her parents' wishes, she followed him to Australia and they married in Sydney's St James Church in 1898.

To supplement the family income, Maggie taught music and German language at home, had a city studio in Palings music centre, then taught piano and music theory at the Conservatorium. She taught her son Charles, Tim's father, to be an accomplished pianist and encouraged her other children to be independent and good at school. Zelie, a twin sister of Charles, was dux of Fort Street High with top State marks, and kept company with the man who would become leader of the NSW Bar, Clive Evatt, QC. As children, Zelie and Charles had the Bible read to them every Sunday.

The wild streak that would soon show out in Tim came through from the Irish landed gentry side that was part of the family background of his mother, Josie O'Sullivan. On that side the family also had a notable past for sporting and personal achievement in the early history of New South Wales.

But amid their success and hard work, the larrikin aspect prevailed. Josie was educated at Santa Sabina, the Dominican college at Strathfield. At one of her speech days there the Cardinal arrived in a shiny limo. Her father Joseph, after deliberately walking across the lawn past a "keep off the grass" sign, said at the top of his voice: "Jesus rode on a donkey. Look at this bastard in a fancy car." Tim is said to have resembled Joseph, his grandfather, who liked fighting, so did Joseph's brother Dan, a good rower and toughie. Both went to private schools, Joseph to St Joseph's College and Dan to the Jesuits at St Ignatius.

Tim's parents met at Collaroy, a seaside spot on the picturesque Peninsula or northern beaches area of Sydney, when Josie, a nurse, went there to work in a children's hospital. She was Catholic but didn't practise. Charles was a Mason who regularly attended lodges, a decent and honourable man who believed in fair play and all the other principles that went with masonry, including family loyalty - blood was thicker than water, stick up for your family no matter what. He insisted Tim and Max always kiss him on the cheek when saying goodbye, a practice the two brothers would always follow themselves and also when meeting.

It was natural for Tim's father to go into the wool industry because economically Australia then rode on the sheep's back and distant relatives on Josie's side were pioneers of the industry. Their names were recorded in copperplate handwriting in a big Bible as the family register - John Lundy Badgery 1794, William Badgery 1796, James 1798, and others, all from the famous Pitt Son and Badgery and Schute Bell Son and Badgery wool firms.

Charles studied at technical college, setting up as a successful wool broker, travelling to the United States, Europe and Bradford mills to build up his business. He became wealthy, but lost a bit of it in the 1940s due to halted German wool sales, although he sold elsewhere.

He and Josie were popular and socially prominent with friends like the Dekyveres, Morells and other socialites on the Peninsula and businessmen in city establishment circles. The family lived at Mosman, their lovely property running down to the water's edge and a boatshed. The lawns were manicured, rockeries perfect, a tidiness that Tim would inherit. They had holiday homes at Collaroy and in the country at trendy Bowral.

From his bed Tim could look out on Middle Harbour and see the sunrise over the quiet retreat of Mosman Bay. He and Max had sailing boats, a swimming pool, fantail and other pigeon lofts and everything they wanted. Apart from fighting, they were brought up in an overtly genteel, orderly and privileged way, taught to compare themselves with the best, not the worst. In an attempt to give the boys some extra culture, Charles played the piano while they stood around singing all the old ballads.

Maggie Bristow tried to teach Tim piano and although he practised under her tuition, he didn't have the patience due to his zeal for the outdoors and sport - fighter, fast bowler, tearaway Rugby Union forward... He would have liked to oblige her due to their close relationship but couldn't sit still long enough to concentrate. But much of his determination and character were derived from her. She lived to age 98.

Although Tim disappointed his grandmother on the practical side of music, every night he and Max went to sleep to the classical piano sounds of their father playing Beethoven's *Moonlight Sonata*, Chopin's *Mazurka No 5* or *Polonaise No 1 in A*, Mozart's *Sonatas*, Brahms' *Ballade in G Minor*, or Debussy's *Clair de Lune*. Debussy was Tim's favourite.

Tim inherited a love of racehorses from his mother's side of the family. Andrew Town, Tim's grandfather, played an important role in improving the breed as owner of the famous Hobartville Stud at Richmond, near Sydney. He built it up into the biggest stud in the world as well as running herds of quality cattle and pigs.

He bought the stud in 1877 and stood some of the greatest sires of the period there, including Grand Flaneur, unbeaten in nine races including the AJC and Victorian Derbies and who remains the only undefeated Melbourne Cup winner. Grand Flaneur, who took out the Cup in 1880, sired the Melbourne Cup winners Bravo and Patron and at least 13 other major thoroughbreds, including Merman which was sent to England and won the 1890 Ascot Gold Cup, the Goodwood and Jockey Club Cups and the Cesarewitch Handicap.

Another of Town's sires was the outstanding Tim Whiffler who scored the 1867 Melbourne Cup, also an Australian Cup and AJC Metropolitan. In 1868 Town inherited from his late father the famous sire Tarragon, winner of the 1866 Australasian Champion Stakes, and he had others such as Trenton and Maribyrnong. The Hobartville Stakes took its name from the stud. Sydney's premier trotting track Harold Park took its name from Town's renowned trotting sire, Childe Harold, which he imported in 1882 from Kentucky, pioneering trotting in Australia.

The racetrack for the Hawkesbury Race Club, Australia's longest-running club going back to 1832, was part of the original Hobartville holding which had been bought in 1816 by William Cox Snr, who among other things, built the road over the Blue Mountains. Mrs Cox became one of the colony's most popular hostesses, young officers boasting that they had "arrived" when invited to stay there. The fine Georgian mansion was set in formal gardens.

Breaker Morant of court martial fame broke in horses there and Colonel William H. Holborow, a member of the Legislative Council, Town's brother-in-law and a great uncle of Tim's, used to get hot under the collar over his friend Breaker being executed for shooting Boer prisoners. He regularly denounced Lord Kitchener and Queen Victoria for making Breaker a political scapegoat over the affair.

Andrew Town was also a community leader in the Richmond-Windsor district. A magistrate, he was chairman, committeeman and judge of the Hawkesbury Race Club, president of the Hawkesbury Agricultural Society, councillor of the Agricultural Society of NSW and committeeman and judge of the AJC, also judge for the Hawkesbury and several other race clubs.

Town began his celebrated annual yearling sales in 1879 under Hobartville's huge oak trees, with hundreds flocking there to be served a splendid lunch under marquees. Even his friend, the NSW Governor Lord Carrington, turned up. Regrettably Town went bust through gambling and the 1890s depression and was forced to sell up to clear his debts. He died soon after, cramming two lives into one. *The Bulletin* said of his passing: "If all men connected with horse racing were as straight and true as was Andrew Town, the turf would indeed be the sport of kings and not a mere spider's web."

Today historic Hobartville is owned by self-made millionaire Graham Mapp. The 1988 Golden Slipper winner Star Watch was bred there.

The Towns, like several other distant relatives of Tim's mother, sprang from convict stock. Sprang, because they obviously formed a good gene pool, working hard and prospering in a remarkable way. Somewhere in there was a highwayman, too.

Andrew Town's grandfather, John Town, was a convict, tried in Warwick in 1796 and convicted for life, arriving in Sydney on the *Royal Admiral* in 1800. He married a convict girl, Mary Pickett, in 1813 and they had three children. Within 30 years they were substantial landholders and Hawkesbury district hotel owners, among other things running the King's Head and the George 1V in Richmond, also the Victoria, the Woolpack Inn and the Traveller's Rest.

But the most remarkable story centres on "Granny" Hale, early forebear of Tim's distant relatives by marriage, including the Durhams, Stewarts, Holborows and McQuades. She was born Mary Lynch of convict parents and baptised in Sydney in 1796, among the first 200 children born in the fledgling colony.

Her father, William Lynch, died in 1804 but her mother never remarried. She had a difficult childhood, was almost certainly destitute at times and had no formal education because even in her last years she could sign her will only by making a mark.

Perhaps in order to survive, Mary Lynch married a convict, Thomas Broughton, at Windsor in 1812 when aged 15 years and 11 months. He died three years later. Six months later in October 1815, aged 19 and not one to watch the grass grow, Mary married William Durham, who had been convicted of highway robbery at Bristol in 1810 and originally sentenced to hang.

Transported to Sydney and arriving in the *Guildford* in 1812, he served only five years and received his pardon just four months before his marriage. He became a man of means as a successful butcher in Richmond. They had four children and were expecting another when he met an untimely end in 1827, knocked from his horse. The *Sydney Gazette,* reporting the funeral, said in part: "It was a rather pitiful sight to see the widow, in an advanced state of pregnancy, with her children, taking a last look at the coffin, peeking into the grave..."

But Mary overcame her grief and difficulties, 13 months later in 1828 marrying James Hale at St. Matthews, Windsor. He too was a convict, having been sentenced to seven years in London in 1815. Described as a farmer's boy, he arrived on the *Mariner* in 1816.

They prospered, at first owning the White Hart Hotel in Windsor, where census records show they gave the underdog a go by employing four convicts, two of them lifers, as servants at the same time - surely a setting for an early *Fawlty Towers* script.

The Hales became pillars of colonial society, regularly entertaining friends at their imposing Victorian mansion on *Fairfield* - a magnificent property where a visiting English cricket team played a match once and the Richmond Golf Club later stood - inviting even those they met casually on the day at Windsor races. They were described in print as one of the most amiable and generous of Windsor families.

The *Fairfield* home, with its high iron columns and intricate wrought iron railings, was the venue of balls and glittering parties when owned by another member of the family ancestry, Henry McQuade, who managed *Her Majesty's Theatre*. A daughter of the Hales, Amelia, was a fine singer and pianist. Old man Hale was chairman of the Hawkesbury Benevolent Society for several years until he died in 1857.

Obviously Granny Hale was a Bristow ancestor to be admired - daughter of convict parents, illiterate, married three times to convicts, rising above it all to lead a full and eventful life, a strong type on which the young Australian Anglo-Saxon nation was founded.

With a background of achievers like that, tossed in with the wild Irish streak of the O'Sullivans and the clinical Germanic efficiency of Maggie Leudesdorf, Tim Bristow was more than likely to be a person of dominating personality. And he didn't disappoint.

Tim's parents spoiled him as a child. He was destructive and troublesome, often causing family holidays to be cancelled at the last minute by outrageous behaviour aimed at upsetting the family. The household revolved around him. What Tim ate, everyone ate. He liked only beef, so they all ate beef. He'd even steal it from younger brother Max's plate, threatening him if he complained. He'd give Max serious hidings at times, once breaking his nose so he couldn't go to school.

More attention was paid to Tim than Max because he was so difficult and unruly. He had a quick temper but soon got over it. In hindsight some family members believed Charles Bristow's insecurities in being rejected for his German background when young, showed out in Tim's disobedience. Charles seemed over-impressed with people of importance, always insisting that Tim and Max say hello to them and shake their hands. But obviously Tim's erratic behaviour was due to more deep-seated reasons than that, although nobody gave much thought to medical analysis in those days.

Charles was usually short on discipline with Tim although Tim always claimed that his father, a perfectionist, was tough on him. Often Josie would tell Charles that he should have given Tim a thrashing. Yet, she too, indulged Tim, especially when as a child he staged tantrums and twice threw all her perfumes out the window without any punishment from her.

Many times Tim beat up some kid in the area and an irate father would come around to complain, bringing his son with a bleeding face. Charles always placated him with soothing words such as saying 'boys will be boys' and poured him a whisky or two. Then he'd say later to Tim: "But did you win?"

Tim insulted a far bigger and older youth one day, a butcher's boy named Headley Hodges. He came round and wanted to fight. Tim had the attitude that he could never back off in any situation and agreed at once. Charles went referee and Tim gave the fellow a real hiding. That's where Tim Bristow grew from - thrashing other kids in the neighbourhood, his dog savaging other dogs and Tim not being disciplined for it.

Kids had to make their own fun then and Tim and his mates formed gangs, throwing rocks at other gangs from neighbouring suburbs, having catapult fights and shooting BB gun pellets at one another. They built a commando course with ropes across a gully and when one of Tim's mates, Peter Easterway, was halfway across, Tim cut the rope and he fell into lantana bushes below. All good clean sport.

Charles sent Tim and Max to Shore for a good education, also believing the private school would give them membership of an old boys' network. They could find themselves sitting alongside someone who would help them professionally later. Errol Flynn and John Newcombe were among the celebrated old boys. Rhodes scholar J.B. "Jika" Travers, who played Rugby for Australia and England, studied there and returned as a master.

Tim made friends with many boys from establishment, moneyed families, others who would become judges, barristers including Alec Shand QC, and top businessmen like transport operator Gordon Barton who later owned Ipec. Tim sat next to Tom Baillieu of BHP mining family fame.

But he didn't kow-tow to anyone. One day he asked top student Barton to do his homework and passed on Barton's answers to several mates. Some answers surprisingly were wrong and Tim and his mates who cribbed were called out by teacher "Digger" Davies, told to bend over and given six of his best downward "cheese-cutters" with the cane. Annoyed, Tim told one of his rugged mates, Butch "The Bull" Lawrence, to belt Barton but he came along as a Samaritan after Barton had copped plenty in the toilets from Butch and said, "Leave him alone." Barton thought he'd saved his life and was ever grateful.

Tim had a ferocious fight in a dressing shed at the school one day with Michael Fomenko, who would become famous as the modern Tarzan. Tim won but it lasted several hours, leaving dried bloodstains on the floor and seats for a long time.

Another colourful character in Tim's class was Charles le Gallien. His parents had a big house and swimming pool on the North Shore and Tim and his mates often went there. But apparently Charlie's father was having an affair with another woman and Charlie stabbed him to death in an argument over it. A mate of Tim's helped the police tie up the murder charge by giving information. Tim was one of the few who visited him in Goulburn Jail and later found him a job in Melbourne as a trumpet player. Tim turned up at Max Bristow's one day with a pale-looking Charlie and said: "He's just come out - give Max a bit of a turn on your trumpet."

As a counter to his aggression, Tim showed a strong sense of justice. He pushed classmates aside at a lunch table one day to make room for a slower kid walking with crutches. He beat up an older pupil named Graham Nock, of Nock and Kirby retail renown, whom he thought had jumped the queue in the tuckshop and took no notice when he told him to move. Tim was always outspoken, sounding off in and out of class if he believed in something. He didn't deliberately set out to stir things up, it just happened as a reaction, surrounding him in controversy in all things, especially sport.

The only time his father strongly disciplined him was when he brought home his usually-adverse school report. Shore headmaster L.C "The Chief" Robson wrote once that Tim was lazy and ostentatious, and neither punishment nor persuasion had any effect on him. Charles Bristow always gave him a hiding with a strap or a belt at the end of every term. Tim retaliated once, punching his father and breaking two ribs.

In the holidays, due to an unusual rapport with animals, Tim toiled at Taronga Park Zoo as an assistant keeper. He saw it as a challenge to be friendly with the animals, feeling sorry to see them in cages. That, too, ended in turmoil. His job was to clean up the animals' droppings and help feed them. Tim used to get in with the cheetahs and jaguars who were as tame as dogs with him, but the leopards and panthers weren't. He tried patting the pumas too and would wear a scar for life where one grabbed him in its claws.

Instead of walking half a mile to pick up the meat for the big cats, Tim would chase them back into the rear of their dens with a broom and take a short cut through their area. Even at Wirth's Circus one day he patted a tiger through the cage, luckily without being mauled.

At the zoo one day Tim jumped on an Indian elephant which was lying down and it took off, bolting instead of skipping along. Tim dug his knees in but was no mahout as the elephant careered along past the bison area until the keeper called out the right commands. It stopped abruptly,

Tim almost taking a nose dive. He was probably the first Australian to ride a rhino. He jumped on it too and it thundered and snorted around the zoo, with the keeper in hot pursuit in a truck. Finally Tim was called in and, in spite of his father being friendly with the zoo patron Sir Edward Hallstrom, the manager told him: "You're a silly bugger. You're sacked."

His father eventually decided that if after five years at Shore he wasn't going to study law, he might as well leave and follow him into the wool industry as a broker - synthetics didn't exist then and wool was still the biggest commodity seller. Charles had stopped him from rowing because of his obsession for sport, but realised he'd encouraged Tim too much in boxing.

Charles started him off at 17 with the wool firm Grazcos, where he began at the bottom handling sheep skins. But he had a dispute with the boss, thumped him, threw him into a wool presser and was sacked. It seemed Tim didn't want anyone in charge of him or dictating to him. Then he was taken under the wing of one of the stalwarts of the industry, John Ure Smith at AML&F, a gentleman of the old school.

He took Tim to the Union Club, probably Australia's top club for members of the establishment, and insisted he dress like a gentleman, wearing a hat and buttoning up his coat. A Beau Brummell, Smith changed his bow ties two or three times a day and had Tim polish his shoes.

Tim also began modelling in a modest way at this time and fellows around the leading Hotel Australia gave him "the bird" as he walked by with Ure Smith - they whistled, called him Fauntleroy and Pretty Boy. He yearned to thump them but couldn't.

That was all too confining for a man of action so he left and went to the Riverina to work as an apprentice wool classer in the woolsheds around there, mainly for the wealthy businessman, rice grower and landholder F.W. Hughes, who owned 1946 Melbourne Cup winner Russia. Always an animal lover, he took a bull terrier with him but trouble erupted when it cleaned up all the shearers' kelpies and cattle dogs.

That caused numerous fights, culminating in a gang battle at the big Coova shearing shed when Tim was asked to fetch water but told the toughest and biggest shearer there to get it himself. The man had bulging muscles and nobody thought anyone would have a go at him. Tim beat him and threw him into the wool in the presser. It developed into a brawl with shearers taking sides but no real damage was done.

Moving around in the area he put together a team of shearers to play a combined Riverina team Australian Rules at Griffith. He knocked out several Italians at a party in a fruit packing house at Hanwood one night, although he met and was friendly with many Italians, among them "Aussie Bob" Trimboli, making contacts for the future with the Italian community. That led to him associating later with Frank Nugan, of CIA bank notoriety. But he didn't like the discipline of the wool industry. Wanting to set his own rules and being in constant trouble didn't help.

His mother had always been against him boxing and now his father was too, refusing him permission to turn professional. That's when he joined the police force hoping to beat their ban. His father told friends: "I have two sons but only one, Max, is normal and does what he's told. With Tim, I've tried everything from thrashing him to being nice, but nothing works. He won't listen to my advice and just goes his own way." Tim was a ying and yang character, tough, but with a soft side to him too.

Josie Bristow, who spoke lovingly of Tim to her friends as "my beautiful boy," was embarrassed beyond words when he turned up in his police uniform wanting to borrow a few quid while she was dining with her socialite friends in Prince's, Romano's or a Double Bay restaurant. She was conscious of her social standing and sensitive to what other people thought. She knew what they were saying - you don't go to a private school to be a policeman.

Charles, who had advised him against joining the force saying he would meet with corruption and there was no future in the job, was more concerned for his future than embarrassed by Tim's present job. "I'm worried about the big fellow," he said.

When Inspector Boswell called Tim in after he'd been a cop for one year and told him brusquely he was transferring him to outback Broken Hill, Tim knew instinctively what his parents would say if he accepted the rebuke. "In that case, sir, I'd rather resign," he said.

He liked the surf and the Sydney beach scene too much, anyway. And the girls.

3

GIRLS, GIRLS ... AND GIRLS

TIM'S affection for a girl was one reason why he left the force. He was sweet on Margaret Kebblewhite, whose father Jack was boss of Beard Watson's, Australia's biggest retail furniture store in the city. They lived in a grand North Shore home and Jack, not keen on his daughter keeping company with a cop, had encouraged him to leave, offering him a job and the chance to do an interior decorator's course.

Tim took it and, as a matter of honour and responsibility because of the father's friendship, made no sexual advances towards the young lady. But soon, she up and left him for another fellow, whom she married. Tim then expounded his simple philosophy to a friend: "It taught me to get in and get it when you can."

He was already an active fornicator. Even at school he was seducing girls, cracking on to them when taking ballroom dancing lessons at Miss Kay's at Killara, Percy Jupp's at Cremorne and a school at Mosman.

In his last year at school, Tim was an inspector at popular Balmoral Beach on the inner Harbour. They were pre-bikini days and his instructions were to put scantily-clad ladies off the beach. Instead, with a wink wink he encouraged them by steering them to the quiet end of the beach.

With lots of beautiful young mums and pretty girls sunbaking at Balmoral, Tim reckoned his job was a beauty.

His physique and charming manner helped him score plenty of times. One was an English singer, older than him. But he greatly offended a police prosecutor by taking his daughter's virginity. That taught him to be careful, at least for a time, realising many of the Balmoral women had fathers or husbands who occupied positions of influence in the community and could cause him trouble. When not eyeing or chatting up the girls, Tim replaced the storm-damaged shark net at Balmoral, diving for fish in his lunch hours.

After joining the force, he continued his womanising ways, dining out on one star performance by seducing the beautiful English actress Jean Simmons. Jean, of the gorgeous blue eyes, pert manner and pretty face, was in Sydney then in 1949 for a segment of the movie, *Blue Lagoon*. She went on to Hollywood to star in more than 50 feature films like *Guys and Dolls* with Brando and Sinatra, and married Stewart Granger.

Tim met her when she opened a surf carnival at Sydney's Queenscliff beach. He won his board race and took her out for a paddle on his ski well beyond the Manly breakers, inviting her out that night to a surfies' entertainment haunt called The Barn at Mosman where Les Welch's jazz band played. He pleasured her in no less a romantic setting than Mosman Bay Park. Motels were not yet on the scene.

He was mainly interested in the three "fs" - feeding, fighting and fornicating, adding a couple of others, football and fishing. But boxing was still uppermost as a potential career. To toughen up after leaving the force he decided to go cane cutting in North Queensland.

That proved to be heavy and laborious work. Cutting it by hand, the best jobs went to the most experienced teams and Tim went in with a team of seven greenhorns. At night, to remove dead leaves, they set fire to the amount of cane they could cut next day before fermentation set in. Then they hacked the stalks at ground level with big knives. As they burnt and toiled, wild pigs and snakes came rushing out. One problem was that a particular cane called Hairy Mary entered the pores of the cutters' skins, causing extreme irritation. After the first two days, five of his co-workers quit but Tim and the other two worked furiously to complete their plantation contract in time.

After a while he left the Cairns area and joined the crew of a tug boat, the Tulley Falls, towing a landing barge called Wewak north to pick up 44-gallon drums of petrol left in the jungle and estuaries in the war by servicemen, mainly American. A team of Aborigines helped him roll them out using an old truck where they could, for a contractor named Johnson.

The ruggedly beautiful Cape York Peninsula area was riddled with crocodiles and snakes, and buffalo were common. Tim hunted and shot crocodiles for the local people. He had a friendly relationship with the Torres Strait islanders, delivering supplies by boat to several outlying islands. Then he moved on to remote Arnhem Land in the Northern Territory, where he again picked up thousands of abandoned drums of petrol.

He dived extensively, including from trochus shell boats, arranging supplies of trochus shell for his Paramount Shirt friend, Freddie Baddrum, who used them for buttons. He also observed the fantastic coloured fish life of the Barrier Reef and other strange creatures like dugong, or sea cow. He dived free and stayed down for almost two minutes by hyperventilating, a skill equalled only by Japanese pearl divers. It caused him ear and sinus problems in later life.

Tim had dived in Sydney Harbour with experts like Marsden Campbell, a backstroke champion who produced the first Australian diving flippers and Malcolm Fuller, inventor of a popular spear gun.

After eight or nine months he returned to Sydney with a big rock python, as thick as a man's arm, which he took into homes and offices where he called, terrifying quite a few people. It took fright one day in Brisbane and bit Tim under his left armpit, locking its jaws. Helpers took at least an hour to prise it off with a screwdriver. The snake wasn't poisonous but the wound turned septic and Tim would bear the scars from the bite forever.

Returning home and again living with his parents in sedate Mosman, Tim the practical joker surreptitiously put the snake in his brother Max's bed one night. Max, not wishing to wake Tim by switching on his light, climbed into bed in the dark and leapt up screaming when he felt the snake. It caused a family row and Charles Bristow barred Tim from the house for several days. He had to sleep in his car out the front. Tim then let the snake live in his car, ostentatiously leaving the doors unlocked as he parked around the city.

A city newsreel ran a film and story showing the snake, saying Tim Bristow doesn't need a burglar alarm, he has one built in. The *Daily Mirror* also ran a story and picture of Tim with the snake wrapped around the steering wheel. Mercifully, he eventually gave it to the zoo.

Tim and a mate were the first to walk across Sydney Harbour between North and South Heads - not exactly on *top* of the water but on the Harbour floor, to test new aqua equipment. Unfortunately, his mate later went to jail for shooting and wounding a policeman who played up with his wife.

Tim started a new career as a designer in the packaging industry, in between surfing, playing rugby, womanising, a bit of modelling and amateur boxing. A sexual athlete, he boasted that he trained for sports by seducing girls.

He competed in surf events up and down the Peninsula and, although others did the formalities, he and four mates did much of the hard work in forming the Long Reef surf club next to Dee Why, raising funds and carrying concrete blocks for the clubhouse. Viewed from the south, the Long Reef headland looks a bit like Diamond Head, the famous extinct volcanic crater on Oahu's Waikiki Beach.

Tim also played a role in forming the Bilgola surf club but was thrown out when sprung for the second time seducing the same girl in the club. That embarrassed him because one of his girlfriends at the time was Sonia Hopkins, a good-looking girl from a wealthy North Shore family, who used to surf there. But she would remain a friend, later becoming Lady Sonia McMahon, wife of the Prime Minister.

He used to visit pretty twins named Gwenda and Evie and one night on coming home their father inquired from just inside the front door "are you in, Gwenda?" Tim called back: "No, Evie." Later he did catch Tim in bed with Gwenda and barred him. Tim thought he'd square up with the father and had a load of blue metal tipped in his driveway.

Tim was competing with a rival for the attentions of a girl named Janine Johnson, whose parents were from the Harden and Johnson Holden agency. One night he went and thumped her escort. Many years later the escort laughed over the incident when they met at a dinner party - he was then NSW Chief Justice Sir Laurence Street, regarded as an all-round good bloke.

Tim also had affairs on the side with the wives of two policemen on the Peninsula, saying they needed a bit of tender loving care. In his Runyonesque way, he even had a special name for his philandering - tooling. In that context, he "tooled" a keen lady one night at a wedding reception at Chatswood on the North Shore after she shed all her clothes in a side room when he made advances to her. Later she married a barrister who became a judge and appearing before him one day, Tim wondered if His Honour knew he'd had a trial run.

Amid all this "tooling," an incident occurred that would put a dampener on his plans to turn professional boxer and, among other things, to fight at Wembley Stadium. He'd boxed in the gyms with many of the leading fighters and beaten them all, including the Combined Services winner and also the man who represented Australia in the heavyweight division at the 1948 London Olympics, but now boxing would have to go on the back burner.

The incident began at a South Narrabeen Carnival where Tim won the classic double of the board and ski event. A boat captain who had bombed out in his race when his boat was swamped in a "Chinese shoot," said to Tim: "You think you're smart, don't you." Tim replied: "Smarter than you."

Later all the surfies met for a beer at the Newport Arms Hotel, the only watering hole on the Peninsula for sportsmen interested in beer, football and surf. As Tim was leaving the hotel on 6 p.m. closing time, the same competitor who had tried to provoke him earlier, approached him in the side bar and said: "You'd like to have a go, wouldn't you?"

"What would I gain by beating you? Who've you ever beaten?" said Tim. With that, the aggressor flexed up but was held back by several companions. Tim walked to his car and claimed the man came at him again, saying: "Right, we're having it here." Tim took off his jacket, a special new one he'd worn in his latest fashion show, and the fellow clouted him. Tim knocked him down with one blow and was putting his jacket on as he walked away when his opponent ripped his jacket and started punching again.

Tim then gave him the mother of a hiding - he wasn't only a good boxer, Marquis of Queensberry style, but a good street brawler, able to hit any way, back or front, with head or elbow as well as his pile-driving fists. Five or six of the man's mates stepped in to attack Tim, but he knocked them out too. The more the merrier. So began his legend as a fighting man.

A doctor who saw the fight stitched the man's facial injuries but refused to provide him with a medical certificate for court purposes. He was admitted to Manly Hospital where he remained for some time.

Later the man charged Tim by summons with assault occasioning actual bodily harm. Tim was represented in Manly Court by Michael Foster, a former school friend from Shore who would later go on the Federal Court Bench. The other man had Jack Thom, an experienced, knockabout city criminal lawyer. Several witnesses gave evidence for Tim, saying the other person was the aggressor and that Tim was forced to defend himself.

Witnesses on the other side gilded the lily, but Tim still expected to win. What he didn't know was that Thom was in cahoots with the magistrate, a man named Gillespie, who Tim believed was the best fixit man he ever saw in a court room, the most "versatile" said Tim. He thought Murray Farquhar, whom he would have dealings with later, was a babe in arms by comparison.

The case went against Tim. He was convicted and had to pay his own legal expenses and the other person's, also a fine plus compensation of about 5,000 pounds, for which his father came to the rescue. The magistrate also declared Tim's fists to be lethal weapons. It showed him how things were not what they seemed. And he began to change his thinking: It wasn't *what* you knew after all.

So, to soothe his mother's anguish and please her social inclinations, he concentrated more on packaging and modelling. He was very successful as a packaging consultant and could have made a permanent career of it, doing successful designs for numerous companies, including the Andronicus and Vittoria coffee people. He worked for various companies including Nugget Polish and had a coup for All Packs in the cigarette industry by convincing Rothmans of Pall Mall to change over to rotogravure printing, enabling them to set their printing much finer on packets.

In another success he put potato chip manufacturers into a new form of wrapping, an innovation still used today that gained all the Woolworths packaging business for his employer. People who knew him then described him as popular and likeable. Tim overdrew on his Nugget bank account one day and his city bank manager, Bob Elliott, in reminding him he was out of funds, found he was the politest person imaginable. "He apologised profusely for not buying me a drink, saying he was a teetotaller," said Bob.

But Tim's employers were using him more often to collect unpaid debts as part of his job. He was ideal for the task - big, loud and persistent. Also his reputation as a fighting man and his ability to handle shearers in the Riverina had spread. He was recalled from the city to settle a dispute out in the central west of New South Wales which was crippling graziers. Shearers were on strike over the width of cutting combs and some sheds were declared black.

He was asked to help by GBS Falkiner, of the famous Haddon Rig merino property at Warren. After sounding out the situation, Tim took a team of 10 heavies out with him to one of the shearing sheds and they belted the trouble-makers who were prolonging the strike. One incident never fully explained was how a man was wounded and fell out of a tree when one of Tim's men fired a shot. The ban was lifted in that area.

But it was as a model that Tim flourished best in the early '50s. He was the leading fashion and photographic model in the last few years before TV came in, modelling every type of male gear, including Akubra and Stetson hats, and featuring in the annual men's wear conventions at the Trocadero in Sydney.

Tim was also one of the first Chesty Bonds, a caricature of his swelling chest and chiselled jaw staring down from billboards around Sydney. He liked walking under one such impression of himself at Wynyard railway ramp. He modelled for all the major manufacturers and brands of the day, including Bond's Industries, Casben, Jantzen, Holeproof, Buffalo Bill products from A.L. Lindsay & Co, Pioneer Distributors, Alpha Knitwear, Katex Fashions, Casual Headwear, Paramount Shirt Co, Coca Cola and many others.

One day at the Trocadero, Vice Squad cops warned him about the prominence of his laughing gear out on the catwalk, telling him he'd have to wear a jock strap underneath his briefs or be arrested for indecency. He was the ideal male clothes horse, a perfect physical specimen, suntanned and good looking, perfect teeth and without a mark on him.

It antagonised others that being a fighter, he didn't have cauliflower ears or a broken nose. Some thought him a pansy and wanted to take him on. Being able to relate to all types, he had no trouble with the poofs in the industry but he had plenty of fights with blokes who thought him one. Call him a siss and it was on. In those times, knives or guns weren't used except by the hard criminal class. Disputes or insults were settled in the old traditional Australian way with fists.

Tim had his shoes hand-made like the American gangsters, and took a shoeshine each day in the Victoria Arcade or the Hotel Australia. A nifty dancer, he frequented the Trocadero while the dream dance palace was still a mecca for lovers and loners looking for fun. Tim was looking for girls. Whenever maestro Frank Coughlan saw him, he'd strike up his 15-piece band with *You Should Have Been in Pictures*.

His reputation as a ladies' man suffered a slight setback one night at the Troc at an artists and models ball. He showed interest in an athletic-looking girl and tried to arrange taking her out - only to find she was a female impersonator. For a lark at the same ball he pulled off the false tit worn by a transvestite and the fellow's mates jumped in to attack him, causing a lively scene at the side of the stage.

But the female models flocked around him. He was tall, handsome, fun to be with, seemed to know everyone and was well connected. He'd built up an image of being a really strong guy and the girls liked that. He was so presentable too.

Jericho's coffee lounge in Rowe Street was *the* meeting place in the centre of the city for the beautiful people. At any time there you'd find barristers, judges, models like Janice Wakely, Michelle Safargy, Jean Newington, Candy Mitchell, Tim and his dancing partner, model Dawn Diedrikson of the shapely tanned legs.

Janice Wakely, one of the leading models of the day - Vogue, David Jones - had exquisite features and was attractive in a chic way, not like a chocolate box blonde. She and Tim were mad about each other and had a long and passionate affair. Later she married a millionaire.

In those days Tim liked to keep himself in the best of company, a man about town who knew socialites and all the top retailers like David Lloyd Jones, the Mark Foys, Horderns. A Governor's daughter at one stage would be one with whom he had an affair, not of the vice-regal kind.

Tim only went out with beautiful women, mostly models. He loved the glamour of being around models who did high fashion or were in the top grade. In those more innocent days, models were held in greater esteem than today. His sexual success with them made him the envy of other men. One of his later girlfriends would be a young Maggie Tabberer, of whom he used to say she had the best boobs of any girl he ever took out.

One model told the story of how Tim would sometimes take a girl into a Hotel Australia lift, stop it in between floors for a time and emerge smiling broadly. Tim's mother found him in bed at their Mosman home or in the boatshed several times with a model. His mother was upset and called him a cad.

He tended to have long, lasting relationships with women and most were still glad to see him or ask for his help after they broke off. One top model from that period wrote to him after calling on him several years later: "Tim Darling, my sincere thanks for helping me when I really needed you, and I only hope when the next hurdle is over I will be able to show you my gratitude. As always..." That's the kind of promise men like to receive.

Another former model said: "It was always strawberries out of season and lots of attention when he was wooing a girl but after he'd won them, he could be a bit domineering. He was really a stalker, very determined in pursuing the women who took his fancy."

That was borne out by one top model who complained to police that Tim had forced his sexual attentions on her. But when they began inquiries with a view to charging him, she withdrew the complaint and the matter went no further.

Other models talking among themselves claimed that Tim had forced himself on them for sex. If he saw a beautiful woman, he would want her. He was really a sucker for glamorous women because he would do almost anything for them to have sex. When he had the urge, he would be soft, cuddly and charming. After winning a woman, he was more the male aggressor, eager to hunt in fresh fields.

But some glamorous women had a different appreciation of him. Jean Newington, a Model of the Year and an international star who made her fame and fortune with the Eileen Ford agency in New York, met Tim at Jericho's when she was very young. She pranced down the stairs in high heels and there was Tim, big and unavoidable. He reached out and firmly felt one of her boobs. She whacked him one in the kisser. There was silence as coffee cups were poised, knives and forks stopped. Then came Tim's deep rumbling laugh: "Ah, so you're a *good* girl, eh? What's your name?"

He evaluated women like that and respected Jean for her action. After that, Tim took it on himself to look after Jean in a brotherly way, making sure nobody was ever rude to her, although they never went out together or were lovers. Soon afterwards she entered a radio station beauty contest at the Sydney Town Hall, the result depending on audience applause. When Jean came out the noise was terrific - Tim had rounded up all the supporters he could find in and near the Hotel Australia, and marched them off to the Town Hall to clap and stamp their feet.

"He would do sweet things like that," Jean explained to me. "I wouldn't know anything about his prowess as a lover, but he was very nice and got to know people quite easily. If a girl brought up a subject and was troubled by something, Tim would say 'I'll fix that for you.'

"He was strong, intelligent, capable of doing everything and of course he had such a sense of humour you could talk to him about anything. He was possessive about the people he liked and I think that basically he always did try to help people. Always had a girl on the arm.

"I was being pestered by a man once and came home to find Tim sitting in my garden at Woollahra. He said he thought he'd call and get rid of the fellow if he was still giving me trouble. He knew how to charm people. Women were attracted to Tim I think because they felt protected by him, that this wonderful big brother would protect them. That was a strong part of his character."

That was one point of view. Another was that women secretly desired to be taken, forcibly restrained and made love to, that there was nothing more pleasurable than the intimacy deriving from the tenderness in a tough guy. If that's what the ladies desired, they received it in ample measure from Tim. And in reality, very few who were romanced by him complained.

But with another "f" word, football, players didn't find him at all pleasurable.

4

COP THIS, MATE

GORDON on Sydney's North Shore was undefeated and leading the 1952 rugby competition and Easts were putting in the dirt. It was a niggling, spiteful game at Woollahra with East players like Perce Newton dishing out the rough stuff in rucks and mauls. Tim Bristow, the big fast Gordon forward, couldn't catch up with Newton, a smart footballer who made sure he kept out of Tim's way.

Came time for the traditional *God Save the King* over the PA system at game's end. All the players stood patriotically still, some with hands over hearts. The strains of the national anthem had hardly died away when Tim walked straight over to Newton and went whack on the chin, laying him out cold. The whistle had gone and the conservative officials controlling the game could do nothing. Bristow was the best get-square man in the game. And he'd wait a season to do it.

Gordon won the 1952 premiership and Tim was their goal kicker as well as ballistic missile. He could put the ball over from 10 metres beyond half way. Fans and players of the rah-rah game in the '50s and '60s regarded him as the roughest, toughest man to play in the code for at least 25 years. That opinion was picked up and reported in the *Daily Telegraph* by sportswriter Mike Gibson.

Tim knocking out Perce Newton was just one of hundreds of incidents in which Bristow figured. He was sent off and disciplined so many times it was hardly worth him continuing. Fans jumped the fence to attack him once and wives hit him with weapons for knocking out their husbands. He was described in the *Sydney Morning Herald* by a NSW Rugby Union delegate as "one of the mad dogs of football," and was suspended for the rest of the season.

In the end, they caught up with him, barring him for the delightfully-expressed offence of "over vigorous play." Yet, he only finished the rough stuff that others started. He was barred from the Rugby League competition too, but for a different reason.

Tim played his last game of rugby for Gordon at Chatswood Oval in 1963. When he applied for reinstatement on 14 July 1969, the Sydney Rugby Football Union refused, notifying him by letter that he still could not play in any matches or become a member of any affiliated club.

He was one of the unluckiest players in the game. The pity is that Tim was an outstanding player who should have represented Australia at both Union and League. Oldtimers still talk of the day he won a match for Gordon by kicking a last-minute goal from 15 metres beyond the halfway mark, right over the black dot. But his lack of discipline was his undoing.

In the view of many people Tim should have been in the 1952 Wallaby team to England and France. Most of the spots went to Gordon players and Tim, forced to play for Northern Suburbs the following year because of residential rules, scored 20 points against the champion Gordon side. He followed that up by being the top points scorer for three years running.

He moved around quite a bit playing for various clubs. Apart from Gordon and Norths, he also played for Easts and Randwick. He switched to League at times, representing Parramatta, Easts, Manly and North Sydney, the grand old club whose traditions went all the way back to the origins of League in Australia and boasted players like Cec Blinkhorn and Harold Horder.

He hardly trained and played for the fun of it, but was still good enough for the big time. Although his reputation and prejudice by officials were his enemies, he did dish it out, never taking a backward step.

Against University for Gordon one day, there were a series of pugilistic encounters (rugby players didn't "fight" but did plenty with their boots), and after Tim elbowed David Brockhoff in the face, sections of the crowd leapt on to University Oval screaming for his blood.

Then there was the donnybrook at Woollahra, Easts against Gordon again. Easts player Norm Storey described it to me as the most outrageous thing he ever saw on a football field when Bristow ran 25 metres to lay out and break the nose of Barry Tilley, later a great friend of Kerry Packer. In the ensuing melee, Tim knocked out eight opponents.

In the confusion, Gordon captain Arthur Summons, who later played League for Australia, sent Tim off - his own player - but was overruled by the coach and Tim came back on to be "second full-back" for the rest of the match. The referee, probably wisely, took no action.

As they came off, the hooker for Easts hid behind some seats and king hit Bristow as he passed by. Before Tim could get quits with the fellow he also encountered the wrath of Barry Tilley's wife, Pat, who vigorously laid into him with a golf club.

As *Sydney Morning Herald* rugby writer Greg Growden later explained in his column, the offending East's forward fled to the safety of his dressing room after landing the haymaker on Tim and was only able to leave several hours later surrounded by the entire Easts' first grade side, who escorted him past the still-waiting Bristow.

A club official put around the story that on the following Monday he sent Tim to a psychiatrist. Later in the day he asked: "Well Tim, are you mad?" Tim replied: "Don't know. I have to go back on Wednesday." Asked again later in the week for the diagnosis, Tim said drolly: "We'll never know - I didn't go back."

But as columnist Growden pointed out, there was a good side to Bristow which impressed the NSW Rugby Union because Tim often helped them out by refereeing schoolboys' matches. However, Tim unnerved the NSWRU staff when picking up his refereeing gear by placing his pistol on the table. He didn't need the pistol to safeguard his salesman's samples on the back seat of his car, his pet python did that.

In numerous other incidents Tim knocked out various players including Wallaby and Randwick's Nick Shehadie, also Col Windon. When forward "Jika" Travers, just back from Oxford to play for Norths and teach at his old Shore school, gratuitously lectured him as they came off the field one day telling him he'd be better if he didn't play the man, Tim said, "Cop this, mate," and clouted him. Peter Coleman, the leader of the NSW Parliamentary Opposition, was hit accidentally one day and the table he sat at was knocked over in a little mixup involving Tim on the sidelines.

Rugby was a more interesting and passionate game then, not marred by today's meticulous rules and technicalities which stop the action.

Frank Dockery, who played with and against Tim and was the all-time champion sportsman from Newington

College, gave this appraisal of Tim: "The unluckiest player of his time not to be picked in a Wallaby side for his country in 1952, and also the side chosen for South Africa in the early sixties.

"He was the fastest second rower I've ever seen in my life, as quick as any winger or centre of the time. He was unlucky because Gordon had such magnificent players, men like Bomber Miles, Snowy Norton and Brian Johnson, but they always picked Tim when a rough one was coming up.

"Unfortunately his reputation went before him. Blokes goaded and sledged him, trying to get him sent off. Fellows boasted that they'd hit Bristow on the chin, but in truth they wouldn't have lasted 10 seconds with him. He spoke his mind too, and you couldn't do that with Rugby Union officials.

"I remember Manly playing Gordon at Chatswood Oval one day and Tony Miller, who played for Australia, had laid out Snowy Norton with a massive punch on the top of his forehead. Snow was off, covered in blood and Tim was trying to get square with Tony, whom he'd played with at Shore. He caught Tony and flattened him.

"The linesman took a hand and ran in trying to hit Tim over the head with his wooden stick with the flag on top. Tim picked him up by the throat, threw him over the fence near the scoreboard and snapped the heavy stick over his knee. In a later match, Tony punched Tim on the head and much to Tim's amusement, broke his hand.

"Tim was tough but had a heart as big as the Harbour Bridge. Once you got into his heart, he was the best friend you could ever have. He'd go out of his way to help a friend and never asked for anything in return. In spite of what everyone said, I knew him since 1949 and regarded him as a lovely bloke."

Tim never started the sledging, having other more effective means of dealing with opponents. But as a private school boy, he was a champion when forced to retort. Modern day exponents of the art such as test cricketers making homosexual jibes or sex allegations against one another's wives, would be mere pikers by comparison. World sporting champs like John McEnroe would simply have been outclassed by Tim first go. One of his favourite opening gambits was to ask: "What festered arse did you drop from?"

His parents said they would never go to see him play because of his reputation, but they did and when some of the crowd began heckling him, Josie Bristow would barrack loudly for him.

Everyone knew Tim would never win an award for genteel play but the toffee-nosed officials didn't show much of the traditional spirit of the game either in the way they treated him at times. The NSWRU once disgracefully caused him to stand down from the Gordon side while they inquired into a false *anonymous* allegation that he had played Rugby League for Manly against the rules. Sports writers ridiculed them for reacting to an unknown fizz gig when it was obvious Bristow was a willing warrior whose presence in the Gordon pack was a source of annoyance and woe to his opponents.

Nor were some of Tim's own club officials without blame for petty behaviour. Tim was late getting on to the field for Gordon one day after misplacing one of his boots. Coach Bob "Captain Bligh" Davidson replaced him and punished him by refusing to let him go on until right near the end of the game, when a steamed-up Tim fell upon the opposition like an angry clansman.

For his non-selection in the team for South Africa, Tim always matter-of-factly blamed the Chief Justice of New South Wales, the Honourable Sir Leslie James Herron, KBE, CMG, K.St.J, who was chairman of the Australian and NSW Rugby Unions and representative on the International Rugby Board. When Tim's mother was dying at home of leukaemia at the early age of 50, on morphine with Tim giving blood to keep her alive, a female relative of Sir Leslie's regularly visited the house. Tim thought that with his mother's illness, she was showing too much attention to his father and he ticked her off. He later claimed to hear from a player who knew the Herrons that Sir Leslie was greatly offended by his action and held it against him. But Tim's reputation for unruly play was more likely to be the reason he missed out.

At the time of selection the Rugby writer Phil Tresidder said in the *Daily Telegraph* that Bristow would be in the team. And readers wrote in saying Australia needed tough, never-say-die forwards, especially against the All-Blacks, so why had they overlooked Gordon's Tim Bristow?

The reason why Bristow was barred from League has been largely lost in the mists of time but it had to do with Tim being rung in to play and also with betting. The betting was done by his friend, Hollywood George Edser, the colourful professional punter known as Holly who had the power of Nostradamus in knowing if Tim would miss a kick at goal (in reality, if Tim pulled up his socks or not before the kick).

Holly rang him in as "Tony Brown" for Parramatta in the main competition at the Sydney Sports Ground one day and Tim was spotted. How could they miss him? Tim was forced to make denials before the committee and scraped through, but it wasn't forgotten.

He was also rung in by Holly in social club games such as in Joe Taylor's Celebrity Club team, and was paid for his efforts. That's when unpleasant rumours began circulating of Hollywood betting on Tim's goal kicking, in the period just before the criminal George Freeman moved in with a system of tickets for organised betting on football games.

Later after his enforced retirement Tim would throw his energies into coaching kids' sub-district junior Rugby Union teams, with great success. When barred from the playing area for running on to the field to encourage his youngsters, the irrepressible Bristow simply did his coaching by walkie-talkie from nearby trees. He also formed and coached a rugby club in his area, revelling in the nickname he gave them, the Newport Nasties.

In the early '50s Bristow showed his all-round sporting ability by starring in surfing events. Fishing and catching sharks were all part of that skill.

Of course, there was still the regular knuckle jousts. Tim, soon after his days as a cop had ended, was beginning to spend some time around Kings Cross where he loved the bohemian atmosphere and nightclub scene, especially Abe Saffron's top Roosevelt club while the Liquor Royal Commission sat to clear up sly grog and to reform the State's liquor laws.

Tim was sitting in the Roosevelt enjoying *When I'm Smiling* sung by a friend called Larry Stellar when a patron who didn't want to hear the song caused a disturbance. One of the bouncers, "Twinkle Toes" Macreadie, backhanded the patron and a second bouncer, Alf Gallagher, joined in the melee. Wanting to hear the song, Tim stepped into the fracas and decked Gallagher and Macreadie, both good footballers.

Gallagher had also been professionally good enough as a boxer to fight Dave Sands for the Australian heavyweight title, when Sands held three Australian titles, also the British Commonwealth light heavyweight title and was natural contender for the world middleweight championship. Gallagher wanted it out with Bristow. Tim didn't want to breach his amateur status but ego was involved and news of the stoush travelled quickly, so he agreed to a city grudge match in the ring at out-of-the-way Grimes' Garage, then owned by newspaper proprietor Ezra Norton. Bristow won the fight.

Tim had been boxing and beating heavyweight ex-servicemen in the Collaroy clubhouse from the age of 15. He had also surfed competitively ever since joining the North Curl Curl club at the age of 8, vying with the men in open carnivals from 12 and taking part in Collaroy march pasts for which that club became renowned.

An all-rounder who excelled at everything, Tim showed great command of the water and anything to do with boats, skis, boards, swimming and diving, And he had no fear of the sea or sharks, feeling almost immune to them, although one day when a huge shark tried to capsize his canoe in Middle Harbour, he reluctantly dropped the fish trap he was trailing at the back of his canoe with its load of dead fish, to avoid an attack by the shark.

While a member of Bilgola surf club he helped a youngster by taking him out in a surf boat and showing him the basics of holding an oar when rowing - it was Stuart Mackenzie, who went on to be one of the world's greatest scullers, an Olympian, the first in history to win the single and doubles sculls at Henley and take six Diamond Scull titles in a row. Obviously Tim *must* have trained Stuart because he outraged Henley officials once by rowing in a bowler hat, another time stopping to adjust his cap and allowing his rival to catch up before powering off.

Apart from showing off generally, Tim had developed a reputation for flashiness by his fashionable gear and his obvious success with women, both in modelling and at the beach - an image well earned and justified. Representing Bilgola surf club at a carnival at Newport, he took great delight in winning the double event, the board and ski race, because Newport had refused him membership. And when officials of the Surf Life Saving Association presented him with the trophy, he embarrassed them by standing on the dais and throwing it to the girls. Other competitors considered it in poor taste.

He had wanted to join Newport to seduce a good-looking girl there but was barred after taking part in the club's championship without being a member. He'd rubbed it in by finishing so far ahead he was sitting on the beach as the next competitor rounded the last buoy. In those days of keen competition it was considered an honour to represent a club.

To add to his image as a flamboyant lair he would borrow his Lebanese friend Freddie Baddrum's car, just about the showiest in Australia at the time, a huge open Ellard Cadillac like Elvis's later pink Caddy but tangerine in colour with twin exhausts and twin carbies that roared like an aeroplane when given the gas. As Tim turned up at a beach with it, the girls would just about swoon. Then he'd pack as many girls as he could into it and tour the beaches, radio music blaring.

Tim's growing surf profile won him a role in a film shot in Sydney, *Long John Silver,* starring Robert Newton and Rod Taylor. Tim with his deep gruff voice was the chief pirate in charge of the long boats. He and Rod Taylor competed off-screen for girls.

Tim's reputation as a fearless, powerful surfer was spreading up and down the coast. Although not competing, he took the buoys out and set them for three northern beaches carnivals when the clubs could not get the boats out to do it in heavy seas. In one case, conditions were so bad nobody could finish the course. He'd do exceptional things like that but hated the drudgery of normal training.

He was always first into the water when a rescue was needed, noted for just dropping his shorts on the beach and plunging in naked. Tim pulled off many brave rescues, including one later regarded as the longest and most difficult in Australian surf history when he was 39, for which he would receive an award for outstanding bravery.

Before that, in the period of the early to mid '50s, a written club tribute was paid to Tim by fellow surfer Ross Renwick, who described his fight to survive after a big wave dislocated a shoulder while he competed in a board race in heavy seas at Warriewood Beach.

Unable to swim or hold on, Ross stepped off his board and hoped for the best, barely able to keep his head up high enough to breathe. Worse, he was circled by a shark. The carnival had been cancelled and officials launched surfboats in a vain rescue attempt.

"Eventually," he wrote in a club circular, "Tim Bristow reached me on a fast double ski and dragged me on to the front of his ski, causing me considerable pain, also great relief. Tim was a reliable man in a big surf and when you think you're going to die, Tim's face is a good one to see..."

A keen topic of conversation in club circles was how Tim could be so good without doing the ordinary training? But he had powerful arms and shoulders, strong knees, a fantastic surf sense and knowledge of currents.

Surfing was gaining in popularity as a sport. With better living standards, more people were able to buy cars, especially the newly-produced Holden, and sponsors were taking an interest. On winning a board event at a Peninsula carnival, Tim was presented with his trophy by Douglas "Tin Legs" Bader of Battle of Britain fame, visiting Sydney with author Paul Brickhill to promote Paul's book on Bader, *Reach for the Sky*.

Bill McCall, an executive of Coca Cola Export Co., introduced himself and offered Tim a contract to feature in the company's advertising, making him the first sponsored surfer in Australia. In future his surfboard would be dominated by a big coke bottle design. He also promoted the product on billboards.

Having just recently got married, to Judy Pointing, a glamorous young model and all-round nice girl who was a member of the wealthy T.A. Field meat industry family, Tim gladly accepted because he needed the extra income.

The Coca Cola company then promoted an international competition for board and ski racing to be held in Sydney, billed as the world championship. From that would grow the Coca Cola Classic, recognised as the world championship until new forms of competition took over. The only formal training Tim did for the big event was to go fishing - by paddling his board and surf ski for hours with the fishing line in his mouth and the cork tucked into his costume. That was the Bristow method of combining trawling and fitness, and he caught some beauties. Young fellows of the future like Midget Farrelly admired his skills and talked about them around the clubs.

The boards Tim and other Australians rode, unlike the lighter polyester ones of later years, were harder to handle then. They were made of solid oregon timber, 16 to 18 feet long. His surf ski was up to 30 feet long, and his costume shoulder length.

An international cast assembled in Sydney for the contest, from Hawaii, California, South Africa, England and Ceylon. The Americans were regarded as the hot-shots because they had surfboard events in California, paddling 26 miles to Catalina Island. The star and supposed world champion was Tommy Zahn, who dined out on the fact that he'd been in the same drama class as a young Marilyn Monroe and had been her first boyfriend. He'd won the Catalina race twice. The Americans introduced short boards for demonstration purposes but used long boards for the competition. These long boards were made of lighter material than the Australian boards.

In the American team was Buzzy Trent, the first man to surf Hawaii's Makaha and Waimea Bays, and Greg Noll, the first man to surf the giant waves of Pipeline. Another was Hobie Alter, then talking about designing a catamaran that could "surf," later called the popular Hobie cat.

In the first event for boards and skis at South Maroubra, Zahn turned up with a board even longer than Tim's, a colourful affair decorated with white stripes, but much lighter in design, and announced he would ride it Hawaiian style, prone or lying down. The sea was big and Zahn only got as far as the sandbar where his board disintegrated as it was pounded by the surf. To the crowd's amazement, Tim was around the three-buoy course and back on the beach almost before the Americans had worked their way through the line of breakers.

Many said it was a fluke and the publicity drew a big crowd for the second event the following Sunday on the Peninsula at Avalon, a beach that tests surfers because in a big sea it has a long wave and a heavy bank at low tide. The seas were up, making it dangerous, with rips at the south end strong enough to almost stop a speedboat.

When Tim arrived on the beach with the other Australian surfers, Serge Denman and Max Watts, the crowd heckled him good naturedly because of the coke bottle ad on his board and ski. Tim won that event too, after Tommy Zahn's board again smashed to pieces. That made Tim rightfully the world board and ski champion. He was in his prime. The Americans achieved one thing though, causing a revolution in Australian surfing - short boards were in.

With the 1956 Melbourne Olympics coming up, Tim decided to give boxing one more shot. The *Daily Mirror* was sponsoring a talent quest in association with the NSW Amateur Boxing and Wrestling Association to find boxers to represent Australia at the Games.

Tim fired in his entry form to quest director Ken Archer, the *Mirror* boxing writer, and the publicity buildup began for the city versus country fights, to be held at the old Sydney Stadium at Rushcutters Bay. The newspaper billed him as "Terrible Tim," describing him in its first article as the wild boy of the North Shore who would rather fight than eat.

"Once," said *The Mirror*," In a street brawl when Tim went to the aid of a man beset by a gang of hooligans, the wild boy from the North Shore flattened 15. Out of a welter of bloody noses, blackened eyes and torn clothing, 'Terrible Tim' emerged unconquered. He has been variously wool valuer, beach inspector, cane cutter, snake catcher, crocodile shooter, seaman on a pearling lugger, professional fisherman, policeman and is now a company representative. Somewhere in 'Terrible Tim's' nature is the irresistible urge to fight..."

He knocked out all his opponents quickly, including the "Man from Snowy River," Frank Negvassy, finishing up winner of the NSW heavyweight division. Officials presented him with a watch in the famous Stadium ring, where Australia's greatest boxers had thrilled fans over the years - and as a boy at ringside with his father he'd seen the epic Stadium bouts between Ron Richards and Fred Henneberry.

One newspaper story describing him as "Terrible Tim the renowned Northern Suburbs Rugby Union forward," said he was the biggest man to be seen in an Australian ring. He stripped at 17½ stone. The official souvenir programme showing all the finalists, signed by secretary Arthur Tunstall, had this to say: "Tim Bristow - from Mosman. Has won all his eliminations in the first round by KOs. Good Olympic prospect."

Then, to give the fans extra for their money and put the issue beyond doubt, Bristow was to fight an inter-services champion to decide who would be the heavyweight to go to the Games. Tim was at the dynamite short odds of 4/1 on to win.

At that stage Hollywood George Edser, the big betting man, put a proposition to him. As a result, to the big crowd's shock, "Terrible Tim" went down for the count in the second round with hardly a blow landed on him. He'd taken a dive. The only "fight" he'd ever lose. Hollywood had arranged some big bets, one with keen boxing fan Ezra Norton, owner of *The Mirror*, and cleaned up nicely.

Back in the showers Bristow took it out on his opponent for the shame he felt when the fellow said: "I didn't think you'd be so easy," biffing him several times. The usual fairweather friends didn't go to his dressing room. Nobody did, except his father. Tim made no reply when Charles

Bristow, puffing on his pipe, said acidly: "That was the lowest thing I've ever seen." He didn't speak to Tim for at least a month. No heavyweight went to the Games. A golden opportunity, a cherished dream was dashed. Who knows? - if Tim had gone, he might have had the chance later instead of Tony Madigan against Cassius Clay.

His only excuse was he needed the money. Tim's thinking had been shattered because his first son had recently died of a congenital heart ailment after living for only nine days. He was renting a dream home at Beauty Point above The Spit on Middle Harbour and was hoping to buy it to please his bride. But he had invested the money he saved towards the home in a business venture run by his partner. His partner went bust and he lost the money. Unable to buy the home, he was due to move out soon because another person had bought it.

For throwing the fight, he was paid 5,000 pounds by Hollywood George, which enabled him to buy a home at Newport.

By accepting the payoff, Tim had proved that the "bile and guile" theory to stimulate the economy, explained to him by Vice Squad cop Ron Walden several years before, was well and truly alive.

5

"EARTHQUAKE'S" LIVERPOOL KISSES

THE Newport Arms is a famous picturesque family hotel in a unique setting on the shores of that superb Sydney inlet of Pittwater. Here on the lovely semi-tropical waterway, yachting is a favourite sport, with hundreds of boats riding jauntily at anchor. The elevated green suburbs overlooking the peaceful blue scene with their forest of native trees and prodigious bird and animal life are among Sydney's most desirable addresses.

From 1800 when first built, the hotel had the reputation as a hangout for bushrangers and smugglers but it was also noted for opening up the beautiful natural northern beaches of Sydney, partly known as the Peninsula. In 1881 it was considered eminent enough to host a visit by Princes Albert and George (later George V), after a wagonette trip to Newport from Manly.

In the late 1950s, The Arms was still the only hotel on the Peninsula and would gain renewed fame for another reason - its colourful bouncer, Big Tim Bristow. In summer and winter The Arms with its indoor and garden bars was often packed with sportsmen, footballers and their fans and surfers from the various carnivals from Collaroy to Palm Beach. It was the place to go for a yarn and a beer, a happy meeting place with music. But, as some also thought, the spot for a fight.

The Ryan family first employed Tim as a manager and guard but his job was really to maintain order and see that the patrons left on closing time. Some objected to any form of restraint and fights were frequent. Bristow quickly showed that violence and hooliganism would not be tolerated. He threw troublemakers out after a warning and drinkers ganged up on him. In the football season fellows who fancied themselves as fighters came to the hotel to test themselves against him, bouncers from King Cross as well. Surfers from other areas attending a Peninsula carnival would call in to have a look at this man with the reputation, many to try themselves out.

Some would just throw glasses against a wall to start a fight. He would ask them politely twice to pick up the pieces, then: "If you don't, you'll pick it up in your teeth." That was it. If they didn't comply, he biffed them and threw them out. Tim dealt with all comers using what he called his hard head and a lack of superstition, even the Bandido bikie gangs who carried chains when their fists weren't good enough, or with other gangs from out of town. The locals supported his efforts to keep the peace and some gave him a hand when he was under siege.

Former boxer Keith Dudley, a three-division amateur champion of Victoria, often pitched in to help. Tim would say: "You whack 'em and I'll stack 'em," and Keith would reply, "No, the other way about."

At times when he knew a fight was developing, he would call his brother Max to assist. If Max was reluctant, Tim would say: "Are you my brother or not?' Max always supported him, often returning home with torn clothing. If Tim had a cut or injury, he couldn't show weakness by bandaging it because that would have encouraged someone to have a go at him.

The stories of his fights there are legion. Peninsula folklore has it that Tim was flattened one day by Tony Madigan, the light heavyweight Olympian who fought eventual gold medallist Cassius Clay (later Muhammad Ali) to a tight finish in Rome in 1960. Some blokes claim to have been present. Well, it never happened. They never fought. Keith Dudley and Max Bristow are just two of dozens who refute the rumour.

At the hotel Tim stood by his mates at all times. Once, when expecting big trouble from tough gangs, he hired several big surfers to patrol the hotel grounds with him. At the end of the day he told the surfers the new owner of the hotel would not pay them because there had not been any trouble. They protested, saying they'd done their job. "All right, I think we should start something, don't you?" said Tim. They got paid.

Tim had several things going for him - fitness, strength, commitment and he didn't drink. Although he'd always taken alcohol lightly, mainly rum and coke, he was now called the Sarsaparilla Kid because that's all he drank. But when he started knocking out gangs of troublemakers, the nicknames Earthquake and Bruiser stuck.

He had two special grips which he'd learned from a heavyweight wrestler, a mate of Bumper Farrell's. One was an arm grip, using the heel of his left hand to hit and grip the other person's shoulder, bringing his arm up under the chin and grabbing the other free arm. Then he'd spin him around and waltz his head into a wall, knocking him out. A second grip enabled him to grab them from behind, pushing their head forward and immobilising their hands and arms.

It looked brutal, but something drastic was needed to counter the violence that broke out at times. He saved an off-duty police sergeant from being kicked to death there one day. It was never the time-honoured cry of "Time gentlemen, please" to close the bars down but rather Tim coming around with a larrikin grin calling out, "Last drinks or I'll knock 'em out of your hands."

He would have some stirring fights there over the next 10 years or so, including one against a group of rugby internationals. That started when Tim noticed a big former rugby forward whom he'd previously barred drinking with a group, one wearing a blazer from the then Wallaby team. He told the former player he was still barred.

"You don't tell me not to come here," said the footballer, crunching Tim on the jaw. Tim knocked him out and the fellow's backstops came at him. Using the big groggy bloke as a shield against those hitting from the side, he poleaxed them all, marching them out into the street one at a time. A friend of Tim's helped by ripping the Australian blazer worn by one of the footballers and pulling it over his head.

Frank Dockery, who had played rugby with Tim, was standing in the bar at the time having a quiet drink with the group when Tim suddenly clocked him. "He mistakenly thought I was there to help the others," said Frank, philosophically.

Tim was upset that his jumper, which his mother gave him, had been torn. He took Max with him to the nearby Clareville house where the footballers were staying for the weekend, some having their faces bathed, and called them out, but they stayed inside, avoiding further pugilistic mayhem.

As if that wasn't enough action for any man, Tim answered the challenge at a buck's party for Max soon after at the Anzac Memorial Club at Cammeray. It was a big do, casually-dressed blokes coming from everywhere and some of Max's mates thought it a good opportunity to get even with Tim for past indiscretions. Tim was dressed in a good suit so they ceremoniously poured a jug of beer over his head.

He took it calmly until they finished, then said "Righto fellers," and started thumping them. As if by magic others joined in, sliding about in the beer swill as food and the contents of glasses were thrown into the combat zone. Max was caught in a bind - should he help his best mates or his brother? Joe, the Norths Rugby Club chef who was doing the barbecue, was so frightened he locked himself in the kitchen with a meat cleaver and wouldn't come out.

It was an all-in bachelor show, like a stoush in an Irish pub, laughter and jibes mixed in with shouts and curses as knuckles hit home. A good time was had by all. Next day some fellows were still staggering around out the front of the club, as pissed as owls.

A little earlier while Max was still courting his future bride, Ann Bellmayne, a glamorous air hostess and daughter of a Macquarie Street specialist, a fellow tried to get under his guard and took her out. "I'll fix him, come with me," said Tim. He took the fellow into a park under threat of a hiding, stripped him naked and left him there.

The night before Max married Ann, Tim gave his brother a good thumping, apparently for old time's sake. Max copped it, taking evasive action without retaliating, knowing it would be far worse if he fought back. It was just another example of Tim's erratic behaviour. But on the wedding day, Tim was on his best manners as an usher.

Tim and Max were as different as the traditional chalk and cheese. By comparison, Max had lived up to his parents' expectations by becoming a wool buyer, exporting to Yorkshire, Japan, Italy and the United States, played first grade rugby for Northern Suburbs at 18 and later A grade tennis. On his father's advice, he would leave the wool trade to study paper wholesaling and marketing, becoming managing director of a privately-owned paper company. He enjoyed duplicate bridge, gardening and painting. To show his gratitude for a good life, he picked drunks up off the streets with St Vincent de Paul for three years and helped out at the Matthew Talbot hostel for the homeless.

Tim continued his bouncing, and stayed in modelling and packaging doing things like cigarette ads on Bondi Beach, partly because it pleased his mother, whom he loved dearly. But when she died in 1957, his attitude to life seemed to harden. One woman friend said she never saw him cry or be sad or melancholy after that. "His feelings seemed to switch off after his mother died," she said. That's when he wanted to break out, when he became a private eye.

He'd seen how the system worked, seen how he could make a quid by dealing with dishonest cops and corrupt politicians, knew how things were and how they could be manipulated. He also knew from the endemic rottenness he'd seen below the surface in the community that he would not survive as a gumshoe by being totally honest - a strain in itself for anyone wanting to succeed.

Already from his days at Shore he'd seen how the sons of the wealthiest and most influential parents were pandered to, how the wealthy had a different yardstick of values and standards to others. He'd seen this demonstrated too in the establishment circles his father had mixed in and in others he'd met through his own friends. Also, he genuinely liked to help people and saw he could do this as well as making himself a quid.

Often he would say in the future that the higher he went in society the lower the morals and ethics, and the bigger the skeletons. And the more larcenous and corrupt the attitudes.

The more money people had, the more they wanted. As a counterpoint to helping some of those people, he would also stand up against them for the underdog, often without charge.

A senior cop who did business with Tim, who understood the generous side of his character and knew him from the early days, had this to say about him for the record: "Tim would walk backwards from Sydney to Darwin to help someone. He always stood up for his mates. He was an Aussie larrikin who appreciated the tradition of mateship. Many are quick to put a bad side to him but the other side is that he did so many good turns for people it was unbelievable, and not for money, but just for the pleasure of helping someone."

His first day as a licensed private dick wasn't a copybook start. He already held a mercantile agent's licence enabling him to collect debts lawfully, but on receiving his private inquiry agent's licence he dropped into Chatswood detectives' office on the North Shore to thank them for their support. He offered a detective sergeant who lived near him a ride home.

On the way Tim stopped his car and said: "Just got to pop in here a moment to serve this summons." The cop waited and soon there were sounds of a scuffle followed by much shouting and screaming and Tim came out the front door with a man punching into him, two kids clinging to his back and a woman flaying him with a frying pan. The cop jumped out of Tim's car and caught a bus.

From day one Tim looked like a well-to-do gangster with the pin-striped suit, black homburg and burnished shoes. He didn't swear often but explained: "If you look like a shit carter, people think they can get you on the cheap."

He loved to affect a colourful Chicago image with a dry Australian sense of humour. On one of his first jobs as security man for the opening of Sydney's Wentworth Hotel, he bumped into an old mate, Keith Dudley, in the lift with several other hotel guests. "Not expecting any trouble are you?" Keith asked. "No, not when you've got one of these," said Tim, pulling out a .38 pistol and waving it around. The others drew back, pressing into the lift padding.

In the best networking tradition of private school boys, Tim already knew a lot of prominent people, but these would soon increase through the new owner of The Arms, a tough-minded Canadian Jew named Ben Cecchik. Tim quickly won his trust and confidence.

While that relationship was developing, Tim was building up his private eye's business, organising credit checks for clients like Jack Thorpe who owned Electronic Rentals, and Barry Tilley from the Joyce Mayne firm. He did fingerprint and other record checks, because if a fellow had "form" when renting or buying a TV set on credit, he was likely to shoot through with the set, same if out on remand. His fingerprint contact was Merv Wood, famous sculler and later Police Commissioner.

Tim helped people clear their records, like the taxation boss who had convictions for offensive behaviour and wanted to join the Masons. Some clients helped in kind, giving Tim information, enabling him to pressure people who had something to hide and were giving other clients a bad time. After a while, Tim could access information wherever it was stored, in social services, banks, electrical companies, retailers, major companies with hire purchase, anywhere. It was easier then in pre-computer days.

The secret in finding out about people's backgrounds from official records was always who Tim knew and how he could relate to them. He charged clients $4 a name for credit checks, putting thousands through and paying the cops and others out of that. He would boast later, in his colourful way, that he'd been bribing cops for 40 years, but he didn't seriously look upon it as bribery, nor did they as he once failed to understand. And he was earning more than the Police Commissioner.

Tim saw that aspect of his work as aiding justice, preventing theft and other crime from happening, stopping cheats and con men from getting a head start. He even had a different view of the cops now. Previously he could make no excuses for them, but now he saw they were seriously underpaid, obliged to deal with the worst people in the community while trying to clean up the community's dirty work and were abused and spat upon by criminals, while the press waited to pounce on them. But that opened an opportunity for Tim - without a badge - to get results while not subject to the same rules and regulations.

Ben Cecchik, the new Arms owner, was part of a syndicate which imported the first of the Bally poker machines into Australia which came, not from Chicago, but from Ireland. The original syndicate was a legitimate group of Sydney friends, among them CJ McKenzie, a good journalist mate of mine, also Keith Jennings and George Clampett. They famously went to Las Vegas to show how they could beat the bandits with a special grip of the pokie handle.

After that, in the mid-1960s, Bally in Chicago offered them the Australian franchise for their poker machines which they accepted. Cecchik, as a partner and financier with Tim as his minder, offered Tim an interest with him, but he hesitated. Sydney businessman Jack Rooklyn, who already had Bally pinballs in Asia, then staged a fightback and took over the franchise. But in the end it would prove a lucky disappointment for those who missed out, with allegations that Bally America was linked to the Mafia and Rooklyn being strongly criticised over those links by Justice Moffitt in his Royal Commission into organised crime in 1973-74.

It didn't matter to Bristow because he had already done well through Cecchik. One of Cecchik's friends, Al Rosen, a heavy gambler from Chicago, had fled to Sydney because his Chicago associates were about to send the boys around to collect his unpaid gambling debts.

But Rosen then ran into trouble in Sydney over gambling debts, owing money to a hotelier who had helped him out. Rosen also had a weakness for young girls. The hotelier set him up with a young girl and called in the Vice Squad. Sgt Ron Walden charged him with carnal knowledge, but he skipped the country before going to court and wasn't seen again.

Rosen had put Cecchik in touch with Lee Gordon, the outstanding American entrepreneur who introduced famous American entertainers to Sydney at the old Rushcutters Bay Stadium from the late 1950s. Gordon's enterprise heralded Sydney's golden age of entertainment and nightclub life in the next decade. Tim would be part of it after Cecchik introduced him to Gordon who hired him as a troubleshooter to look after his artists.

In the early to mid '60s, Gordon brought out Judy Garland and about 600 other legendary performers One of his first Stadium acts was Bob Hope and Betty Hutton, the crowd throwing eggs at them because they couldn't understand their American jokes.

A brilliant American from Los Angeles, Gordon had toured Elvis Presley in North America for Presley's manager, Colonel Parker. His one regret was never bringing Elvis to Australia. Eccentric, a hustler and a visionary wearing skin-tight pants, he staged shows by such names as Louis Armstrong, Sammy Davis, Sinatra, Gene Krupa, Crash Craddock, Chubby Checker, Johnnie Ray (who held the record for numbers of Stadium appearances), Wayne Newton, Nat King Cole, and just about everyone you could think of who was a star, even if some were a little faded. The old Stadium was then Sydney's only venue for a big crowd.

The two most elegant nightclubs were Chequers in Goulburn Street and the Silver Spade in the Chevron at the Cross. Sydney's movers and shakers gathered there to be seen and make contact cheek-by-jowl with the city's notorious and colourful characters in what was the most cosmopolitan atmosphere outside Royal Randwick racecourse - Eric O'Farrell, Lennie McPherson, Dr Reginald Stuart-Jones, Prime Minister John Gorton, the Police Commissioner, officials from the Pope's tour...

In Chequers, the Wong brothers featured acts like Shirley Bassey, Liza Minnelli, Kathryn Grayson, Nelson Eddy, Jane Russell, Esther Williams. Credit cards didn't exist then and lots of company accounts and blackmarket money were thrown around.

The strip clubs were big time in the Cross, places like the Pink Pussycat, Pink Panther, the Pigalle Club in Bayswater Road run by Lee Gordon, and other popular clubs the Tabou and the Paradise Room, also Crazy Horse and Staccato. Miss Subtle Sex was a negress who swung her boobs and Madam Lash was one of the strippers, as was Sandra Nelson (who went topless on a Bondi tram) with lesser lights Eurasian Sex Kitten and Sexy Sabra.

One of the characters Tim kept in touch with at the Cross was Wayne Martin, known as "Morals" or "Scandalous" Martin because of an incident at Palm Beach in the mid '50s when he and three other identities were charged by Bumper Farrell with scandalous conduct.

Wayne ran Saffron's Pink Pussycat with Last Card Louie Benedetto, so named by radio star Jack Davey when beaten by a last hand in Joe Taylor's Carlisle Club. Often when Wayne and Louie walked around the streets from the Pussycat, Louie would put 100 quid in various notes in different pockets and when those down on their luck came along he'd shake hands and leave a note in their hand.

Those charged with "Morals" Martin over the Palm Beach affair were Abe Saffron, hotel broker Max Murrell and caterer Hilton Kincaid. It was alleged that at Murrell's mansion, *Orcades*, in Whale Beach Road, they "openly outraged public decency by taking part in lewd, obscene and disgusting exhibitions."

Wayne was questioned by two of Tim's mates, Rocky Walden and Bumper Farrell. Rocky said: "Jesus Wayne, the girls have given you up - they've told us everything." Streetwise Wayne replied: "I don't know what you're talking about." While that was happening, Bumper was belting him with two phone books or punching him in the gut through one phone book so as not to leave a bruise.

Truth ran pages of the sensational evidence and pictures of the girls with blacked-out faces under the heading "Girls' Lurid Stories of Nude Sex Party." One girl, Jean, admitted to have intimately known 32 men in one night but denied she had led an immoral life. Witnesses described how men and girls allegedly stripped and committed acts of indecency, giving an insight into unsuspected goings-on in the Peninsula retreat of the rich and famous, known as "Palmie."

The newspaper didn't publish the nitty gritty of the case, involving the girls and the partaking of oysters by the men.

But a heavyweight battery of lawyers, including QCs Jack Shand and Jack Smyth, were able to show that the only person outraged was Bumper, who had to climb up on a garbage tin on tip toe to peer in the windows. The men were discharged.

Bumper could never get evidence of another well-known Palm Beach affair, a "daisy chain" of gays who met regularly from some of Sydney's most prominent families, including retailing and architecture circles. Tim knew them because they drank at The Arms. Homosexuality was then a morals offence.

The morals of some of the artists Tim and Wayne had to look after left a lot to be desired. Johnnie Ray injured a local gay while performing a sex act too forcibly and the fellow needed hospital treatment and wanted him charged. The cops went to Ray's room, saw champagne and glasses, broke a glass and said "Ray did it with this accidentally." Cleared, Ray appeared that night before 11,000 screaming fans at the Stadium.

Sinatra was as bad as his vulgar reputation dictated. One night, 20 minutes before going on stage to a full house, he ordered Wayne to summon Lee Gordon. Sinatra told Gordon he would not perform unless oral sex was arranged. In a panic Gordon gave Wayne some money and said "see if you can find someone."

He ran outside and saw a model he knew. Asked what she was doing, she said: "I'm selling programmes here because I'm hoping to meet Frankie." Wayne said: "Come with me, I'll introduce you." He did so, and seeing Sinatra sitting there in his specially reinforced underpants, he knew why he was called the King. Later during the show the model told Wayne: "You're to pick me up when you drop Mr Sinatra off at the hotel and take me to the Tabou where's he's coming to have supper."

Sinatra wanted to play baccarat so Tim took him to an illegal game run by Eli Rose and Perce Galea at a spot that later became the site of the Kings Cross police station.

Tim felt sorry for Judy Garland, an alcoholic who had to be high on drugs before performing, a victim of showbiz pressure. But Wayne Martin was adamant Lee Gordon was not responsible for bringing in drugs. He said the artists brought them in or obtained them from local musicians. Gordon, a millionaire who went broke three times staging his Sydney shows, didn't own a thing, leasing or renting everything and living only for the entertainment world. He died almost a pauper in a little pub in London.

Every time Tim went to the Cross he was likely to bump into various characters, among them Racoon Roy who always wore a fur coat, Two Storey Ted who robbed bedrooms on second floors, The Fox who was always sneaking around corners or George the Fibber. But it was still basically the innocent place he remembered as a cop in 1949.

Morals Martin would also prove there was substance in Rocky Walden's "bile and guile" theory to lubricate the economy. While in London he ran into two old Sydney pals, Sir Edward (Eddie) Valleous and Sir Ivan Markovics. Both had become knights of the oldest charity order in the world, the Knights of Malta. Valleous was a Greek businessman and Markovics, who claimed to be a doctor, had taken over Dr Stuart-Jones's abortion practice following his death in 1961, running it with Det Sgt Ray Kelly and standover man Dick Reilly. Markovics had left Sydney when abortion became a hot issue.

"Listen Wayne," said Eddie, "you know those big American stars Lee Gordon used to import? Would they be interested in donating money to charity? If so, we can get them knighthoods through the Vatican, back door. It's a papal thing, not from the Queen."

Wayne said he'd see what he could do when he went on to the States. He made some calls from there, contacting Markovics who had returned from London to his office in the United Nations building in New York, giving him home numbers for Sinatra, Ernest Borgnine and Sammy Davis Jnr.

The upshot was that home in Sydney again, Wayne received a call from Eddie Valleous in London telling him they had received $100,000 from each of the stars for a knighthood. But he said he would skim $25,000 from each of their donations to make up $75,000 for a knighthood for Wayne as well. Lovely, said Wayne. All the regalia duly arrived, the robes and medals, diplomatic passport, the lot, making "Morals" Martin a Knight of Malta. He had great fun on his travels, getting himself paged in hotel and casino lobbies as Sir Wayne to impress visiting friends.

Prior to him becoming minder to the stars, Tim Bristow as a new private eye didn't knock off when the whistle blew at five o'clock. Being successful quickly, he had so much work to do he often went around the clock. Sometimes he worked for several days without sleep.

In addition to all his inquiries, he was a nocturnal animal who kept up his social contacts, calling in at clubs and restaurants, checking, meeting friends, totally enmeshed in his work. There simply weren't enough hours in the day, or night. Often he would arrive home near dawn and find his phone ringing within the hour for the new day

He often felt he couldn't afford to sleep because people were paying to get results. To avoid mistakes, he was popping pills to keep awake. He was still affected by the heartache of his first son dying, although that had been nearly two years earlier, and he'd just been through the trauma of his mother dying. His concern for her in giving enormous amounts of blood had probably weakened his physical condition.

On top of those worries, his relationship with his wife was shaky. He had married Judy Pointing only two years before because he was attracted by her glamour and sophistication. He liked her shapely legs too after seeing her win a beach beauty pageant. Friends doubted that he really loved her as a person. His parents had been against him marrying Judy. Josie Bristow did not think any woman was good enough for her son. The parents also didn't think the marriage would last and refused to attend the wedding, held at trendy St Mark's at Darling Point on 6 February 1956.

Tim's line of work wasn't making him good marriage material at the best of times, but also Judy was emotionally churned up with stories from her friends in the fashion world that Tim was having affairs with other women.

In the wake of those troubles he had competed in a surf race at Bilgola in 1958, and won it. Then, trying to prove he was still as good as any of the younger fellows, he showed off by jumping on a board and going out to crack a few waves. Suddenly he felt unwell, had to be helped back in by a friend and collapsed on reaching the beach. Treated by a local doctor, he was unconscious for several days. Tim had had a stroke.

It left him with Bell's Palsy, paralysing the left side of his face, resulting from damage to the seventh cranial, or facial, nerve. Nobody was home there any more. It caused that side of his face to drop, leaving the once handsome features looking slightly deformed. It affected some other facial functions too, giving the impression he was deliberately talking out of the side of his mouth, like a gangster in the old movies.

Although he felt sensitive about losing his good looks, he tried to put a positive spin on the situation by joking about it, saying it was a great help. "People hit me on the numb side of my face and I can't feel a thing," he told everyone with a crooked grin which could be mistaken for a leer.

When hit there at times, he would laugh mockingly at his assailants, adding to his image of toughness. That was the side of his head he used when delivering Liverpool kisses to violent opponents at The Arms.

But he needed more than sheer toughness for some of the tricky work that lay ahead.

6

CELEBRITY RAIDS

NOTHING was calculated to cause more fear and loathing, anger and hatred or to create more enemies than the divorce raid.

The technique was all about catching errant husbands and wives with their pants down. The stakes were high. A husband caught in bed with another woman could lose half his wealth in a cash and property settlement. That was the law. Men were in jail all over Australia for being "wife starvers" - failing to pay alimony ordered by the courts.

Adultery was a ground for divorce in the '50s, '60s and early '70s under the *Matrimonial Causes Bill*. All you had to do was catch the guilty couple and obtain evidence through photos, confessions, observations or by listening devices. People's lives and reputations could be ruined by a visit to the Divorce Court. And the costs were crippling.

As a result, offenders went to great trouble to avoid detection and if caught, even greater pains to wriggle out of it. Many settled out of court to avoid the scandal of publicity. So a lot of cheating went on, in bed and out, by the hunted and their pursuers. And on the other side of the coin, some couples anxious for a speedy divorce, even engaged private inquiry agents to stage apparent adultery scenes, photographed with bogus lovers to obtain a quick settlement.

But when a private eye dropped in at an inconvenient moment, the Adonis often came out fighting or even shooting - which is why Tim Bristow was the king of the divorce raiders, being tough, fearless and efficient. He was shot in the skull while bursting into an apartment at Darling Point one night, was attacked with knives and other weapons and charged with assault several times. On every raid he was likely to be charged with assault or causing malicious damage to a door. So he employed off-duty police to accompany him as a leverage against the arresting cops who may be called to the scene.

Often he had to restrain his client who wanted to pull the head off the male fornicator. Tim employed all sorts of methods to meet the various situations, but usually he just burst in with a photographer and a witness or two. To do so at the wrong time opened him up to charges at once, so he had to be spot on with his team's leadup surveillance before making a raid. As technology improved, he used listening devices and waited for the sound of rhythmical movement before moving in.

His methods were not always brushed with the thin veneer of legality. Hotels didn't like their name damaged by having doors kicked in, so Tim bribed staff to tell him when to move. He had such a primal quality about him that lovers were mostly intimidated by his physical presence and did what he ordered. If told to get back into bed so a picture could be taken, many did so for fear of what might happen if they refused.

He didn't particularly like that kind of work, publicly advocating divorce law reform, but it was the law and he had a wronged client to represent. He hated to see the manipulation that went on in the courts, with some lawyers manoeuvring to gain advantages by appearing before certain judges. He saw that as collusion and corruption. And he didn't like to see the wide disparity ordered in alimony amounts.

While one or two judges sneered at him for being a keyhole operator, most judges in the Divorce Court smiled or actually laughed at the pictures of startled lovers he presented from the witness box in contested cases. They pored over the shots. Mr Justice Dovey, the Judge in Divorce, was an old perv and often asked witnesses to repeat juicy bits of evidence to bring out every salacious feature of the divorce raid. His Honour, a pompous man, hated private eyes but he would lean forward on the bench and look alert when the pervy bits came out.

When Tim gave divorce evidence he never lost a case because he was always on top of the facts, even if a little persuasion had been used. Jim Hulbert, a private eye who worked with Tim in divorce and other jobs in those early days, said of him: "Jesus, he was a hard man, as in a tough bastard. He would never back off. Many examples are unmentionable.

"If there was ever an argument, you'd have to be on Tim's side, never against him. He was a forgiving sort of person, but if you mouthed off, you'd be knocked arse over head very quickly. That's the simplest way to put it. He was that sort of bloke. I would have hated being one of those blokes behind the doors he kicked in who wanted to fight him because rest assured, they'd finish up on their arse.

"Repossessing goods had to be done the hard way without much help from the law. If there was a dispute, Tim would be there, fronting up. Someone would shape up and I'd close my eyes. Next thing, they'd be knocked arse over head, Tim still standing there. Didn't matter who or how many. He wasn't a thug but a renowned heavy."

Divorce work was competitive and costly because it often took a long time to target co-respondents. Some suspected *femme fatales* turned out to be blokes who were regarded then as closet poofs. For 20 years Tim made raids all over Australia and in many other countries. He did the celebrities, the TV and radio stars, entertainers and big businessmen, the daughters of judges.

One that nobody else would dared have taken on was a raid on Warwick Fairfax and the former Mary Symonds, wife of leading Sydney lawyer, Cedric Symonds. Warwick was chairman of John Fairfax Limited, publisher of the *Sydney Morning Herald* and, as a member of the ruling class, one of the most powerful men in the nation, capable of causing grief to a private eye. Only a man of fearless temperament would poke his nose into the private lives of such potent people, busting into what was the heart of the establishment. Fairfax had inherited a million pounds, control of the *Herald*, more than 100 years of newspaper tradition and 500 years of family tradition. Heritage and trusteeship had been the main influences in his life.

Previously Warwick's first wife, attractive, titian-haired-Betty Fairfax, had divorced him in 1945 when he left the marital home, moved two doors away and refused to obey a court order to return to her. Around this time Warwick had a passionate affair with a voluptuous Russian ballerina, Madame Helena Kirsova, building a Sydney home for her on the waterfront at Clifton Gardens.

He was one of the most private and retiring men in the land, yet his relationship with Mary Symonds made flaring headlines - not in the *Herald* or in Frank Packer's *Telegraph* but in *Truth* and the *Daily Mirror* owned by renegade publisher Ezra Norton.

Late one night Tim and a couple of his boys climbed over a neighbour's fence and raided *Fairwater,* the baronial two-storied late Victorian Fairfax mansion overlooking extensive gardens at Double Bay. The raid would touch off a crisis later in the Fairfax boardroom in 1961.

The background began in 1957 when Warwick Fairfax and his second wife, Hanne Fairfax, had become friendly with Cedric Symonds and his wife, Mary. As described in evidence in the Divorce Court before Mr Justice Dovey, the Symondses had a dispute while Mrs Fairfax was overseas and Mary left the marital home to stay with her father.

Cedric Symonds divorced his wife in August 1958 for her failure to comply with an order for restitution of conjugal rights. Some months later Mrs Hanne Fairfax obtained a divorce from Warwick on the same ground. That one made the headlines. A young lawyer in Warwick's team was Gough Whitlam appearing before his father-in-law, Mr Justice Dovey.

The most intimate details from both marriages were read to the court as evidence in letters exchanged between Warwick and his wife while she was away in Europe in 1957-58. In one, Warwick referred to Symonds flying into a jealous rage because of Warwick's friendship with Mary Symonds. Mary had left him, afraid for her life.

Warwick wrote of Symonds: "He is a neurotic and unbalanced person and some years ago tried to kill himself with an overdose of sedatives. Finding that Mary was friendly enough with me was enough to put him into a jealous rage in one of which he tried to kill her by strangling her with a scarf."

Other letters were read, referring to the tender feelings Warwick and his wife had for each other. In one Mrs Fairfax referred to gossip she had heard but Warwick told her it wasn't true. In another, Warwick wrote: "My dearest Hanne, you have sent me a very sweet and loving letter and it means more to me than I can say..."

And again: "Well, darling, it is very hard to say what I feel in writing, except that I have never forgotten what we meant to each other and the good times we had together, and maybe we don't know how much we feel or how much we can do till we try..." Then, while still abroad visiting her parents, Mrs Fairfax received the biggest bombshell from faraway Sydney - a note from Warwick telling her it was all over, that he could not take up married life with her again. The day was 5 February 1958.

Mrs Fairfax told the judge she did not think her husband was guilty of impropriety with Mary Symonds. Justice Dovey ordered Warwick to return to his wife within 21 days.

All editions of the *Mirror* ran columns of it, *Truth* gave it a double page spread, the *Sun* buried a small paragraph on page 7, Packer's *Telegraphs* suppressed it and the *Herald* ran it for those with keen eyesight as a small paragraph on page 11 in the least noticeable heading typeface, placed under four other items on irrigation, onion and pumpkin prices, real estate and betting fines. When the order was not obeyed, the judge granted Mrs Fairfax a *decree nisi* for divorce.

Sometime in this period Tim and his boys burst into *Fairwater* and Warwick and Mary were found together but apparently not *in flagrante*. Pictures were taken and the details from that raid encouraged Symonds to issue a Supreme Court writ against Warwick Fairfax in February 1959 alleging that Warwick had induced Mrs Symonds to leave him. And he claimed 100,000 pounds in damages.

Warwick and the former Mary Symonds were married at *Barford*, his Bellevue Hill home, soon after midnight on 4 July 1959. But the impending writ, which took some time to develop, caused serious strife in the Fairfax boardroom. The dire situation brought about by the Bristow raid, was referred to obliquely by Gavin Souter in his authoritative history of John Fairfax Limited, *Company of Heralds*. Souter wrote:

"As the time for Cedric Symonds's suit grew nearer, it came to the company's knowledge that Symonds was proposing to make allegations and call evidence which might reflect adversely upon the chairman and consequently also upon the company.

"By that time Warwick and Mary Fairfax had been married for 18 months and had a son born on 2 December 1960. Symonds had also remarried in October 1960. Fairfax's own view was that Symonds's chances of success were not great and that at an appropriate time a settlement could be effected.

"Henderson [managing director] discussed the suit with McLachlan, James Fairfax and Vincent Fairfax, and decided with them that until the matter was concluded satisfactorily, Warwick Fairfax should cease to be chairman and Henderson should take his place.

"When he conveyed their decision to the chairman on 5 January 1961, Fairfax reacted with an angry sense of betrayal. He called James into his office and in the course of a very heated discussion accused James of betraying him and alleged that Henderson was using the situation in order to advance his own position..."

The crisis came to a head on 13 January 1961 with Warwick forced to resign "for private and personal reasons," the board accepting his resignation "with regret." Warwick remained on the board, although he refused to attend meetings. However, the Symonds proceedings didn't see the light of day because Warwick settled out of court for what was generally believed in legal circles to be 90,000 pounds, a fortune at the time. This would have a sequel in the ill-fated 1987 bid by young Warwick Fairfax, son of Warwick and Mary, to seize control of the Fairfax empire in revenge for Warwick (later Sir) being voted off the Fairfax board, causing the long Fairfax proprietorship of the *Herald* to end abruptly.

With successful cases like that under his belt, Bristow quickly developed a reputation for delivering results and would soon have the biggest private eye divorce operation in Australia. Ted France was the main solicitor referring cases to him but clients also rang him directly. He sometimes did as many as eight divorce raids a night and had 20 operatives under him.

As an aftermath of the *Fairwater* raid, Warwick was paranoid about eavesdropping devices and phone tapping. One of Tim's friends and co-operators, "Tropical John" Petford, was regularly called in to debug the *Barford* and *Fairwater* residences, Sir Warwick's office in Hunter Street in the city and also their home in the Blue Mountains.

Mary Fairfax, born Mary Wein in Warsaw, had arrived from Poland with her parents to be educated at the Presbyterian Ladies College and Sydney University. She was informal and effusive, far different from the generations of Fairfax women who preceded her. As Lady Mary, she gave Sir Warwick a new lease of life and would become one of Sydney's best known and wealthiest women, a generous charity donor and the hostess with the mostest.

Sydney was always a city that loved its horse racing. The 1959 AJC Spring Carnival at Randwick had been well up to standard as a spectacle - big crowd, sparkling track, brilliant day and lots of money flowing in and out of the bookies' bags.

The bookies had a good day on Saturday the first day of the carnival with Noholme winning the Epsom Handicap, and their bags were stashed with cash. As usual many bookies completed their tax sheets and stowed their bags under lock and key in various lockers in City Tattersalls Club in Pitt Street where some of the settling with credit punters customarily took place the following Tuesday after the carnival.

But when the bookmakers called at the club on Monday morning to retrieve their bags for the Metropolitan Handicap meeting, they were dismayed to find that the unthinkable had occurred - they'd been robbed. The cupboards were bare in a robbery so daring they were left stunned.

Shocked officials of the venerable old club were reluctant to call in the CIB and bookmakers weren't keen either. Nothing like this had ever happened and officials didn't want the solid reputation of their club tarnished by the news becoming public. And the bookies didn't want their takings put under investigation. No telling where it might end.

Cool thinking soon replaced the bookies' anger and frustration as they borrowed from other fielders to carry them over for Monday's racing. Jockey Club committee men, some of them among the richest and most influential men in the State, did not want to see the image of racing brought into disrepute either, so it was generally agreed to keep the incident under wraps to avoid ridicule and scandal.

The police were never officially called in although numerous unofficial inquires were held. But the culprit was never officially identified. Not even a solitary fingerprint was left behind. However, the robbery was of such magnitude that it was impossible to keep it confidential, and gradually news of it leaked out at the track and in sporting circles.

Something like 250,000 pounds had been ripped off, then Australia's biggest heist.

Bristow knew one of the committee men who briefed him on the theft and asked him to make a few discreet inquiries. The person who had planned the scam so meticulously had obviously enlisted the aid of a professional burglar and somehow obtained a key to the safe deposit room, obviously with some inside help. After the club shut at midnight following a quiet Sunday's trading, the thief entered the room and using keys to the lockers, rifled the bookies' bags.

It didn't take Bristow long to pinpoint the man who planned it. He learned that the organiser had obtained soap imprints of the bookies' keys while they swam at Neilsen Park in the eastern suburbs.

Once he knew that, he followed the trail to his old betting mate, Hollywood George Edser with whom he had played handball at Neilsen Park. He was convinced of it. Hollywood never admitted it, knowing how to hold his guard up, but Bristow joked with him about it. He knew that as a colossal punter up one minute, down the next, Hollywood took the view that the bookmakers owed him plenty and he was getting some of his own back. Besides, Hollywood had a lovely wife and family and Tim didn't intend causing them any undeserved anguish. He carried the secret with him and mentioned it to close friends only after Hollywood died.

A few months after the great bookie robbery at City Tatts, Tim was out with Hollywood and his wife the night he met Ava Gardner in the Silver Spade nightclub at the Kings Cross Chevron. She was in town for the filming of *On the Beach*. He simply had to have Ava, one of the world's most beautiful women who became a star from the cotton fields in Grabtown, North Carolina, and later ended up married to Mickey Rooney, Artie Shaw and Frank Sinatra.

Turning on the charm, Tim had a one-night stand with Ava in the Macquarie Street apartment of his friend, Freddie Baddrum. She was a live one sexually, but having a full diary of ladies at the time he passed her over to a mate, Jackie "The Crooner" King, a doorman at Prince's nightclub, to look after.

Always unfailingly courteous to women when out socially by standing when they stood and pulling out their chairs to seat them, Tim was thrown off by Ava's crudity at their only meeting. He'd mixed with all types but had never met anyone with so filthy a tongue, using all the swear words in the book. When with Tim at the Silver Spade she told one fellow, "Cross your legs, your breath smells," and to another who was balding, she told him he needed a zom, explaining it was a wig for a bald ——, referring to a woman's private parts. But he admired her for not being a kiss and tell type.

At the time Tim had a girlfriend, Elle Body, his favourite pinup girl whom he regarded as more beautiful than Ava. Older than Tim, she was temporarily parted from her husband, Ted Body, who owned Bundemar Stud at Trangie in central western New South Wales. Her family, the Moses, were socially connected with the Packers.

At one stage when Ted Body came to Sydney and was pestering Elle to return to him, Tim gave him a hiding, put him in a hire car and said to the driver, "Take him to Trangie." He was so infatuated with Elle that after she died, he sentimentally arranged through Body's second wife to take possession of Elle's double bed, which he would sleep on always.

With women, Tim believed in the principle of *droit de seigneur*, literally the right of the master, as in the right of the feudal lord of the manor to deflower the virgins on his lands before they were married. This translated into having a head wife but with freedom to have multiple affairs at the same time, like a bull elephant or bull moose on the loose. He could never be with just one person.

Complementing his charm and handsome appearance, Tim's private schoolboy manners with parents, especially mothers, were superb - "What a lovely dog you have there..." All the women he bedded knew he was an incorrigible player and strangely most loved it, or at least tolerated it - perhaps a reflection of their own rebelliousness. He could be jealous of a friend who came to the beach with a beautiful woman and would become overbearing towards him, wanting to wrestle him to show his superiority. He always wanted to show he was the best, and that meant "tooling" as many women as possible and boasting about it.

There was no doubt he loved his mother, an emotion that had no affinity with sex. But some of the more thoughtful of his lovers speculated in conversation that with his women he could not distinguish between sex and love. They thought he might have loved his stunning first wife Judy, who was eight years younger than him.

While he continued his divorce raids on other unfaithful men, his relationship with Judy would be put fully to the test.

7

RAIDING CLOSE TO HOME

THE war over Sydney suburban newspapers between the Packers, Fairfaxes and "boy publisher" Rupert Murdoch in the early '60s was as exciting and violent as anything that happened in the pitched battles for tabloid circulation in Chicago, as highlighted to some extent in Ben Hecht's film *Front Page*.

Right up there with the best of them was the battle for the Anglican Press printing plant when a combined force representing Packer and Fairfax clashed violently with roughnecks from the Murdoch camp.

Bristow was called in by *Telegraph* owner Sir Frank Packer at the last minute to see what was happening to his sons, Clyde and Kerry, caught up in the thick of the fight. The punching, kicking and wielding of wrenches and lumps of timber were over when he got there, but he was able to calm some murderous tempers.

Tim was a good friend of Clyde, Sir Frank's eldest son, being groomed to take over the Packer publishing and TV empire. They often dined together at Beppi's upmarket restaurant in east Sydney. Clyde knew Tim so well he rang him one evening to remove an uninvited knight's son who gatecrashed a party at Clyde's home.

Clyde had joined Tim at a David Jones' fashion show one night where two top French mannequins paraded Dior garments. That night, encouraged by a businessman who put on a party for the models at his luxury Elizabeth Bay townhouse, Tim - to use his popular phrase - tooled one of the mannequins in the bedroom while the party giver, a voyeur, peeped through the window by arrangement with Tim.

Next day Clyde took the models to Bondi beach in his father's Merc, meeting Tim who arranged for tough beach inspector Aub Laidlaw to turn a blind eye to the models' brief bikinis. No longer in fashion garments, the girls looked thin and hardly drew a glance from the "cliff rats" who perved on girls lying on the beach below.

Soon after that party and beach outing, the Anglican Press stoush occurred. It resulted from a carve-up of the suburban advertising market which newcomer Murdoch, fresh from Adelaide, was muscling into. Murdoch had bought Cumberland Newspapers at Parramatta and began publishing new free sheets in the city's western suburbs. Fairfax and Packer joined together through Suburban Publications Pty Ltd to fight him in the suburbs, planning to use idle press time at the *Daily Mirror*, then owned by a subsidiary company of Fairfax.

But then, out of the blue, Murdoch bought the *Mirror* and suddenly the Fairfax-Packer group, under the chairmanship of Clyde Packer, had to find an alternative printing plant. The Anglican Press, in seedy inner-city Chippendale, was the best bet. It was already in receivership and Clyde was a director.

The Packers made a bid and were told it would be accepted. But another offer had also been made to the receiver by a company whose directors were Murdoch and eccentric POW-escapee and journalist Francis James. Clyde was foolish enough to boastfully tell James he had the deal stitched up the evening before it was to be signed. Within hours, Francis James moved in and persuaded the bishops who controlled the Anglican Press to sack the receiver who was about to sell to Sir Frank, and the deal was off.

The Packers were furious, deciding to seize possession of the premises. Clyde and Kerry pulled up outside the premises at 9.15 on the night of 7 June 1960, with company lawyer Fred Millar and two or three *Telegraph* employees, brandishing documents claiming the premises were theirs. The new receiver, Harry Reid, refused them entry.

Clyde and Kerry strolled around the back and got in the back door. When Reid walked back in through the front, he found Clyde ensconced in his office chair and was told he couldn't make any calls because the lines had been cut. Reid left to call for help and returned to find himself locked out. Windows were barricaded and locks had been changed. The cops arrived but went away after talking to Clyde.

Meanwhile Francis James had mustered old air force mates and told Murdoch what was afoot. Murdoch contacted Frank Browne, a tough, pugnacious ex-boxer who was still a columnist on the *Mirror*, and he organised some heavies to storm the barricades. They all met outside Sydney Town Hall just after midnight for an update on events and Murdoch handed out a fistful of banknotes to Browne to pay his gorilla-like toughs.

Reaching the locked-up Anglican Press building, all was quiet before the storm. They found an unlocked toilet window at the rear which the smallest one among them was able to squeeze through, hopefully to open the back door. While that was going on, Browne and his gang noisily battered on the front door, eventually smashing it in.

The Packer team, greatly outnumbered, were attacked from front and rear, their attackers wielding wrenches, tyre levers and thick lumps of wood. Punches and kicks were delivered amid much yelling and cursing and the two Packer boys, under siege, were chased around inside the building as they tried to defend themselves. They had no chance of repelling the invaders and were forced out into the street, where the fracas continued. Clyde and Kerry put up a good show but were clearly beaten.

Back in the *Telegraph* boardroom in the city, Sir Frank was gathered with several executives, listening to two-way radio reports from a staff reporter in an office car. Murdoch was doing the same in his office in Kippax Street, Surry Hills. When things looked grim, Packer rang Bristow and asked him to get there quickly to see what could be done to rescue his sons. Tim rushed in from his Newport home, but too late to turn the tide.

He met Browne, whom he knew, and said to him: "You must be mad. You won't get away with this." Still fired up by the heat of battle and gripping a thick piece of timber, Browne said: "I'll fix these c——s." Tim calmed Browne down. Clyde and his defeated troops were still at the scene vainly hoping to re-enter the building.

Then Tim talked to the heavies, led by Hal Morgan, who used to wrestle under the name of The Phantom. He knew Morgan too and advised him to lay off and not go on with it or there could be further trouble. Tim had in mind that Sir Frank had connections to the underworld through Det-Sgt Ray Kelly, who was close to criminal Lennie McPherson and standover merchant Dick Reilly. If Sir Frank had given Tim more time, he could have done his usual trick of rounding up a truckload of rugged footballers to meet the trouble, but events moved too quickly. In a way he was glad he didn't have to because of his friendship with Browne.

That morning Murdoch's *Mirror* ran a sensational front page headed "Knight's Sons in City Brawl," the front page showing

Clyde on his back in the gutter with Browne on top of him trying to wield a wrench. That was changed to a less violent picture. In spite of their defeat in the punchup, the Packers with the Fairfaxes managed to publish scheduled suburban papers on time and a year later came to an arrangement with Murdoch to share the market on a rational basis.

Kerry, who would later become Australia's richest man after taking over the Packer empire and rebuilding it, received a black eye in that escapade. At the time I boxed with Pat Burgess and a few other journalists in a gym near the *Telegraph* office where I worked and Kerry asked if he could come and box with us to sharpen his technique. He showed himself to be a heavy puncher but could take it too.

As if divorce raids didn't provide enough adrenalin rush, Tim in between private eye jobs kept up his exploits with sharks and rescues of drowning surfers and stranded boats.

When New York Governor Nelson Rockefeller's 23-year-old son Michael, heir to the vast family fortune, went missing off the rugged coast of Dutch New Guinea in 1961, Nelson chartered a plane and brought in dozens of international journalists, also an American anthropologist to head the search team. Billing it as "one of the enduring unsolved mysteries of the 20th century," the Americans thought Michael may still be alive.

The anthropologist contacted Tim to see if he could help. Tim didn't go to New Guinea but made some inquiries, concluding that young Rockefeller was eaten by crocodiles or sharks after his trading canoe was swamped by heavy seas in the Arafura Sea. Rockefeller had clung to the wreckage all night, then set out to swim for the distant shore, telling his expedition companions, "I think I can make it." Bristow was certain he was taken before reaching land. I had flown over that same area earlier by helicopter while reporting on the discovery of oil in New Guinea and you could see the white pointers lying in the sea like big logs.

Always friendly to visitors, Tim introduced the anthropologist to friends in country New South Wales and they gave him a good time. The American didn't find any trace of Rockefeller but he made a fortune in New York selling Asmat primitive art from New Guinea's Sepik River area.

When out in his boat from Pittwater, Bristow rescued dozens of boats that were dismasted or broken down off Barrenjoey at the northern tip of Palm Beach or in the general area of Broken Bay, taking them in tow. Some weren't registered, the owners didn't want publicity, so few people knew about most of his efforts. But some rescues were so dramatic that everyone knew about them.

After a sand bank collapsed at Bilgola, he figured in a massive rescue one day with another surfer, Michael Bartlett. Using a line, they saved 17 swimmers in trouble, bringing them in from as far as 100 yards out. Many panicked, making the rescue more difficult. The rescued needed resuscitating with oxygen.

The police didn't have a diving squad then and because of Tim's skill as a diver, they often called on him to recover bodies along the Peninsula shoreline. The police enjoyed a good rapport with him and he never minded helping them. When some person was missing, parents would be hanging on the beach looking for their loved ones and frustrated police, without their own divers, would have to wait until the seas subsided or use grappling irons from boats.

Usually a sunken body would float to the surface in five days unless wedged in a cave or crevice, where it was likely to be attacked by sharks. To avoid that happening, Tim would dive and recover the bodies. Hard to find bodies, particularly those trapped or wedged between grey or white stones at North Bilgola, proved another challenge for Tim to overcome. But he recovered bodies from there, too.

In another incident, Tim saw a distress signal go up about two miles off Bilgola beach while out on his ski. He paddled out to the cruiser, *Kallina*, which had sprung a plank and was taking water. It was part-owned by Theo Kelly, boss of Woolworths. Tim helped two people aboard into a dinghy and they reached shore.

The police launch *Nemesis* came out and took the cruiser in tow to Palm Beach. As they turned around Barrenjoey to come into Pittwater, the cruiser nose dived. They called for Tim by radio to come out again, to dive and attach a rope from *Nemesis* to the *Kallina*. It was already night and they were powerless to do anything else.

Knowing fishermen who operated in the area and realising the number of sharks that frequented the mouth of the nearby Hawkesbury River, Tim knew the dangers. Shortly before, a whaler shark had attacked the outboard motor on his cousin's boat. In spite of the risks, he didn't hesitate when asked. But it would be a frightening experience.

In inky blackness, he free-dived in fairly deep water, about 40 feet down, where fortunately the cruiser had stuck on a ledge. He retied a rope to the cruiser, cutting his hands on broken glass in the cabin, then skied back to the shore. The *Nemesis* towed it into Pittwater where it was refloated later with 44-gallon drums. In gratitude, Theo Kelly donated equipment to local surf clubs.

Tim's fearlessness was demonstrated to me one day when out with him in his boat a mile or two off Barrenjoey. His propeller fouled and he simply leapt overboard in his shorts and spent five minutes fixing it, regardless of possible sharks.

His rescue of round-the-world lone English sailor and grandmother, Mrs Anne Gash, was one of his more courageous efforts. After sailing around the world she turned too sharply coming into Pittwater and was catapulted into the foaming bombora water. Her boat was sucked in and went down, smashed on rocks. A lot of boats had come to grief in the bombora and unwary people had drowned there.

Luckily for Mrs Gash, Tim was going past in his speed boat at his usual speed, flat out, when he saw her go in and realised she would drown unless he acted quickly. The bombora was just off the rocks and she was in the whitewater being tossed about. He switched off his motor, attached a long line to himself and dived in, leaving his boat floating about near the bombora - a dangerous operation.

To reach her he had to swim right into the bombora, a boiling swirling torrent of water about 200 metres across. She was in tears, crying out in distress. Telling her she was OK, he swam back with her to his boat and helped her in. Still shaking with fear, she said: "I've come around Cape Horn and all the bloody world to wreck my boat here." Mrs Gash hugged him in relief when he dropped her off at a wharf at Paradise Beach and went on his way. He built up a lot of goodwill with his diving and rescues and was just as well known on the northern beaches for his courage and help as he was for his reputation of toughness and daring.

His courage in water was not confined to Sydney's northern beaches. Driving to the NSW snowfields one day he noticed some activity just up ahead near Jindabyne. Reaching the spot at a bridge he asked other travellers who like him had just stopped: "What's happening here?" Someone said a car had just skidded off and gone into the river. "Is anyone doing anything?" he demanded, already stripping off his clothes. He dived into freezing water, rescued a woman and her child, had a chat and went on his way.

Nobody ever drowned while Tim was in the water close at hand or on the beach except at Palm Beach one day. Out on his board with a girl, Sue Phillips, he spotted a ski upside down and saw a man floating face down. He quickly brought him in and helped carry him to the Cabbage Tree Club for oxygen, but he was already dead. He was an honorary doctor from Tim's old Shore school.

Three times a week Tim swam along the Pacific shore from Bilgola to Newport catching lobsters, carrying a hand spear in case of sharks. He always saw sharks but in those circumstances they didn't worry him. He knew every lobster hole on the coast from Manly to Palm Beach and could free-dive to the extraordinary depth of more than 100 feet.

Whenever he speared a lobster he believed it must have sent out some kind of call because carpet sharks up to 10 feet long would suddenly appear from every crevice and cave nearby. Just like blowing a whistle. He knew that more people were bitten by carpet sharks than any other species in Australia. More often they took his lobsters. A carpet shark bit him once but fortunately when it opened its mouth to cough, he pulled his forearm out. His hands were often lacerated when carpet sharks grabbed him from caves, but luckily the sharks always coughed.

He didn't wear gloves, believing he had a better chance of pulling his hand out if grabbed by a shark. On spearing a lobster in a cave one day, he spotted a shark about five feet long and grabbed it by the back of the head near the gills to stop it biting him. His diving companion couldn't believe his fearlessness. Max Bristow often went lobster diving with Tim and carpet and wobbegong sharks taking their catches drove him mad too. Max didn't wear gloves either. These guys were crazy!

Diving with Max one day Tim hit a shark with a spear gun apparently in the wrong place and it went into a frenzy, biting a rock and smashing its teeth. In another experience on Newport Reef he had a lucky escape when a shark attacked and crushed the side of his ski - if his foot had been in the chock, he'd have lost it.

Tim put lots of fruit on the sideboard by catching fish and sharks and selling them to a professional fisherman who supplied the city markets. One day he caught 12 sharks ranging from five to eight feet in a nylon net off The Peak at Newport, swimming them to the beach with only flippers on and with some help from two boardriders. A mighty feat.

He fished about a mile off Newport reef on grounds known to his father, who used to take him there in an old surf boat. They didn't have a depth finder to tell when they were over the reef but Tim learned from his father to find the spot by lining up land markings in Bungan Head Road and Bilgola surf club. Here he speared kingfish and jewfish up to 50 kilos.

Tim was unsurpassed as a shark catcher. One method was to tie his boat to a buoy with rope weighted by a bag of sand, with a second rope attached to a marlin swivel underneath tied to another buoy. He'd put snapper or red bream on the marlin hook through the tail so it still flashed and sharks couldn't miss seeing it. He brought a tiger shark 9 feet 7 inches long into Newport beach on the flat of his surf ski, holding up his oar to indicate there was a shark around. Another day at Newport, he caught a tiger shark 13 feet 4 inches long, a local record.

When actress Marcia Hathaway was taken by a shark at Sugarloaf Bay in Middle Harbour in 1963, a reward was posted for its capture in a one-day competition. Tim knew the area backwards, having fished and hunted sharks there previously with radioman Bob Dyer in his *Tennesee* boat. Tim caught a hammer head shark about 9 feet long, the only one landed on the day, an event reported in the *Sydney Morning Herald*.

He went on entertainer Don Lane's show on TV and offered to fight a shark in a cage for $1 million. Some viewers thought him mad. Nobody put up the money, but if they had he'd have been committed. He simply could not back away from a challenge. Passing the aquarium at Manly one day, he bumped into an acquaintance who bet him five pounds he wasn't game to get in the tank with a grey nurse shark. Bristow stripped down to his underpants, slipped into the tank and swam around, collecting the bet.

He couldn't resist a prank, either. A Mona Vale boat crewman leapt into the water in sheer fright when Tim caught a 10-foot bronze whaler shark in pre-metric days and tossed it into the boat. Early one morning a 7 -foot shark turned up in the sea pool at Bilgola, terrorising swimmers and causing them to flee. Bristow was the culprit and the local council wanted to prosecute him. Another day a smaller shark suddenly appeared in the saltwater pool of the Newport Arms Hotel, circling an hysterical female swimmer. Perpetrator Big Tim thought it a great joke.

After four years of marriage, Tim and Judy had reached an impasse.

Judy Pointing was only 15 when she met Tim. They were engaged when she was 16 and he married her at 17. She was pregnant at the time. She always said if she'd been older, it would never have happened. Their separation would be a traumatic affair for both of them, marked by drama, stalking, restraining orders and some violence. Their warfare would last for several years before they were finally legally divorced.

Some fellows smile when they lose. Tim wasn't like that. He was a poor loser, not being one to share his wife with anyone. Tim and Judy later gave sharply divided versions of what happened between them. According to Tim, the son of one of Australia's wealthiest families whom he befriended and allowed to stay in his home when the man was having personal difficulties, was responsible for his wife leaving him.

Judy maintained that the marriage was over before she began keeping company with the man. The marriage failed, she said, because of Tim's behaviour with other women, and there was little doubt about that being a key factor. If she had stayed, she believed the relationship could have ended in some kind of personal disaster or tragedy.

Their second son, Stephen, was two when they parted in 1960. It was difficult enough for Tim trying to cope as a single parent, but trouble erupted because he would not give up, pursuing Judy in her new relationship and wanting her back. That was part of the *droit de seigneur* principle, the lord of the manor not yielding up his head wife. But any woman who lived with him had to live by his rules.

Tim knew the father of Judy's friend well, having done packaging work for his company. He realised he was up against money and at the time was limited financially himself. But passion ruled the day. Not only was it a blow to his pride but he was also ropable in believing, rightly or wrongly, that the man to whom he had shown goodwill had taken advantage of him.

Max Bristow and his wife Ann assisted by looking after Stephen and their help was greatly appreciated for some time, but eventually the arrangement needed to change because Tim would call on them in the early hours on his way home to see Stephen, disrupting the household.

Like a reporter with a good nose for news, Tim had an uncanny ability to sniff out information. He was shocked to learn that the man had gone to Queensland with Judy, and ringing the father in a friendly manner he found out when the son would return. He waited at Sydney Airport. Two acquaintances he bumped into saw how stretched his nerves were and waited with him. As passengers came off a plane and walked across the open tarmac, he spotted Judy and the man, arm in arm.

He waited as an air hostess checked them at the gate, then growled, "keep walking." A scuffle broke out and the man hit Tim on the jaw - on the numb side. Tim punched him back, and down he went. Several Federal police and security men raced in to arrest or restrain Bristow, now in full flight and somewhat out of control. Passengers were held up as the fight ensued. In the melee Judy was punched by Tim and finished up hanging over the fence. He claimed later that he had miscued as she intervened while he was trying to hit her escort.

Then came the crunch. Tim's opponent got to his feet and grabbed him by the orchestra stalls, causing him to grunt with pain. Bristow did a Mike Tyson and bit off one of the man's ears, spitting it out.

Security men were thumped too but somehow an uneasy peace returned before Tim helped his injured wife into his car and took her home. Then he rang the man's father and told him what had happened. The wealthy businessman asked Tim to locate his son. Tim found him heavily bandaged at Double Bay after having his ear stitched back on with micro surgery.

He took the injured man to the city to see his father, who asked him for the truth. His son swore on his mother's honour that nothing improper had taken place, that he had merely taken Judy for a holiday. He then charged Bristow with causing him grievous bodily harm. Andrew Leary, regarded as one of Sydney's best instinctive criminal lawyers, went to Paddington Court to defend Tim on the basis he was in such pain when grabbed that he had to do something drastic. But the man didn't turn up and the charge was withdrawn.

For Judy the marriage was over and she wanted to get away from Tim. She left home for the second time to be with her lover, never to return. However, Tim would still not accept the inevitable. He rang contacts in various places, asking them to keep an eye out for his wife. Eventually he heard of Judy's whereabouts from Jimmy "Numbers" Knowles, son of a leading stockbroker who ran a nightclub in Melbourne and claimed to have discovered the talents of singer Diana Trask.

Bristow flew to Melbourne and was met by "Numbers" who took him to his mansion at Toorak to give him the details about Judy. "Numbers" assigned a couple of fellows to help him and Tim set out for a Palm Lake Motel just out of Melbourne. Here Tim caused a scene at night right out of the best of *Fawlty Towers*.

Tim knocked on the door of a suite and was met by a person he took to be a bodyguard. Trouble erupted at once. As Tim and the bodyguard traded blows, Judy's lover ran out minus his pyjama pants and Tim stopped punching the bodyguard to confront him. Judy moved between them trying to stop Tim from assaulting him. Once again, Judy was injured and this time would need hospital treatment. Tim claimed it was an accident but obviously he had lost his cool.

The man ran down the stairs calling out, "Help, Help." Bristow gave chase and startled guests looked on as Tim pursued him around the vestibule, dodging pot plants. More fisticuffs took place on the run. The police were called as confused staff ran around after them. Tim was lucky not to be charged and no doubt would have been if "Numbers" had not pulled a few strings at the local police station.

Bristow still wouldn't give up and restraining orders were taken out against him. But the law on individual rights was less rigid then and the orders had little effect. Then, one night in 1962, an attempt was made to kill Bristow which he linked directly to his divorce troubles. It was the only time in his life he ran but he remained alive because of it.

He was doing his security job at the Newport Arms when he was called to the beer garden because of a disturbance. At the time Tim was chatting to several chaps in a lounge area, including Kevin Schubert, a senior off-duty policeman on the Peninsula and a former Australian Rugby League forward who toured England with two Kangaroo teams and played with the legendary Clive Churchill.

Bristow moved in to stop three men fighting, but he was suspicious because somehow it didn't seem like a genuine brawl. They were strangers but one seemed familiar. As he approached they turned on him and one threw a punch and Bristow knocked him down. Schubert moved in and one of the remaining two stepped in front of him, demanding, "Who are you?" Schubert said: "I'm a police officer," and the other laughed at him and replied: "You keep out of this."

Schubert replied: "I'll keep out of it if you do." By this time, the third member of the trio had joined his companion in attacking Bristow. Tim flattened the second attacker and, using one of his special grips, turned the first man around and speared his head into the bar causing glasses to smash and cut one of the barmaid's legs.

Tim's attacker was a tough rooster. Staggering up, he rasped to a woman holding a bag: "Quick, give me the gun."

Bristow ran, slamming a door behind him as he went for his car. It was the only healthy thing to do. The attacker ran after him, waving the gun but Bristow was too quick. Later, when he returned and conferred with the police who'd been called, he realised that the main aggressor was Duckie, or "Machine Gun" Ray O'Connor, a vicious standover man and killer, whom police said had taken part in nine murders.

O'Connor's cohorts were John Andrew Stuart and John Stuart Regan, both underworld killers. They had staged the phoney fight to draw Bristow in. One had given a false name to Inspector Schubert. Stuart would later be convicted of murdering 15 people in the fire bombing of the Whisky Au Go Go nightclub in Brisbane in 1973. All three would die violent deaths as a result of underworld feuds.

Kevin Schubert said later: "I happened to be there that day and it was a dicey situation. O'Connor was tough but so was Tim who gave him a terrible hiding and I thought he'd killed him, but he got up and asked for a gun. It was a nasty episode and Tim is not exaggerating it. I can tell you this - Tim could handle himself. He'd get a forfeit from me any time in an argument. But he liked to help people and many don't give him credit for some of the good things he did."

Two days later on returning home Bristow found his Alsatian dog, King, dead. His throat had been cut. One of Tim's phone numbers had always been listed in the directory and he received a gloating call from O'Connor saying, "I've squared up with you with the dog."

Tim had loved the dog and went looking for O'Connor. He turned up an address in Double Bay through Hollywood George and called at night a few days later. He felt like belting O'Connor but decided it was better to neutralise him to get to the bottom of it. O'Connor told him that the father of the man involved in Tim's marital problems had paid O'Connor 5,000 pounds to kill Tim to avoid a scandal for the family through publicity in the courts. Tim was convinced the son was unaware of the plot and that the father was acting on his own.

O'Connor also told Bristow he didn't really want to kill him and they parted amicably. Bristow walked out into the darkness.

The shadows near the gate moved. "I'm gone," he murmured, thinking O'Connor had outfoxed him. He was unarmed and there was nothing he could do except continue on the narrow pathway, alert but seemingly unafraid. Two figures stepped forward. "CIB," they said. One was Det. Kelly Welles, and both were from the Consorting Squad. They must have tailed him there. They booked him for consorting with a known criminal. He tried to explain but to no avail.

Tim rang Det.-Sgt Ray Kelly at his home and told him what had happened. He'd built up a good relationship with Kelly over the past few years. Kelly said simply: "See me at 8 a.m. at the CIB tomorrow." When he saw Kelly at the old city CIB office in Central Lane, the famous detective said: "I'll get you to come upstairs and we'll take a statement."

Tim felt comfortable in familiar surroundings because his old mate, Ron Walden, was now in charge, laying down the edict that every detective was to wear a hat and nobody was to wear suede shoes. Det. Bob Day typed the statement explaining the circumstances and Kelly squared it away with Det. Welles. That was the end of the matter. Kelly told Tim: "I'd better speak to Lennie about you because Duckie O'Connor is a dangerous bastard." Later he told Tim that McPherson had said to O'Connor: "If you see me in a bar, don't come in, and if I walk into a bar where you're drinking, you'd better leave."

The feud between Tim, his wife and her companion had to end. After four years Tim was still taking out injunctions against Judy's lover to prevent him leaving Australia until he had lodged 1,000 pounds as security with the Divorce Registrar - the amount he was claiming as damages in a pending divorce suit.

Eventually on 19 August 1964 Tim filed for divorce on the ground of his wife's adultery with Robert Gordon Edgell as co-respondent. Judy cross petitioned for divorce, citing Tim's new companion Glenda Roberts. Mr Justice Selby dismissed the cross petition and granted Tim a *decree nisi* to be absolute in 21 days. Tim was awarded custody of their six-year-old son, Stephen, with reasonable access allowed to Judy.

But the Court ordered that Tim be restrained from interfering with, molesting or telephoning Judy, her mother or the co-respondent, or from entering Judy's home or place of employment.

He had seen the drama of divorce from both sides of the witness box and would feature in many more scenes with influential people before the archaic divorce laws were eventually reformed.

8

BOGLE-CHANDLER WAS MURDER

ALTHOUGH divorce inquiries and raids remained his staple work, Bristow by now had developed an encyclopaedic knowledge of the city and the people who pulled the strings.

As a knockabout on the road day and night, he knew the honest politicians and those on the take, honest and dishonest cops, big-time gangsters, thieves, crooks and racketeers, murderers and hit men, cons, crooked businessmen, bookies, jockeys, gamblers and gambling joints and sportsmen. He also knew many of the influential people from the big end of town like judges and other power figures.

He moved in a dangerous world of intrigue, threats and dark deeds. Knowing someone and how they related to a situation, could save his life. He mixed with all types, treating everyone as he found them.

But the more people he helped, the more enemies he made. To gain justice for a client, he had to tread on someone's toes. There were no half measures with Bristow. People either loved or hated him. He was either a saviour or a menace. Hardly a week went by without a death threat against him, usually anonymous.

There never was a better networker. He kept in touch with old friends from the surfing, sporting and police worlds and from Shore and other private schools for contacts that could help with a client's problem. He set out to make friends with everyone he met and his informants ranged through all levels of society, tradesmen, doormen, garbagemen, shopkeepers, journalists. A walk along a city street with Tim was slow progress as he stopped to talk. A visit to the Supreme or criminal courts was always delayed as he chatted to barristers and solicitors, prosecutors, popping his head into sitting courts to wave or call out to judges on the Bench. In that sense, he was accepted as a character about town.

Bristow's wide knowledge of people brought him an incredible range of inquiries, not just on the most publicised crimes of the day but the most baffling, extending from the theft of art works to one of Australia's most intriguing unsolved crimes.

Bristow prowled the city by day but as a nocturnal creature he always roamed well into the night and even the dawn, carrying his office with him, an attache case with diary notes and a minimum of documents, meeting and briefing his agents on the run, in offices, cafes, cars. Aware that cops liked to go through his diaries for information whenever they questioned him, he wrote down only the barest details, storing the rest in his incredible memory, names, numbers, dates, clues. His memory also made him a good card player.

His agile brain became a who's who of crimes, infamy and wrongdoing, a reservoir of dirty linen of the rich and famous who feared that once Bristow was aware of their infidelity, corruption or dishonesty, they might be exposed. Hence, after he did their dirty work for them, many prominent people condemned him privately as a cover-up for their peccadillos.

Some influential clients simply wanted results to hide a shameful past without raising scandal or going to the police, others had been to the police or lawyers and spent their money without result and their only chance of getting justice was through Bristow bending the law and taking the risks.

With his opponents, it was always the same. Those with the most money were able to buy the best protection through the best lawyers, the most powerful politicians or corrupt cops. People with police and political pull were the toughest to beat - he could forget the law working for him in those cases.

One of Bristow's maxims was: Don't expect to meet an honest man. "What's an honest man?" he would ask when the question of integrity in society was raised. "I've always found that when the chips are down and someone's family or even friends are about to be shown in a bad light, they will want you to break the law to get them out of trouble. So where's the honesty?"

As one of his main newspaper contacts, I was aware how cleverly Bristow protected himself and his clients by using the media to expose crooks and rackets. It was good newspaper business and in the public interest. At first I kept his name out of my newspaper stories to confuse his enemies and throw other reporters off the scent, but as his reputation grew he wanted to see his name in print.

His efforts alerted the public on dishonest practices in the community and put pressure on the cops and politicians to do something about it. It wasn't a one-way street with him either. In return he made inquiries for pressmen to help them and he kept political friends on side. For instance, when Labor politician George Neilly got hopelessly pissed in parliament, Tim would receive a call and drive him home to Cessnock in the country.

At times he rescued a hard-drinking lawyer from gambling joints, sweeping aside threats from bouncers or the management who demanded the lawyer settle his losses before leaving. A security guard who pulled a gun on him in a Kings Cross casino once when he picked up the lawyer got the usual response: "If that goes off, it'll go off in your arse."

An agent who began working for Bristow in the '60s and remained with him for many years, was impressed at how he controlled his operatives in difficult situations. "He had a good brain," the agent said. "That's the first thing I noticed. He had a hawk-eye and saw everything, even if there were 10 people in a room. If one person failed to follow his instructions or made a wrong move, he'd remind you at once. He never forgot a breach of discipline.

"Tim was so bloody primal, and that's the part people hated about him. He could be an animal. If he told you to go and do something and you said no or hung back, he'd say what! And he was so witty he could often motivate you to do something hard by the jovial way he talked to you. But if you crossed that line and refused, he would deal with you on the spot. But he could do a lot without using his fists.

"Some people suggested Tim was mad. He wasn't. He simply could not be bent over to other people's wills and he liked to keep full control.

"He had a bad Irish-German cross in him, the worst you can find for precision and exactitude. If he said 'be told,' and you weren't told, you were in trouble. If you didn't sit when he told you to, he'd punch you. If you lit a cigarette in his non-smoking house, you were punched. He did it to heavy crims, killers.

"Tim had a little kingdom that he ran and if you worked with him, you had to follow his rules, live by them, dance to them, or else not associate with him. But people who worked with him will all tell you that anyone who obeyed his rules, including his clients, all got what they wanted. The man was justifiably a legend."

Bristow never asked an agent to do anything he wasn't prepared to do himself. In a confrontation he insisted on taking control. Walking into a public restaurant with several burly assistants, Tongans or Maoris or Australians, he would ask his chief operative: "Is that the guy?" Then he would extend both arms to hold the others back and say "I'll take care of this." The others would stand back, impotent. He would pull away the chair the fellow was sitting on and that person would fall over. In extreme cases where the fellow was threatening violence to Tim's client, Tim would put his foot on his head and say: "Fancy yourself?"

If the fellow was offensive and abusive, Tim was known several times to drag him off to the toilet and push his head into the bowl. Once, a well-dressed lawyer had his bald head caught in the bowl due to suction after Tim pulled the chain. This happened in upmarket Eliza's restaurant, while the tricky lawyer had Bristow's client in court on a false premise. "That", said the agent, "was Bristow the man. Others would have said you go and do it, but he said he would get it done and took full responsibility."

In a discussion group one day the agent rated Bristow the best private eye he ever knew, first because of his intelligence and ability to put people and situations together and to rectify a problem with a phone call. Also, except for names and telephone numbers, he rarely wrote anything down.

Second, he was the best because he was so fearless. "I don't think he knew fear," the agent said. "I never saw him intimidated by any situation. Cunning? I don't think that's the right word, or shrewdness either. It was more perception, although that has elements of cunning and shrewdness. He was a fellow of such intelligence and experience that he could assess you and the situation quickly. He would know you after a few words.

"A lot of people thought Tim was a crim but he wasn't, although he associated with them. Crims are cunning and sneaky, with a mentality to molest and harass people until they force them into a situation. That wasn't Tim. He was always upfront, always laid it on the line.

"Some said he was a bully, but I could never see that. A bully is usually a coward who folds up when challenged. That wasn't Tim. Also, bullies don't usually have friends, but Tim had friends everywhere and he always helped them. Many of them were prominent people who were regarded as icons of Australia and they respected him.

"But he was a bit of a bully at times when paying his operatives after a job, especially if they were crims. The crims didn't have the brains to make a deal with him first, and in those cases he could be a crocodile and take the lion's share, so to speak. It was his show, his brains and contacts, and he might sit there for hours talking on different things before paying them.

"Some of these fellows were heavy crims who would shoot you, but if they broke discipline and demanded their money, Tim would tell them they were getting nothing and showed them the door. What did they do? They just walked out. If they complained, he would say, 'Fancy yourself?'

"That's how primitive he was. I could see what he was doing - testing their discipline to maintain control, because he was betrayed so many times by people who could not be trusted. I saw it happen many times. And later if they came back and tried to belt him or shoot him, he loved it and would fight them on the spot. He did it for one thing -

control. He didn't have a badge and it was his way of court martialling you. He was the law. You had no rights except those under your allegiance to him.

"But if you did the right thing, he protected you and stood by you, not like some weak bastard when things went wrong who might say, 'oh I made a mistake.' In my view that made him a man.

"It was known that he got the job done. He did so because he was a force. The people around him were trained to do as he said. If he said stand over there or punch that guy, you did it. He was paid only on results. That's why he tested people. The undisciplined ones fell by the wayside.

"If you caused trouble, Tim would assess it. He knew he was right and would tell you to your face. If you denied it, he'd go whack. That's why a lot of people hated him. A lot of people couldn't deal with him because of his naked upfront manner. Any who opposed him were usually given one chance - then it was 'fancy yourself'?

"The fellow had a strong social conscience. In his sense of right and wrong, he didn't contradict himself as the law does, allowing crooks and their lawyers to twist this way and that on technical grounds. Tim's way was if you're wrong, I'll deal with you now.

"That was the essence of the man. And he never backed down from a challenge. In his early days as a private eye, he always jumped to the call wanting to do everything because he had the mental and physical powers to do it. That was his main fault, responding too often and too quickly. Later he learned to listen to all claims but act only on a few."

In every sense Bristow was a cross between Damon Runyan and Attila the Hun because of his knockabout humour and his ideas on summary justice. Clearly in his early years Bristow was a law unto himself, in that he did things his way - a situation those sworn to uphold the law like cops and legal people profess not to like, even if often powerless to deliver justice themselves. Their traditional attitude against a private eye like Bristow ignored the fact that life is usually not black or white but a shade of grey.

It raised the logical question of whether there is a need in society for someone like Tim Bristow and his associates who got things done outside the strict parameters of the law. One of Bristow's chief agents often debated the point with cops and solicitors.

In his experience, and also in mine as a journalist, it is difficult for many people to get justice by going to court (mostly a lottery anyway) or the police, either because they often cannot afford lawyers or the system is loaded against them. The crooks or wrongdoers opposing them have deep pockets, can hire the best lawyers and can afford to hold out, even intimidating them with threats.

And, as the agent said, "There are many people out there we can't call criminals because they've never been to jail but they are educated bastards who know the law, they have money and methodically rip people off to the extent that the law allows and beyond, and they're never beaten by the poor people whom they leave destitute.

"The beaten people are mostly the ones who come to us for help, usually after all else has failed. Bristow was not like a lot of men who walk this land allowing themselves to be told what to do, who bow down and let others get on with their corruption and whatever else they want.

"He wasn't one of those who turns a blind eye, goes home to his family, says and does nothing as others are robbed and stabbed and killed, looted rooted and raped, divorced and harassed, with people left destitute by con men. We help them, that's what we do.

"That's what goes on out there on the mean streets. People are being bashed and robbed and conned by sneaky, dishonest, violent, thieving bastards, some of them out of their minds on drugs and alcohol, who have no purpose in life except to take advantage of someone trying to earn an honest living. Violence and intimidation are close to the skin with many people. Decent law-abiding people can't walk around the streets at night any more without the fear of being beaten up or stabbed. There's menace in the shadows of the city and suburbs, even in well lit areas. People are terrified of being maimed in home invasions.

"Why is there a need for a fellow like Bristow? I'll tell you. It doesn't matter how many laws the Government draws up to protect or control society, there's a certain inbred quality of dishonesty among many people to do the wrong thing, and there's always some arsehole out there who will find a loophole. And when he gets through that loophole, and the law can't handle it, we deal with him."

Bristow would walk that grey area all his life, stretching it but trying not to break it. Most people don't even go to the threshold of that grey area once in their life because of fear or insecurity, a feeling of oppression or intimidation. They would like to but don't have it inside them to do it. So they asked a man like Bristow to do it for them.

Tim Bristow learned the value of informants while in the police force. He saw it at work not only with Det-Sgt Ray Kelly and his fizz gig Lennie McPherson but also with others. Kelly was contemptuous of certain detectives, saying: "The untouchables arrest few and convict less." He said of one well-known detective that the few he did arrest were all acquitted.

His observation wasn't strictly correct, but he had a point. Some untouchables like Jack Bateman and Brian Doyle were just as tough as Kelly, with different styles. The distinction between Kelly and Doyle was shown by one incident in the CIB's general detective office known as the "Bull Ring," where rookie detectives were assessed to work with the old hands.

Kelly was known as The Gunner because of his quick trigger finger and Doyle as The Cardinal because of his Catholic solidarity. Interviewing some young aspirants one day, Kelly asked one: "Would you be prepared to load up a suspect? He replied: "Oh no, certainly not, sir." Kelly told the young fellow: "Go back to the Cardinal - you're no f—ing good to me.""

Kelly, a former jackeroo in outback New South Wales and Queensland, was flamboyant, the sort of bloke who if he went to a murder and couldn't solve it in 24 hours, would pass it on to someone else like Jack Bateman, a plodder by comparison but a terrific investigator who solved many of the big murders like the Bega bombing case in the late '50s by spending months on the job, then giving skilful court evidence. In that case, a local man murdered a constable by blowing up his house with gelignite, simply because the constable had booked him for a traffic offence.

The Gunner had no fear, did a lot of daring things in capturing and arresting criminals and was the first to kick down doors in sieges, as when a crazed Maltese gunman named Charles Spiteri fought a gun battle with police at Darlinghurst on 24 May 1957 before being shot dead.

In his career Kelly wounded several criminals and shot two dead, including one near Darling Harbour who was sitting next to Lennie McPherson in a car - no prizes for guessing how Kelly arranged that one. Brian Doyle was unlucky to have missed out on being Police Commissioner, but he was unwise enough to say once that if he became commissioner, the interfering politicians wouldn't last five minutes before he told them where to go. It was a disgrace that such good investigators as Kelly and Bateman, two of the best, should have retired at career's end on lowly ranks - Kelly as a third class inspector, Bateman as a first class sergeant - because of the then promotion system mainly by seniority.

Bristow knew most of the leading detectives. Some were corrupt, some weren't, but the tough-minded ones all had one thing in common - they were well informed and had their criminal contacts. That's how the system worked in those days. The cops were permitted to have their informants and when there were murders or big robberies, they went to them for information.

Sure, there was some corruption, especially in the old-style squads, but they built up intelligence for when it was needed. And there was some injustice. But the system of control worked. Criminals knew that if they stepped out of line they would be dealt with, that fire would be met with fire. Young hoods weren't running around willy-nilly brandishing guns, shooting people with abandon as they do today, showing no respect for the law and getting away with it as if cops were a bunch of pansies.

Under the old system of policing, with fellows like Bumper Farrell running the Cross and tough dicks cracking down on crims who overstepped the mark, pulling them in and booking them for consorting, trouble was usually nipped in the bud before it got out of hand. There was a certain order, and politicians and courts generally supported the cops.

Cops were taught to be polite, but if someone wanted to punch them, they punched 'em back. People don't seem to realise today that you can't have a police force made up of Sunday school teachers and theorists and expect them to deal effectively with violent and criminal behaviour. Bristow knew all that first hand and espoused it many times.

The value of having informants helped him solve one of the most intriguing art thefts of the 1960s. His fizz gig was the dangerous criminal and notorious escapee, Keith Joseph Hahn. Known as The Fox, Hahn was at large for more than 18 months and through a homosexual friend of Tim's, gave him the tip where to find some missing paintings of Sir William Dobell. They belonged to Sydney art fancier and Dobell collector Emil Gheysens, who contacted Tim. A thief had stolen several Dobells from his Mosman home, hoping to do a deal with the insurers.

Tim discovered a gay had the paintings and made a deal with the man who was not charged. In mysterious circumstances, the paintings were left in shrubbery in the Sydney Domain. Tim had contacted his old friend, Ray Kelly, who was believed to have co-opted the services of Len McPherson to arrange leaving the paintings in the shrubbery. The whole affair was a public mystery, with three policemen demoted for misconduct in being paid $7,000 reward for their return.

Kelly could not officially take part in the case because he had retired shortly before, in 1966, with almost 1,000 people farewelling him, including Premier Bob Askin, judges and known crims. Tim was there too, causing a slight disturbance by head-butting an offensive senior CIB cop who, as Tim observed later, was full of "piss and indignation" and made the mistake of trying to manhandle him.

The pilfering of Dobells became a popular pastime for larcenous art fanciers. Even Dobell himself lost one to a light-fingered house painter. Tim was also called in to locate the whereabouts of one of Dobell's most famous paintings, *Wangi Boy,* or as it was originally called, *The Narrows Beach,* one of many Dobell painted of his idyllic Wangi landscape on the NSW central coast.

The artist had borrowed the painting from its owner, Mrs Thelma Clune, the gallery owner and widow of Australiana author Frank Clune, to exhibit at the 1948 Exhibition of the Society of Artists, at the Education Department's Art Gallery in Sydney. It was stolen from there on 4 September 1948, and has never been recovered.

Mrs Clune, after a fruitless search, taking out ads and even posting a reward on Qantas planes, commissioned Dobell to paint another one of the Wangi boy with the turned-up trousers and knitted beanie alongside Lake Macquarie, one of the great talking points of Australian art. Produced in 1956, it was substantially the same as the stolen work.

Thelma Clune did not give up even after the insurance company had paid her out for the stolen first version of *Wangi Boy.* She asked Tim to see if he could find it. Knowing that many gays were attracted to art, Tim sought help from a gay friend, Neil Taylor, who ran a slimming business and two male bordellos in Sydney.

Taylor, who also figured behind-the-scenes in the recovery of the Gheysens paintings, eventually gave Tim a tip. He then went to an address in Curlewis Street Bondi where "an old poofter" lived. He knocked and as there was no answer, he gained entry. There on a wall, among other paintings, was the missing Dobell. He left it there and quietly let himself out. In Thelma Clune's interests, he checked discreetly with his good contact, Police Commissioner Norman "The Foreman" Allan, who told him the painting, if it turned up, would officially belong to the insurance company.

Mrs Clune, satisfied to know where the painting had finished up, instructed Tim to leave it on the Bondi wall. Even if she could buy it from the insurance company, it would now cost a great deal more. It went against Tim's grain to leave the theft unresolved, but he respected her wishes and that's where the matter rested.

The second painting, bought from Mr James Fairfax by stockbroker Rene Rivkin for the then Australian record auction price of $264,000, would be sold by Rivkin at auction in 2001 for a disappointing $200,000.

The bizarre unsolved deaths of scientist Dr Gilbert Bogle and former nurse Mrs Margaret Chandler, whose semi-nude bodies were found on a track in Sydney's Lane Cove National Park on the North Shore on New Year's Day, 1963, have been described in police records as "the most baffling mystery of the 20th century." Some mystery!

But in truth those deaths still nag at the peace of mind and professionalism of medical experts and pathologists around the world. Many have contributed their theories, even uninvited, but nothing has been proved to achieve a solution.

The Japanese sex drug theory has been advanced, shellfish poison, toadfish poison, neurotoxic gas capsules, a conspiracy alliance involving the Russians and the American CIA, murder, skulduggery by MI6, death rays, death by accident or misadventure, motives ranging from jealousy to a Le Carre-style conspiracy involving Bogle's work...but there is still no proven reason why these two people died from acute circulatory failure after a happy New Year's Eve party.

Bristow, always fascinated by murder, violence and mystery, took a close interest in the strange affair.

The mystery began when two youths looking for stray golf balls found the bodies of attractive mother of two

Margaret Chandler, 29 and Dr Bogle, 38, well apart on the banks of the Lane Cove River between 8 and 9 a.m. With 20 other society guests they had attended a party at the Chatswood home of Ken and Ruth Nash. Scientific examination showed that after leaving the home they had made love at around dawn.

Among questions posed by the discovery: Did Margaret Chandler neatly cover Bogle's face-down body with his suit coat and trousers before she removed him 15 metres down the river bank to die? Or was there a third person at the scene who was implicated in their deaths?

Margaret Chandler was found lying on her back, naked except for her floral frock bunched up around her waist. Her feet and knees were mud-stained and a pair of men's underpants was between her legs. She had been covered with three flattened-out beer cartons. There were indications that both victim's had been violently ill.

Margaret was the wife of Bogle's CSIRO colleague and friend, Dr Geoffrey Chandler, a specialist in solar radiometry. He also was at the New Year's Eve party. Dr Bogle, born in New Zealand, was a Rhodes scholar who came to Sydney in 1956 to work for the CSIRO. He had a master's degree in science and arts, a doctorate in physics from Oxford and was soon to take up a two-year fellowship at the Bell Telephone laboratories in the United States.

Bogle, a man with a strong sexual appetite, apparently found rich pickings in an intellectual group called The Push who met in pubs and talked about various issues, including who was sleeping with whom. He was also into one of the diversions of the swinging '60s, wife swapping.

He met the vivacious Margaret Chandler at a Christmas party a few days before the Nashes' New Year's Eve party in Chatswood. Chandler said later that his wife commented to him the next day that "the thought of going to bed with Gil Bogle" appealed to her. Chandler later wrote in his 1970 book *So You Think I Did It,* that he and his wife had an understanding that each could engage in extramarital affairs without disturbing the essential solidity of their marriage.

Police established that Chandler left the Nashes' party about 11 p.m. for a beatnik party at Balmain where he met up with a secretary named Pam Logan before driving to her flat where they had sex. He returned to the Nashes' party between 2 and 3 a.m. and chatted with his wife and Bogle for a while before leaving about 4 a.m. Margaret remained with the doctor.

Bogle and Mrs Chandler left the party together about 15 minutes after Chandler left and drove into the Lane Cove River Park where four hours later the first of two youths, Michael McCormack, 16, found what he thought was a hobo sleeping off a New Year's hangover.

The big problem with the case was that it happened on New Year's Day when everybody was relaxed and there was no real sense of urgency. It took time for everyone to focus on the investigation. Police trudged clumsily all over the area before a thorough scientific examination could be made and even reporters and photographers tramped the area where the bodies were found.

Even more unfortunate, the Coroner could not be found on that public holiday, no doctor was available at the City Morgue and it was more than 24 hours before an autopsy could be carried out. By then, based on the methods used at the time, no traces of any drugs or poisons that may have been used could be found in the bodies.

The inquest was a sensation with "other woman" allegations and stories of unconventional sexual attitudes. Press attention focused on Geoffrey Chandler as one of the main suspects, but nothing in the evidence linked him in any way to the deaths. Indeed, all 22 guests were suspects. Millions of extra newspapers were sold from the inquest. Many people expected a finding of murder, but were disappointed when Coroner J.J. Loomes found that "each of the unfortunate persons died an unnatural death...from acute circulatory failure, the cause of which is unknown."

The police hierarchy even brought in the painstaking Det-Sgt Jack Bateman in the hope he might turn up something, but every theory, even the most outlandish from abroad, was blown out. There were even suggestions that party host Ken Nash was jealous of Bogle's prowess with women and that his wife Ruth may also have succumbed to the scientist's womanising charms. But in the end, neither could answer the gossipy claims. On New Year's Day, 1974, Ruth Nash died and two years later, on New Year's Day, Ken Nash shot himself dead.

Bristow knew one of the male guests at the Nash party and he questioned him closely, also a woman claiming to have some knowledge of the mystery, but he was still really on the periphery until one of the police squad asked him if he could help.

That brought him up to date with everything that had happened. He went into print in the *Daily Mirror* adding to the range of exotic theories by saying that a veterinary drug, a hormone substance used for bringing horses into season, could have caused the deaths. But as the autopsy already showed, no traces of that or any other drug would have been left in the body.

As colourful as it sounded, it was fairly close to what Sgt Bateman believed privately. Crime reporter Bill Jenkings revealed in his book *As Crime Goes By* that Bateman thought the deaths were due to a prankster who, knowing the pair were likely to have sex that night, slipped a popular brand of dog worming tablets into cups of coffee drunk by Dr Bogle and Mrs Chandler which would have disrupted their sexual interlude.

Bristow knew about that one too, but discounted it. As his therapeutic knowledge of drugs improved due to his anti-drug work on the northern beaches, Bristow came to the conclusion that the painful symptoms they suffered just before dawn that day were caused by an overdose of the drug LSD. He made his belief known publicly. Later, in 1996 when new testing methods became available, 33 years after their deaths, his opinion was proved when traces of LSD were found in tissue samples from their bodies. After the lapse of time it could not be shown how much LSD they had ingested.

But did Bogle take LSD and maybe slip a hallucinogenic Mickey Finn to Mrs Chandler before their first sexual encounter? Or was it slipped to them at the party? Bristow sensibly debunked all those theories, including the dog worming tablets prank. He put it down to murder firstly on the simple basis that a third party had clearly been at the scene. That person probably covered up Mrs Chandler.

The post-mortem did show that Bogle could have died as early as 5 a.m. and Mrs Chandler probably died an hour or more later. It was therefore unlikely that Bogle could have covered her with the flattened beer cartons or that she did it herself. Abrasions on her torso indicated that she either crawled or stumbled around - or someone dragged her.

But that still left the intriguing question of how was the drug administered? With Bogle's knowledge of science, it was highly unlikely he would have knowingly taken a lethal dose or given such a dose to Mrs Chandler, the woman he was wanting to woo. So that means someone else gave it to them. But how?

Putting himself in the mind of a criminal, Bristow concluded - and at least one detective on the case agreed with him - that the perpetrator of the crime arranged for one or two accomplices to follow them to the Lane Cove scene, perhaps hold them up with a pistol as apparent lover's lane bandits, then say something along these lines: "What the hell, you seem like a nice couple, let's have a drink and forget about it. After all, it's New Year's Eve."

Producing a bottle laced with LSD, they offered it to the lovers, with disastrous results, while drinking from a safe bottle themselves or pretending to swig from the bottle handed to the lovers in the semi darkness of what was then early New Year's Day. Margaret Chandler and Dr Bogle, having already had a fair amount to drink, were likely in the circumstances to have accepted the invitation from strangers to have another drink in sheer relief at no longer being held up at gunpoint and likely to suffer harm at the hands of two apparently crazy gunmen.

It was a more believable, practical and realistic theory than any other put up, and cut across all the objections investigators had to the many outlandish theories floated. In the end it had to be something simple and cunning like that which led to those bizarre deaths.

The person whom Bristow suspected to be guilty of plotting the deaths was still alive at the time of publication. One day a vital clue or denouement by someone involved may flush out this person.

9

DANGEROUS LIAISONS

THE strong voice was unmistakable. Lennie McPherson was on the line as Bristow stood naked, dripping with a towel around him after leaving the shower at his Newport home. "Tim," said McPherson, "I thought you might be interested to know that I've been offered $40,000 to knock you off."

Bristow stood blinking into the phone, suddenly feeling vulnerable at the chilling message. He knew Lennie was a killer feared and respected in the underworld as a man who could get things done. Not sure if this was a threat or a friendly tip, Bristow thought he'd act tough anyway. "You'd better make the first move a good one," he said.

Big Lennie laughed. "I didn't say I was going to do it. But you've got to admit, it's a lot of loot for a job." That took the pressure off. The friendly introduction from Ray Kelly had stood him well so far. Kelly had said at the time: "Lennie is one man I can trust."

Then Lennie gave him the part that worried him. "I told him to do his own dirty work. The trouble is, someone else might take it up." Bristow said: "I think I know who's behind this. Could we meet to discuss it?" McPherson agreed. They met later that afternoon at The Spit on Sydney's Middle Harbour.

He told McPherson about the man who wanted him killed, an Englishman who claimed to be a Battle of Britain hero with a DFC and Bar but who was in Dartmoor prison at the time, as New Scotland Yard told Bristow. The man, who Bristow had confronted on debt jobs, was now involved in a messy Sydney divorce action in which Bristow was acting for his wife. She was almost penniless and living apart from her well-to-do husband.

Bristow told McPherson the man had pulled a pistol on him. He'd taken it from him and unloaded it. McPherson confirmed he was the person who wanted him to kill Bristow. He offered to put the word out that nobody should take up the offer. Bristow took McPherson to his car to meet his client the wife, who was now extremely agitated but the big fellow put her mind at rest, offering to help her if she was threatened.

Bristow was greatly relieved to have McPherson's friendship and assurances. Although Lennie was mainly into protection rackets and organising robberies, he was a kind of repository of underworld knowledge whose opinion was usually sought by smart criminals if planning any underworld killings. It didn't pay to upset him. After that, they began ringing each other. Bristow always contacted him if he had a job that touched on the underworld.

Another attempt had been made to kill Bristow shortly before, in 1966, when he took on a job several other private eyes had turned down to serve divorce papers on a ruthless criminal turned respectable businessman on the North Shore.

He took the wife along to identify the man, knocked on his door in the evening and when he came out, served the papers on him. The fellow went berserk, screaming "I'll kill you, you bastard," and ran inside. The wife panicked and in trying to jump off the porch, fell into a rose bush, calling out: "Oh god, he's got a gun."

Unarmed, and with the wife noisily trying to extricate herself from the rose thorns, Bristow could do nothing except move behind the side of the door jamb and hold the door shut with the fingers of one hand. Inside, the criminal yelled and ranted with a pistol in one hand, wrenching at the door with the other.

Finally, the woman jumped into Tim's white Merc, revved the motor to let him know she was ready to go and Tim was over the porch and down the drive before the crim realised what was happening. As the car moved off, he waved his pistol and shouted: "I'll get you, Bristow."

The terrified woman hired a bodyguard. About a month later when the bodyguard parked his car in her garage around midnight, a hit man shot and wounded him, obviously mistaking him for Bristow.

Another time he went close to being killed on a raid in a block of flats at Rosa Gully at Vaucluse. Trying to force open the door, he found it wouldn't yield against a strong chain and suddenly a man inside fired through the opening. A bullet creased his scalp on the left side, causing blood to flow. Bristow forced his way in, knocked the nude man over in a flying tackle and took the revolver from him.

Usually Bristow took his pictures and was gone by the time the cops came but this time in the commotion someone in the flats rang them quickly and they arrived before he left. Ignoring Tim's bleeding wound, they wanted to charge him with causing grievous bodily harm for "touching up" the gunman, although Bristow considered he'd gone lightly on him after the fellow burst into tears. A divorce resulted from it.

In other raids he was stabbed twice, in an arm and the stomach. He accepted that a private eye bursting into a love nest always had to watch out for repercussions. Those violent incidents convinced him of the need to take off-duty cops along with him as a bargaining point against being arrested.

Bristow believed that if you had enough money, came from the right background and had the right connections, you could get away with murder. Although he wasn't one to lose sleep over it, that was always at the back of his mind.

He always expected trouble if he raided a policeman's daughter or someone with authority, but he came to worry more about those regarded as pillars of respectability. They were capable of the worst treachery and violence. So, without his client knowing, he always tried to check to see if enemy action was likely. Also, to see if he was being used, because warring couples could reconcile and leave him in no man's land.

Threats to kill him were common and he had to weigh up whether they would pay to make an attempt on his life. But he knew that those who didn't show anger or make threats were the dangerous ones. He was always wary when occasionally finding two men instead of a man and woman - gays, he found, were unpredictable and usually handy with their fists.

At rare times he discovered that a husband would not be having an affair of the heart, but was into bondage. He was amazed that one of Sydney's best-known men and a top businessman, whom he knew well, was a bondage fiend, who sometimes visited Madam Lash. The person's bondage activities elsewhere led to him being blackmailed by a man, a situation brought into sharp focus when Lennie McPherson was called in to assist. Big Lennie simply said to the blackmailer: "Give me all the pictures you have and the negatives, or you're dead." The sleazebag, deciding life was real and earnest, took Lennie's "advice."

Survival, especially for those working with him, was vital to Bristow. That's why he felt justified in bribing cops to protect himself and help his clients against repercussions. He was liable to be arrested for every door he kicked in and indeed, he was charged several times. He bought his way out through one senior cop who would remain a lifelong friend.

The extent of dishonest practices he saw in the divorce field was enough for Bristow to give himself the benefit of the doubt when it came to his own faults. He saw them as minor by comparison - but they were to cause him serious trouble.

The contract on his life for which McPherson came to his aid was brought about by Tim's habit of falling for his beautiful female clients. Usually he upheld a client's rights - double dealing was always the big worry for anyone using a private eye - and he'd seen how money and "tooling" had got men into trouble. But when it came to his own sexual interests, he threw caution to the winds, even somersaulting on some male divorce clients to throw his lot in with their ladies.

If Tim got a divorce job and the lady he was raiding was a stunner, a few days later he'd literally be in bed with her. He loved blondes and if they were German, so much the better. Germans were real women, and strong.

Di Parkinson, a model who knew Tim from the '50s and worked with his first and second wives, was familiar with all his serious ladies. She was not one of his lovers but a friend. Di at age 15 didn't know what he meant when he asked her: "Do you have a lover?"

But later, with more experience, she realised there were always two sets of rules with Tim when it came to ladies. He didn't like his own women playing around but it was OK for Tim. While out sleuthing at night, he called in at various places for cups of tea and sex. And he always claimed that a man wasn't a man unless he "tooled" lots of women. She blamed his mother for his attitude by always letting him have his own way.

Di was one woman who believed Tim could not distinguish between love and sex. "He once said to me 'if you marry someone, you love them, but what is love?' He was really two characters in the one head and body. One moment he would be the tough guy, the would-be gangster prepared to punch the lights out of someone. Next he would be feeding the birds and admiring the flowers, roses especially and everything that was beautiful, like a golden sunset.

"With children, he would tell them lovely stories, wanting to give them a drink or a lolly, and just watch them to enjoy the beauty of their youth and innocence. But he also liked to create drama and chaos around him. When he insulted me once, I did wheelies in my car all over his immaculate lawn and he was going to murder me. Another time, he rode his horse into my kitchen for fun.

"His was always a dual life. He took whatever women he wanted without any real thought for the person with whom he was supposed to be a partner. Women could manipulate him, but only for a certain time, until he could seduce them, then he'd go back to being himself.

"But Tim had another side to him, the funniest side. People had a lot of laughs from Tim because he was outrageous. He was a great story teller and would tell stories against himself.

"I was one of his dancing partners and like him, loved it for the sheer joy and exhilaration of the music and rhythm. For all his faults, I don't think there'll be another like him. I especially liked him for the way he helped people. He was so much larger than life and there was always excitement and something new happening around Tim."

In the background to the $40,000 murder contract that had been offered to McPherson, Bristow had made some powerful enemies. The husband wanting to kill Tim had made a lot of money as a developer, but his wife wasn't sharing in it. She hired Bristow to help her obtain evidence for a divorce, although she couldn't afford it. Tim genuinely wanted to help, and he was also struck by her beauty. A blonde, she had been an English beauty queen winner who did airline ads. To help her with money, he hired her as his secretary.

The case became complicated and fuelled by emotion. The husband petitioned for divorce, naming another man as co-respondent, but he admitted in a discretionary statement to the court that he had committed adultery a number of times with a younger woman. He claimed he was living apart from his wife at the time and that their marriage was at an end.

The husband's action followed a raid on him by Tim, accompanied by the man's wife. In the raid Tim gained evidence of misconduct by listening outside the bedroom window with bugging devices. A typescript of that evidence contained some prurient conversation. On Tim entering the home with the wife and taking pictures, a gun was pulled on him and a scuffle took place.

The businessman summonsed Tim alleging damage to a door, trespassing and assault but although the allegations went to court, they didn't proceed. Then Tim was accused of having an affair with the wife, but ultimately that didn't go to a court hearing. If proved, it would have meant an immediate divorce for the man with Tim paying all the costs.

An Australian wartime air ace, a friend of the husband's, called on Tim at his home and aggressively threatened him with the evidence he intended giving. Tim threw him down the stairs.

That person summonsed Tim alleging assault occasioning actual bodily harm but, although surrounded by five or six bodyguards from the rival Websters private inquiry agency, he decided not to get out of his car at the court to give evidence and that matter lapsed too. Tim then sued him in the District Court for damages of $6,030 for "falsely and maliciously and without reason or probable cause" alleging assault and ill-treatment. Tim's counsel was the aggressive Tony Bellanto, QC. It was then that the husband approached McPherson to kill Tim.

The would-be murderer had some powerful friends, including Justice Minister John Maddison, whose legal firm was profiting from the husband's business. He complained to Maddison about Tim raiding him.

Asked privately if he was intimate with the wife, Bristow admitted he was, explaining she was dependant on him, relying on his ability to help her establish a home for herself and her daughters, and in the circumstances he had to be close to her. She won her divorce, custody of the children and an allowance. No doubt Tim was a saviour to the lady, but he wasn't missing out in the process.

He needed to be close to clients because in a real life situation if he miscued with the wrong information or raided the wrong people, he could have ruined someone's future as well as being liable for damages. He also had to be on guard against betrayal by a client. In kicking down that door, there was always a feeling of anxiety over what might happen.

One sensational divorce case, in which Bristow did a somersault to go with the lady, involved a Macquarie Street

eye specialist, Dr Edwin Trenerry and his beautiful North
Shore wife, Averil. The doctor alleged his wife was having an
affair with Irish-born, American-accented Chuck Faulkner.
Averil, of Killara, was a former model and fashion consultant
who worked for some of Europe's more exclusive fashion
houses, and Chuck, of Double Bay, was the first of
Australia's big-name TV personalities and the first man to
read the news on Sydney television on Channel 9.

The doctor wanted Tim to raid Mrs Trenerry to obtain
evidence, but Tim preferred to befriend her. A raid was
eventually carried out by Websters inquiry agency at the
Florida Hotel in Terrigal after undercover work.

The case, a lawyer's picnic, was raised in parliament and
made frequent headlines, but Tim kept in the background.
Among the heavyweight legal eagles was Mr P W
Woodward, QC, a later Royal Commissioner.

The facts were that Mrs Trenerry petitioned for divorce
in the mid 1960s on the ground of her husband's cruelty and
he cross-petitioned for his freedom, alleging she had
committed adultery with Faulkner. Mrs Trenerry and
Faulkner both contested the allegation.

The upshot was that after 18 high-profile days in the
Divorce Court, Mr Justice Jenkyn found in favour of Averil
and Chuck, deciding she had not committed adultery with
him and granted her a divorce. The doctor sued Chuck for
$20,000 damages. Chuck had to pay his own divorce costs
and the doctor his own and Averil's costs. Chuck's wife
divorced him.

The judge commented that Faulkner had played a
dangerous game by misleading private inquiry agents into
believing he was committing adultery with Mrs Trenerry, both
conceding they had occasionally kissed and embraced.
Faulkner had freely admitted falling in love with Mrs Trenerry.

But that wasn't the end of it. Amid uproar, Dr Trenerry claimed in a statutory declaration read out in the NSW Parliament by MP Rex "Buckets" Jackson, that he had been the victim of a vicious conspiracy by the Divorce Court proceedings being spread out, instead of lasting only the expected four days after his father agreed to pay any outstanding costs, and he was subjected to legal costs of $34,169.92 plus fees of $6,062 to the agents, Websters.

The doctor also alleged his legal team had instructed him to give false evidence, that vital facts had been deliberately suppressed and that his wife had repeatedly given false testimony in the court. His declaration said Faulkner's legal representatives had approached his counsel admitting adultery by Faulkner with his wife on condition that the doctor drop his $20,000 damages claim. On his threatening to sue, Websters had repaid the money he paid them.

Mr Jackson demanded a full inquiry to obtain justice for Dr Trenerry but that was defeated on party political lines. The former Mrs Trenerry issued a statement denying the allegations. Tim was smart to keep his head out of that one. But after the divorce he won the lady and had a fling with Averil.

Tim's colourful way of expressing his attitude to such complicated situations was: "I didn't want the lady to feel lonely. If they were good sorts, I didn't bother trying to find a replacement for their lovers. I helped them out by standing in as a tooler."

That well-publicised case would have one or two echoes soon after. Faulkner continued a turbulent career bouncing between peaks of triumph and dark lows. He was charged with complicity in an $8,000 payroll robbery at Channel 10 in 1967, but was acquitted. The costs from his legal cases caused him to be bankrupted a year later. Chuck died on the east coast of the United States in December, 2000. Averil would marry the widowed Sir Percy Spender, former Federal Government Minister and President of the International Court of Justice.

But the somersault job Bristow would regret came after his liaison with Averil. A well-to-do businessman asked him to raid his wife, a German girl named Renate. Normally if Tim knew the people, he tried to avoid getting involved in their divorce proceedings. He'd met Renate with friends at the Newport Arms, and his brother Max had met her and her husband as well. Reluctantly he took on the job.

But Tim didn't want to proceed and the husband engaged other agents to obtain evidence. After the husband filed for divorce, Tim began working for Renate against the husband and in the wake of much drama, a settlement was negotiated in which Renate received a substantial amount of money.

Renate was pretty and Tim began a long affair with her. But she was something of a sex kitten and he engaged in a furious fight over her affections with a Kings Cross bouncer, ending in a court case that would later have disastrous consequences for Tim.

Meanwhile, Tim's liking for stylish divorced ladies continued. One attractive divorcee named Peggy from a town in western New South Wales even bought an apartment near his home so he could call late at night. He did a raid for beautiful model Maggi Eckardt and fell for her.

He turned down one request to raid a leading barrister who kept a mistress in an apartment near Manly, because he knew him well. The chap was so grateful he gave him free legal advice afterwards.

But Tim did most of the professional sneak jobs on celebrities and entertainers, including one for blue nightclub comedian Joe Martin on Joe's wife, who had left him a year or so earlier. Joe insisted on taking part in the raid, at a Rose

Bay flat, but had to be restrained from thumping the co-re, a television executive. The wife had known one of Tim's team intimately in earlier days and said in surprise when he started taking photos: "Well well, what are you doing here?" He said: "Small world."

Bristow was the only private eye in the world who went on divorce raids with cops and his own locksmith. It would save him many embarrassing moments like the time he and three others couldn't get though the security door of a big block at Manly and they elephant-walked it, flattening it to the mosaic floor. As the four of them stood there guiltily with brief cases, absurdly trying to look like serious businessmen, the concierge rushed in screaming: "What have you done! What have you done!"

The cops he usually took along were only there for insurance and didn't wish to get too involved, although they helped behind the scenes. They could not be counted on up front when the going got tough, as was the case when Tim took a senior detective from the Peninsula with him one day on a raid near Collaroy police station.

The co-re pulled a gun and threatened to shoot them. The cop left Tim to it and ran and hid behind a flame tree. Tim never let him forget it, embarrassing him with robust humour in the presence of others by saying whenever they met: "Remember that day you shit yourself outside Collaroy police station?..." Subtlety was not Tim's forte.

But it was a lucky day when Tim employed a little chap named Richard Wigglesworth, a genius at picking locks and for making things mechanical from a generator to a steam engine. Looking like a suburban doctor, he went around with Tim carrying a little black bag. But when he opened it, various board layers popped into position with enough gadgets to attempt a break and enter at the Bank of England - lock-picking devices, scopes, listening apparatus, all manner of picks and other manipulating devices, even a miniature oxy-acetylene torch.

A locksmith by profession and a firearms collector, Wigglesworth was being harassed by the cops who wrongly thought him to be a crim. He was sick of it and reading in the paper that Bristow was on the side of the underdog, rang him. Tim told to come to his house at nine next day.

"I arrived on time," he said later, "And a voice thundered from the bedroom 'in here.' Tim was in bed with some lady. He pointed to the bed and said 'sit.' I told him my problem and without a word he lifted the phone, asked for Ross Nixon, the head of ballistics at the CIB, and began bellowing at him. Christ, I thought, I'm going to be arrested and I was crapping myself. He finished up telling Nixon 'I want you to stop hassling this mate of mine, now,' and to my amazement the cops did.'

The lady in bed with Tim was Baroness Rita Dobronyi, a Playboy bunny from Miami, Florida, and former wife of Baron Sepy Dobronyi, who had financed Hugh Hefner into the Playboy business.

Tim then shocked the somewhat coy Rick Wigglesworth by suddenly pulling down the sheets to display a nude, unblushing Baroness. "Have a look at these for melons," he joked, laughing uproariously. Rita, measuring up at 37-23-36 on the old scale, lay there sensuously, making no attempt to cover up. Tim had already shown her off topless at a surf carnival where she bared her bulbous boobs on his boat, disrupting the competition by causing the males to ogle her instead of watching the races.

Looking anywhere but at Rita, Rick told Tim he was a locksmith and Tim said: "'I'm sick of kicking in doors. I'll handle your case and you'll work for me'. Right, I said. Later we'd go to all these places at night, get to the door and Tim would say 'righto Fingers, open it up'. It was always an adrenalin trip and I kept low down at doors in case of bullets."

The work often had its light moments. One of the first raids they did together was at Rose Bay, on a gentleman called Viscount Palmer, an English biscuit manufacturer, although on this occasion he was trying out some crumpet, the wife of an Australian shipping magnate. Also on the raid was "Tropical John" Petford for a bit of backup and "Iron Bar" Freddy, who wrapped newspaper around a steel bar in case a little Russian anaesthesia was needed.

They caught the biscuit man in bed with the wife, took shots and the shipping magnate, obviously a man of the old school, said to the fornicator with admirable composure: "You sir, are a cad and a bounder."

That was rich enough in the circumstances, but the Englishman, standing there starkers, tried to show that he too was a man of refinement, saying: "This is an outrageous invasion of one's privacy." In the circumstances, Tim delivered one of his great one liners: "That's the way the cookie crumbles."

Wigglesworth couldn't stop laughing and even Tropical John lost his usual Sphinx-like demeanour and laughed. His job completed, Tim's personal locksmith went and sat in Tim's car for about three hours until Tim came out - with the lady, whom he dropped home. "He certainly had a way with women," said Wigglesworth, "I think he got on to her too."

Another time a separated wife temporarily living at the home of a Supreme Court judge wanted Tim to raid her husband. The job came from Frank Pittard's inquiry agency - the husband was a fitness fanatic and Pittard's men weren't game to tackle him.

The fit husband had one flaw, a glass eye, and when Tim and his boys went in he was missing the peeper - he'd apparently popped it into a tumbler of water beside the bed while doing the trick. His estranged wife, who accompanied Tim, hurled the tumbler at him, hitting him on the forehead, saying scornfully: "Get your eye in." The romantic lover, glaringly naked, was forced to crawl around the floor looking for his glass eye, so humiliated he proved to be a real pussycat.

Then there was the musician at Asquith, on Sydney's North Shore. Given instructions by a solicitor acting for the musician's wife to raid him, Tim and Tropical John and one or two others went on their "milk run" of several jobs one night, but had trouble reaching the musician's house.

The detective whom Tim had head-butted at Ray Kelly's sendoff was in charge of the local Hornsby division and had heard Tim intended doing a raid somewhere in his area. He had set up several road blocks, hoping to charge Tim with some offence. So Tim had to use the back streets.

That night Tim had about 12 operators running around Sydney doing surveillance and it wasn't always easy for them to find a public telephone to say they had a target and things were right for the job. Usually they removed the light fuses so the occupants couldn't switch on the lights and identify them. And often they let down the tyres of a target's car so he couldn't follow them. They also put singlets over the number plates of their own cars which they removed after a raid when a few hundred metres away.

So Tim wasn't in the mood for horseplay when they entered the musician's house in the early hours. In the hallway they saw the instruments the two musos in the house had used for their gig earlier that night. Suddenly there was a commotion as two men and two women came out yelling. The musician who was the target wanted to fight Tim and next thing, Tim upended a big bass drum, smashing it over the fellow's head who ended up wearing it around with his head sticking out, bellowing.

One night, to snap some shots of a wayward husband, they went to Sydney's North Head, a spacious and desolate spot looking across to the city lights and a favourite trysting place for motorists in pre-motel days. They pulled open the doors of a targeted car, their camera flashes went off and soon after, the car's headlights and tail-lights went on and the bonker sped off.

As if a starting gun had gone off, car lights went on all over the place and about 50 drivers took off. Talk about *coitus interruptus!* It reminded Tim of an old Laurel and Hardy comedy film in which Hardy leapt out a window in a block of flats after a husband returned unexpectedly, found him in bed with his wife and fired a shot at him as he fled. Within seconds every window in the block opened and men in various stages of undress jumped out.

Tim joked to his companions: "How can professionals make a living when there are so many ladies of amateur status about?"

Doing a raid for a female friend late one afternoon in the Ranelagh skyscraper unit block at Darling Point, Tim found the target, an American con man posing as a millionaire but who was trying to rob Tim's friend of her cash, to be offensive and troublesome. Tim held him out by the ankles from the top floor balcony until he stopped struggling and came to heel, saying to him suggestively: "I think you have suicidal tendencies."

He successfully raided the MP and ABC sports commentator Dick Healey in a car, appropriately, at Balls Head and did several at equally appropriate Rooty Hill. In one of those, Tropical John was shot in a hand and Tim went into the house, took a .22 rifle from the assailant and belted him. That was a job sub-contracted by another agent, Frank Monte, who Tim claimed would meekly sit outside in his car "holding his client's hands" while Tim and his team did some of his tough ones.

But Tim got square with Monte for not levelling with him that guns were likely to be produced. Before handing over his incriminating photos to Monte on other jobs that were without major incident, he'd say: "The fellow produced a gun. You owe me another five hundred."

A Sydney shipping bigwig, not as polite as the one who thought his wife's lover was a cad and bounder, had a morally loose wife and wanted her caught quickly. But she was vigilant and Tim's surveillance team didn't have any luck. The shipping man was a bit of a skinflint and didn't want to keep paying out without positive results.

Not wanting to fail, Tim brought in his secret weapon, a stand-in co-re, like a professional stud, whom he'd used several times. The stud got to know the wife, went water skiing with her, took her to bed and bingo. Again, not the Marquis of Queensberry, but effective in a tricky world.

Some of the women on these raids screamed, others smiled and with their futures in mind appeared silently pleased because they were caught with the right man. But one woman threw every vase and piece of crockery she could find at Tim until he could quieten her down. On another raid Tim and his team gracefully withdrew after entering a block of flats one day when a co-re grabbed his clothes and leapt out the back window to the car park below, injuring himself.

Over the years Tim successfully raided one man three times on behalf of different women. A former private school boy, he was a wealthy Jewish entrepreneur - "a good pants man and a good customer," Tim said, dryly. Tim did a raid in Bowral at Craigieburn, the private hotel where a bell rang melodiously at 5 a.m. on weekends to remind some of the guests it was time to return to their own rooms, if they wished. When not using his own name, Tim always booked in as John Watson, and his agents were Watsons.

He also did one in Singapore, at the Hilton on a frequently visiting Sydney businessman. Staying at the Shangri La, Tim dined splendidly at Raffles in between trailing the man around. Then he generously tipped the Hilton's concierge to plant a bug in the man's room and to lend him a key. When he heard the right sounds, he went in and took the action shots.

Another favourite spot known to lovers as "The Place" was a motel at Rushcutters Bay, where many of Sydney's eastern suburbs set thought they were safe from prying eyes, not realising that Tim had connections with the management and could arrange a discreet job there. He never used those premises for his own philandering, preferring a room at the Sydney Hilton. This motel was where Sir Billy Snedden, who came within a few hundred votes of being prime minister, later died of a heart attack after enjoying a vigorous intimacy with a well-known eastern suburbs lady.

It opened up a fascinating new world to Rick Wigglesworth, who loved going to the Divorce Court and listening while Tim or Tropical gave evidence. Rick laughingly told friends how the judges ogled the pictures, imagining Justice Dovey saying to himself, "Hmnnn, nice knockers...".

Not all Rick's lock pickings were for cheating spouses. One of Tim's clients, a Mrs Benson, had an ancient Japanese scroll stolen by a Taiwanese man, a martial arts expert who was supposed to be a known killer. Richard had to open his door while Tim recovered it. "Sure this bloke's away?" he asked nervously. Tim simply replied: "Yeah."

In the same suburb, Ashfield, a male client wanted to recover his passport so he could leave the country. He and his wife had separated but she wanted to keep him in Australia. So Tim had Wigglesworth get out his bag of tricks and go to work on the safe in their home. After much exertion and sweating in the summer heat, he drilled through the half-plate safe and found the passport. Also in there was a mummified human finger and a shrunken human head.

Bristow's fame spread to the extent that he was asked by solicitors in Los Angeles to do a raid for a prominent lady whose husband was a bigshot financier in Hollywood, despite the fact that plenty of Pinkerton agents were available there.

Tim flew to LA, was introduced to the financier's wife and promised to keep it confidential. She went to a theatre with her husband and arranged for Tim to go incognito to identify him for later. He glimpsed him - and enjoyed the terrific dancing in the show, *Sophisticated Lady*. He thought the name also suited his client, a refined person who was nicely mannered. She laid down two conditions: "I want you to catch my husband with his girlfriend, but please do not hurt him."

The raid had to take place at Newport on the opposite side of the country, where the America's Cup was run and the tycoon had a girlfriend. Tim flew to the east coast with the wife. Entry to the raid venue was easy because Tim was given a key. He went in and took some shots but the fellow carried on a treat. While his wife stood there triumphant and serene, he punched and kicked as Tim held him at arm's length. When he caught Tim one or two glancing blows, it was time to apply one of his Newport Arms grips, turning him around and making his efforts impotent. "Tell me when you want to change the script," Tim said cynically.

He never heard the result but didn't think they parted. The lady just wanted to put a stop to it. She was delighted with Tim's effort, hugging him, paying him handsomely and giving him a fashionable blue and cream sports shirt decorated with a Newport yachting motif.

Nobody is better qualified to give an assessment of the Bristow of those days than Tropical John, a man of achievement in several directions before taking up PI work, including being a pharmaceutical chemist. He went to private schools too, Cranbrook and Scots. The many jobs he did with Tim depended on complete trust and respect between them.

"I always found Tim to be a straight shooter and a good operator," he said. "For looking after the clients, in handling the 'bread' and for counting it correctly, I take my hat off to him as being the best in the business. But he didn't worry too much about the paperwork and typed a lousy report.

"Without taking anything away from him, he was more like the old-fashioned movie-type of PI who didn't go in for sophisticated reports. I think his typewriter had cobwebs. His idea of accountancy was, I know what I've got in this pocket and what I have to pay out in the other pocket.

"He was very hands on, straight up, confrontational. Loved conflicts where someone was being stood over or threatened and would take it further. Never known to shy away from confrontation. Had a terrific knack for doubling the fee in those situations, and when you mentioned he was doing a double ender, he'd laugh deep and long.

"He was intelligent, had lots of natural courage and street nous. He was known as The Enforcer in those days but there was more to him than that suggests. Also he was far more than a standover man. He was quite generous and good hearted. Like all PIs he talked out of the side of his mouth and acted like a wise guy at some stage - it's the nature of the jobs we did.

"I don't think he trusted many people, which is why he put on such a hard exterior. I used to get a bit weary of waiting for him while he dined and wined his female clients, and waiting on instructions for jobs in the mornings while he rode one of his horses up and down Newport Beach nodding and chatting to the girls.

"He always said it was dangerous to talk on the phones, but talked anyway. Whenever I offered to debug his phones, he said 'ah, don't bother.' He was very vain and had a big ego. I used to tell him, you've got more mirrors than windows in your house, and I posed like him in front of them. He just laughed."

Bristow would lead the last of the celebrity raids before Federal Attorney-General Lionel Murphy eventually introduced the *Family Law Bill,* removing adultery as a ground for divorce and replacing it with an irretrievable breakdown of marriage and a separation of one year.

It would do away with private snoops in the divorce area. But it didn't matter to Bristow - other clients were always knocking with strange jobs.

10

DIAMOND JIM AND THE DOCTOR'S WIFE

BRISTOW'S reputation for fearlessly leading from the front brought him numerous clients. The big private eye, in spite of having to deal ruthlessly with some scammers and con men to get justice for clients, didn't go out of his way to create enemies. In many cases he recommended compromise to his clients and approached opponents in a friendly way, suggesting they act sensibly.

It was better, for instance, to discount a debt and get something back rather than drag it through the courts at great expense and inconvenience. But if it had to be done the hard way, okay. One thing Bristow demanded was that clients level with him. He'd usually help, provided they told him the truth and he knew what was afoot. He could make enough enemies in strictly legitimate situations.

The trouble was many misjudged him, expecting him to do their dirty work without question, not realising he was a man who had principles and could not be used as just a hired toady. He made thousands of friends by helping out in difficult situations, more often with battlers than prominent identities. But one powerful friend he made was former SP bookie Bob Askin when he ran into serious political trouble and Tim was asked to help. As a youth he'd known Askin when Askin and his father were together in the Collaroy Surf Club.

After becoming Leader of the NSW Liberal Opposition in 1959, Askin was making a bold bid to become Premier in 1965. But just before the State election, a close relative of Askin was charged by police with sexual assault. If it had hit the press, it would almost certainly have ruined his chances of being Premier. Tim fixed it with cops for the charge to be dropped, avoiding what would have been whipped up as a scandal.

But Tim made some powerful enemies by being lured into cases before realising their full implications, then standing up for the wronged party. One of the worst scenarios began quietly enough about 7.30 p.m. on 19 December 1966. The details would be set out by Bristow in a statement he prepared at the time as evidence.

The manager of a Sydney inquiry agency, Frank Pittard, rang Tim asking him to be at the Circular Quay shipping terminal early next morning to meet the liner *Himalaya* for a special job. Pittard said a "violent character" was coming in who had earlier shot the managing director of a company in Sydney. He'd also been the "number one suspect" in the horrific Sydney mutilation murders of the early 1960s. Tim was advised to come armed.

Next morning at the wharf Pittard gave him more details. The person was a Dr Shane Watson whom he described as "a dangerous man, suspected of bringing drugs back into the country." Police and Customs men were watching his arrival. Pittard handed Tim pictures of the doctor taken on the *Himalaya's* voyage.

He mentioned the legal firm handling the matter, including a heavyweight QC. Pittard's job was to serve a divorce petition on Dr Watson. Tim's job after the doctor left the ship was to go to the doctor's home at Longueville on Sydney's lower North Shore where his wife lived, but to get there before him. He said police were waiting outside the house and "we have an armed guard inside the house and if he attempts to force an entry, he will be shot."

After the ship arrived Tim hurried to the house and saw two senior CIB detectives sitting in a car nearby. Pittard arrived and gave him further instructions: "He should be here any minute now. He'll walk to the house and, we hope, try to force an entry. If he doesn't, but puts on a turn, the police will lumber him and take him to Ryde Psychiatric Centre where two special doctors are waiting to certify him. I'm going to serve the petition on him as soon as he turns away so as to annoy him. That should do it. But I want you to follow him and aggravate him when you get the chance."

Tim asked: "What happens if he sees me?" Pittard said: "I hope he does, as we want him to pick up a gun. If he does, we've got him." Tim's clear understanding was that he should deliberately aggravate the doctor so he would have an excuse to shoot him in self defence.

The doctor arrived, knocked at the door and on being refused entry, began to walk back to his hire car in the rain. Pittard served his wife Freda's divorce petition on him alleging desertion, which the doctor accepted quietly. Then the doctor drove to the Shore Motel. Tim followed and, feeling uneasy by this time, approached Dr Watson at the motel to gauge his reaction. Watson asked Tim to join him for lunch but he declined, saying he was working for Mrs Watson.

Then the doctor said: "I can't understand this. I was forced to leave the country three years ago. I went to England for further research and gained an extra degree there and picked up another one in Glasgow. I've been interested in underwater weapons in England and America, where I worked on cancer research."

After seeking advice on the phone from a barrister and solicitor, Tim went to the wharf with Dr Watson to help him retrieve his belongings, which were still being searched. Tim questioned a senior Customs officer who told him: "I've thoroughly checked out Dr Watson, and he's not the man they're making him out to be. He successfully performed a major operation on the ship on the way here and the ship's captain and officers speak highly of him."

Tim noticed toys and other presents the doctor had brought for his children and, noting how upset he was, said he'd assist him in seeing the children. He spoke to the doctor's solicitor, Brian Nagel, then rang Pittard and told him what he'd done and that he'd no longer be working for the agent's client, Mrs Watson.

Convinced the doctor was the victim of a conspiracy, Tim then threw a big cat among the pigeons by going around all the legal people concerned in the case and questioning them. Imagine their chagrin on realising that the bulldozer they thought they had plunging ahead for them had now turned about, charging full speed at them and raising awkward questions.

He called on them all. They included influential legal people who would go on to achieve important positions. Two of them would become judges and several others, QCs. At the centre of his inquiries was the solicitor J R McClelland, then a leading industrial advocate for the unions with strong political connections who would later become famous as Diamond Jim, Federal Labor Senator, Whitlam Government Minister and a NSW judge.

At one stage as Tim was doing the rounds of city legal offices with two operatives, a man in a dark suit and hat yelled to him on the footpath in Bathurst Street: "I'm the man you're looking for, I'm the man you want," and he kept walking. It was McClelland, letting Tim know he was aware of his inquiries.

Next day a detective rang Tim and told him to report to the CIB at 9 a.m. the following Monday for a conference with the two detectives he'd seen outside Mrs Watson's home. The senior cop told him: "Keep well away from Watson and drop off McClelland as he's a friend of mine. And this Dr Watson is a dangerous man. We'll get him but there's no need for you to make it harder."

Tim's legal adviser told him to hold off for a while, but after a week Tim turned up at Longueville making inquiries among Mrs Watson's neighbours. One told him he'd found the doctor to be a decent man and he was upset that three detectives had been waiting in the locality for Watson. Another, a doctor, said the only thing wrong with Dr Watson's marriage was that he had appeared to be obsessed with underwater weapons research.

Still on the trail, Bristow spoke to people in charge of the Navy diving unit like Commander Cuthbert and Bill Wilcox, who described Watson as a brilliant diver, doctor and surgeon who was skilful in all aspects of underwater biology and weaponry. Watson was on loan to them from the Royal Navy.

Then Bristow discovered that Shane Watson was a Second World War hero who was decorated for his bravery for diving into the dark, oily, waterlogged innards of HMAS *Nestor* to bring out the bodies of four shipmates. He tried to revive them after the ship had been strafed and crippled by German bombers in the Mediterranean in 1942, not far from Tobruk. For his gallantry he was awarded the Distinguished Service Cross.

As surgeon lieutenant on the *Nestor*, he was engaged in a convoy operation with other N class destroyers to take urgent supplies from Gibraltar to embattled Malta in the gloomiest days of the war. The *Nestor* was taken in tow but was a sitting duck at night to U-boats and bombers because of light from the fires below deck. The crew tried to douse the light with hammocks. Knowing they would never make it back to Alexandria, the RAN sank the *Nestor* by depth charge.

Commodore Red Merson, a shipmate of Watson's on the *Nestor* who today lives at Clifton Gardens in Sydney, said of him: "He was a normal fellow and as brave as they come. The worst you could say of him is that he could have been a bit eccentric."

It didn't take Bristow long to discover the truth: Diamond Jim was having an affair with Dr Watson's wife and, believing the doctor before going to England had shot the managing director of a large electrical company in the backside on finding him climbing out his wife's bathroom window, he feared he might suffer the same fate. Hence, all the elaborate protection and Diamond Jim's loose plot to kill the doctor or have him certified if he showed the slightest aggression, was simply because McClelland fancied the doctor's wife.

Tim learned that the doctor was lucky not to have been arrested as the madman known as The Mutilator, who terrorised Sydney by knifing to death four down-and-outs in 1961 and 1962. He was one of the suspects as the city was gripped by fear with the newspapers demanding results. The Mutilator always left behind his gruesome calling card, the severed penis of each of his hapless victims.

If the real killer, William Macdonald, had not been arrested by chance in Melbourne in 1963 and convicted for life, Dr Watson might well have been in trouble for the mutilation murders through sheer prejudice, paranoia and injustice.

Dr Watson might have been eccentric, but he certainly wasn't the dangerous lunatic his enemies were painting him.

After his return to Sydney he went to Melbourne to practice but the fear trail created by McClelland followed him there too. They tried to take his practising certificate away and at one stage the police Special Branch grabbed him and committed him to the Royal Park mental institution there, but he was quickly released when his legal representatives got on the job.

In the divorce action brought by Mrs Freda Watson, the doctor named Diamond Jim as the party cited. The divorce went through and later McClelland married Freda. After Diamond Jim McClelland's death in 1999, the *Sydney Morning Herald* described him as "a man of charm, wit and erudition." The newspaper went on to say "all sorts of dreadful secrets died with him." McClelland's dark fixation about Dr Watson, to satisfy his own selfish interests, was one.

Bristow liked and respected Dr Watson, diving with him at Balmoral and helping him test his underwater hand-spear explosives to stun sharks, also to study the effects of the bends. But although Tim knew what he'd done was right, he regretted upsetting so many people with clout, some of whom never missed an opportunity to denounce him as being "mad," fearing he would damage their credibility by speaking out.

McClelland wasn't the only one posing as a pillar of society whom Bristow sorted out in that period of the 1960s. He got stuck into a crop of crooked solicitors, brokers and businessmen who stole millions of dollars through bogus land deals, manipulating company scams and keeping one jump ahead of inadequate laws. His clients were investors ripped off for worthless "land in paradise."

One Bristow client had been taken for a total of $360,000 by two con men. Standing to gain nothing, he offered Tim a third of what he could recover. Walking straight into the first con's office unannounced, Bristow said: "You owe my client $180,000. He'll settle for half. Now."

The fellow laughed. He denied it and said he didn't have any money, anyway. Bristow told him how much money he had and where he banked. He also said if he went to the police he'd be up for fraud, no matter what connections he had. But the con man still bluffed and Tim had to leave empty handed.

As the man left the building later that day, a limo drew up beside him, two big men jumped out, one grabbed him as the other opened the boot. Tim loomed up and said: "Put him in - he's going for a ride." The con man turned pale and said: "I'll pay." Next morning Tim picked up a bank cheque for $90,000.

An hour or so later Tim was on his way to Brisbane by plane and walked in on a third generation solicitor who owed his client the same amount. He put the same deal and met a similar response. "All right," said Tim, "If you don't pay I'll go into the clubs you belong to at lunchtime today and tell people what you've been up to." Soon after, he picked up $90,000 in cash and stashed it in his airline bag. His client was glad to pay him $60,000.

Bristow often used variations of the "take you for a ride" tactic. Some of the corporate rogues he had to deal with lived in fortresses, secured behind high walls and electronic devices and were impregnable in their homes. They bred the criminality into their families, their wives lying for them ("no, he's not here"). One of Sydney's wealthiest men, a developer, lived in such a fortress with cameras everywhere and Tim's men could not get in.

He owed $50,000 to an Italian sub-contractor who carted sand, and refused to pay, dishonestly alleging some fault in quality to avoid payment. He often used this ruse, growing rich at the expense of small suppliers. He brushed aside legal letters and in desperation, the Italian came to Tim.

As Tim's boys couldn't get into the businessman's home, one of them tried to jump into the back seat of his car as he backed out into the street one morning, but he was too quick and drove off. They appeared to give up, but followed at a discreet distance, knowing where his office was and hoping to catch him there as he arrived.

They drew close behind him in city traffic and saw a chance when he stopped at traffic lights in Pitt Street. "Don't hurt him," said Tim's chief operator as one of Tim's tough boys, Tom, leapt out, pulled the businessman out of his car and in full view of all the peak-hour passersby, sat him up on top of the vehicle. The chief said to him: "Fix this bill up, or you won't be so lucky next time."

The businessman went straight to the cops and had such pull that at one stage he had 12 cops on the investigation. Tim told Tom to make himself scarce, so he went to Melbourne. Tim's Italian client, whom he'd wised up, would not admit to anything and "knew nothing" and things gradually quietened down.

Then Tim, still in the background, played his trump. He would do this type of thing many times, coming on the scene as a friend after the event. Dressed fashionably with black homburg and with his best manners, he called at the businessman's office and courteously asked to see him. "I hear you've had some trouble with some Italians," he began. "I've got some good contacts in that area. Most of them have muscle behind them but I think I can help you there..."

And in the friendliest possible manner, he arranged a settlement on the spot. The businessman, although hard, mean and tough, was oblivious of the fact that Bristow had set it up in the first place. It was for cleverness of that kind that Tim's regular operators respected him so much.

Bristow often used bugs and at first bought his own, but as they became more sophisticated he relied on Tropical John, who went to America to study the latest developments. A wealthy Arab sheik who wanted to invest in Australia was propositioned by an Australian politician while on a junket through his kingdom. When the sheik came to Australia, the politician pressured him to appoint him as his secret business consultant - and he wasn't even in Government. The Arab didn't want that, but didn't know how to avoid the situation either.

He saw Bristow. After discussing the problem, Tim said: "Next time you see him, have this tape recorder on you and wear this tie-clip to record his conversation. Get him to say it all, then we'll give him the message." That was done and Tim, staying well in the background, arranged for an offsider to approach the politician in the street and tell him damaging evidence of his proposal had been obtained and would be used unless he dropped off. Nothing more was heard from him.

Bugging was the only way to gain evidence in cases that were incredibly complicated, reflecting the worst side of human nature by people of social standing. In one, a prominent solicitor who was a social snob, disapproved of his son-in-law on the ground of status, and arranged for him to be posted overseas, while his daughter remained in Sydney with the children.

Not suspecting treachery, the son-in-law transferred all his property into the name of his wife who meanwhile began an affair with her father's encouragement. When he returned to Sydney a few months later he was confronted with an appalling situation - the solicitor told him that unless he quietly gave his wife a divorce on the ground of *his* adultery, which wasn't true, he would see to it that he was refused access to his children.

That's when he saw Bristow, who out of compassion took the job on without a fee. Bristow gave him a bug and as smart as the solicitor thought he was, he repeated it all for the son-in-law who taped him. Then, with Bristow's strength behind him and accompanying him, he called on the solicitor again and revealed all, threatening to sue and put the evidence into court unless he was given a divorce, access to his children and his property back.

It worked out like that, although not without some trouble. The solicitor put the Crime Squad on to Bristow but he was able to show that as the law stood, he'd acted legally with the bug because his client had approved.

It was nothing for Bristow to disguise himself as a doctor wearing a white coat, or as a cleaner as he did one morning, entering a lawyer's office before dawn to search the files for an agreement of stealth between two businessmen who had sold their business and agreed not to start up in competition, but were in fact double-crossing the new management by competing incognito. Taking the document, he photographed it, picked up a mop and bucket and returned the document before dawn the next morning.

Bristow couldn't remember how many women he'd saved from a certain life of prostitution after con men offered to make them stars as models or entertainers in Asia. They were bound for whorehouses and drug addiction without knowing it. He had to talk roughly to some of those girls who didn't want to listen. Many parents were forever grateful to him.

Although his reputation was fearsome, he tried to avoid physical clashes where possible. But if it was necessary or inevitable, he didn't flinch. He was known to single-handedly throw 10 security guards out of a building where his client had a valid right in a property dispute.

In the midst of all this frenetic activity and detailed planning, Bristow still had time for friends and mates who might have felt depressed or worried about something. He would always lend a sympathetic ear to their problems, meet them or have a meal and, as one well-known barrister said, he could speak freely to Tim without having to watch what he said.

A footballer mate referred a desperate Sydney woman to Tim. Her businessman husband, a rotter and scoundrel, had taken all her money and kicked her out. She still part-owned some property but he had a court order out to seize that too. The footballer said to her: "You need Tim Bristow."

The woman, who cannot be named for legal reasons, described what happened: "I was in a bad way. My husband was banking on my suiciding. Then Tim became involved. He took me to a chiropractor friend of his, Verne Powell, and stood there for an hour stroking one of my hands while I was massaged. There was no sexual connotation. He helped solve my problems and sent two big blokes around to my marital home to get my personal belongings.

"He rang me every day to ask how I was feeling. I had never met such a kind man. And he never charged me a cent. That proved to me he was not the bad man many people said he was."

Perhaps the funniest episode of Tim's life arose from his involvement in one of the most unusual sieges the world had seen. Indeed, without his backroom dealing, the Glenfield Siege in the '60s would not have happened.

Tim was indirectly responsible for causing the siege by arranging for some car-stripping racketeers to escape being dealt with by the law. Another racketeer objected to being made the fall guy and set the chain of events in motion.

Wally Mellish, at 23, was a very ordinary and minor criminal, yet for seven days he staged a "comic opera" engaging the full attention of the NSW Police Commissioner, a senior superintendent, two inspectors, six sergeants, three senior constables, five first class constables and 15 ordinary constables.

The cast was large enough to have staged the *Pirates of Penzance*, and Gilbert and Sullivan would have been proud of their performance. Before it was over the script would change to the Theatre of the Absurd, with a bridal party of 32 cops standing by while a real shotgun wedding took place. It was high farce, and to add to the fun, the bride's name was Muddle.

A factual report in the *Australian* newspaper gave no real clue to the drama about to follow. It said an unarmed detective the previous evening had talked for 90 minutes to a man who had defied police for 15 hours holed up in a house at sleepy Glenfield, 22 miles south of Sydney. While talking, the man had nervously cocked and uncocked a double-barrelled shotgun. Det-Supt Don Fergusson had emerged saying: "The barrels of a shotgun look about a foot wide when pointed at your stomach."

The man with his hand on the trigger was Mellish. With him was his companion, Beryl Muddle, 19 and her 10-week-old son, Leslie. He was refusing to come out after police tried to serve a warrant on him and he'd driven them off with seven shotgun blasts.

After Fergusson left, a Presbyterian clergyman, Reverend Clyde Paton, who had known Mellish, entered the shabby fibro cottage with Beryl's young sister, bearing food and medicine for the baby. Mellish said he would not harm Beryl or the child during the night. Enter Gilbert and Sullivan in the person of "Norman the Foreman," or Commissioner Norman Allan. He turned up and stopping the Emergency Squad from storming the house with teargas, went inside with Reverend Paton to marry Wally and Beryl.

What had brought about this ludicrous situation? Nobody could work it out at the time. It was known the police wanted to question Mellish and that Allen had rushed to the scene after Mellish phoned Police HQ and "complained." Bristow knew the truth, that Mellish threatened to blow the gaff on police involvement in car stealing rackets and Allan went to the scene trying to keep the lid on a police scandal.

At the time car rackets were reaching epidemic proportions. Many panel-beating businesses were fronts for stripping stolen cars which were sold off for parts, stolen cars were being touched up and resold, and luxury sedans from the United States which were stolen after being bought there on low deposit and imported into Australia, were also being handled by local thieves.

Mellish was in a panel-beaters' car-stripping business with four others. They were investigated by Motor Squad cops and about to be arrested and charged. One of the four men had an uncle at Palm Beach who knew Bristow and approached him to see if they could buy their way out. Tim arranged it through the Motor Squad and they paid handsomely.

Mellish's four companions escaped being charged but Wally couldn't afford the bribe. When the cops then tried to arrest him on warrant and charge him with a major car stealing racket in which he was only a minor player, he became upset at the injustice of it and staged the siege. To prove his knowledge of those events at the time, Tim took this writer to the panel-beating shop and introduced him, in confidence, to Wally's lucky accomplices.

Meanwhile, the wedding proceeded. Wally arranged a makeshift altar using a table with flowers on it, Beryl wore a yellow dress and held the baby, Don Fergusson was witness and Wally momentarily put his shotgun and pistol on a chair after the Commissioner and best man said loftily: "You can't get married in a house of God while bearing arms, and we are in fact in the presence of God."

The ceremony over, Fergusson signed the marriage certificate, they shook hands all round and had a simple wedding breakfast of soft drink, sandwiches and chocolate biscuits, courtesy of the gendarmes, topped off with a wedding cake.

But Wally still wouldn't come out. "Norman the Foreman" went home for the night, a constable brought in nappies and the newlyweds dined on a hot meal from the nearby police canteen. Next day Commissioner Allan went in again but Wally was in a dangerous mood, holding a pistol at his wife's head while swigging from a flagon of wine. After several phone calls were made to the police operations centre in the next street, Fergusson arrived with a transistor radio and something wrapped in a pink bunny rug. It turned out to be a powerful Armalite rifle with 200 rounds of armour-piercing ammunition. A grave looking Fergusson came out saying: "The position is very, very serious."

The siege cops outside the house were furious and what they were saying about their Commissioner was nobody's business, especially when speaking of the state of his underpants as Wally held a gun to his head in the house at one stage. Here was an unstable man provided with one of the most dangerous weapons in the game, and they weren't allowed to grab him. Allan, another of the Government political appointments, had never come up through the ranks, spending his time in administration and as a prosecutor. Even Premier Bob Askin was forced to admit that Allan's tactics were "unusual." Allan claimed his actions were based on "psychiatric advice."

The cops outside eventually restored some commonsense, refusing to send in more food or cigarettes for Beryl and cut off the power. Finally, after one week, Mellish came out with Beryl saying "I'm finished with him for good."

But the farce wasn't over yet. Instead of charging him, police were ordered to drive him in the Commissioner's car to Ingleburn Military Base to keep a promise of helping him join the Army. That didn't work out, so they then drove him to Morisset Psychiatric Hospital where he remained for some time, often ringing reporters to boast of his exploits.

Later Mellish was sentenced to three years in prison on another matter for demanding money with menaces, then slipped quietly back into obscurity, except for a film they made on the weird week in which he made Glenfield almost as famous as Glenrowan, where Ned Kelly made his last stand.

But it still wasn't the end. Detectives who complained about not being able to arrest Mellish during the siege, including one who got inside and confronted him, were transferred to uniform duty. And "Norman the Foreman" rewarded himself with a medal for "bravery."

Tim always kept his head low on that one, not wanting his friend Norman Allan to know he was responsible for sending Wally off the rails. But he laughed about it in private among friends and associates.

In the early hours of 28 May 1967, the Latin Lovelies were dancing erotically on the stage at the *Latin Quarter* nightclub to finish the night's entertainment when a shot rang out - they didn't miss a beat as the band played on but the music stopped for Raymond Patrick O'Connor. "Ducky" or "Machine Gun Ray" lay dead on the floor from a .32 bullet to the head.

The killing took place in the nightclub in the basement at 250 Pitt Street at 3.25 a.m. when about 60 patrons were swallowing their last drinks just before going home. Versions varied as to what happened but O'Connor came in late apparently to seek - if that is the right word - money from the owners, Sammy Lee and Reg Boom, so he could defend a charge of murdering a Melbourne woman, a Mrs Bowker.

At 29, the man who tried to kill Bristow five years earlier at the Newport Arms, had come to the end of his short but vicious criminal career in an obviously arranged underworld killing. He would not be mourned, nor would anyone be charged with his murder, although it was carried out in public execution style.

About 3 a.m. two detectives from the Safe Breaking Squad, Maurie Wild and Jack Whelan, had wandered into the nightclub at the end of their shifts and sat down to have a drink. They saw three men sitting together at another table, Lennie McPherson, John "Chocka" Clark and Tony Williams.

Wild said in evidence at the inquest he heard someone shout, "watch out, he's got a gun," and he drew his gun and pushed through the crowd. O'Connor was slumped on the floor, a bullet wound to his head. Two guns, a .25 and a .32 automatic pistol with a spent cartridge in the breech, lay on the floor nearby. They had been wiped clean of fingerprints by what one newspaper described as "the fastest handkerchief in Sydney."

Det. Wild said he told the three men to keep their hands on the table and McPherson said: "It's OK Mr Wild, the —

—tried to knock us." McPherson also said O'Connor had tried to murder him because he'd refused to help finance his murder defence. McPherson further said that O'Connor had come to the table and, pulling a gun from his coat, said: "This is for you." Clark, said McPherson, had grabbed O'Connor's arm and as it went up the gun went off and O'Connor "sort of shot himself."

None of the three knew anything about the other pistol, the .25. But a woman who also gave evidence at the inquest, Annette Robyn Maddern, said that before the shooting she was standing near the three men when something dropped on to one of her feet. It was a small pistol. McPherson bent down and picked it up and she said: "That's a funny thing to drop." McPherson didn't reply.

After the shooting, McPherson, Clark and Williams had been taken to the CIB and questioned, but none would make a statement. In an open finding, the Coroner said the evidence didn't show whether O'Connor shot himself accidentally, or whether someone else shot him.

"Morals" Martin, or rather Sir Wayne Martin who ran the Pink Pussycat, was there that night with a couple of girls to catch the late floor show. He told me that shortly before the club closed the owner's son, Terry Boom, came up and said: "Wayne, piss off, there's going to be trouble. Ducky O'Connor is coming in to demand money from the owners."

"Next minute," said Sir Wayne, "there's a voice, 'Wayne, you old ——.' I turned round and said 'ah, hello, Ducky boy.' He put his arms around me on the edge of the dance floor and I did the same to return his greeting. Then bang! - a shot went off almost right in my ear. I fainted with surprise and fear, and not only that, I soiled myself.

"Then I see Terry Boom standing above me saying 'Wayne Wayne, are you all right?' I said what happened? He said 'Ducky O'Connor's been shot." I said oh shit, where? He said 'there.' And there he was lying on the floor, blood oozing from him. I said I've shit myself, where are the toilets?

"He said 'I'll take you.' I went and cleaned myself up and Terry was showing me out the back way. Two detectives stood in the way. 'Nobody is allowed to leave.' So I started taking deep breaths saying mmmmy heart, mmmmy heart. One of the cops said 'go round the front.'

"We went to the front and there were two cops there. I said could I just stand out in the fresh air? 'No.' So I went through my heart attack routine again and one of the cops said 'go over there,' indicating a detective sitting at a desk, 'and give him your name and address.'

"I went over to him. 'Yeah? What's your name?' Johnny Robertson. 'Where do you live?' I said, ah, 16 Ocean Street Woollahra. And he looked up at me and said, 'Wayne Martin. Still bloody telling lies.'"

So who pulled the trigger? Sir Wayne said: "Wouldn't have a clue. I want to live a bit longer." But Tim Bristow had no doubt who pulled the trigger, In fact, he knew. So did most of the cops and everyone else. Big Lennie.

In the manner of how things were conducted then, certain cops and underworld heavies agreed that Mad Dog O'Connor had pushed his luck too far and his time was up. Bristow firmly believed that Ray Kelly, although retired by then, was in on the decision with McPherson, although others like Fred Krahe were also calling the shots, so to speak.

Since O'Connor had come to Sydney in the early 1960's, eight or nine underworld killings had occurred in the few years leading up to his death as rising criminals like him upset the established scene by attempting to take over the city's lucrative rackets in gambling, prostitution and the new craze of drugs. O'Connor had gone on a rampage of protection demands, forcing himself on casinos and businessmen. At least McPherson did provide protection for the people who paid him money for the purpose.

O'Connor and other interloping criminals were like the Mafia which had moved away from its original ideals to resist invaders and by the 19th century had deteriorated into a criminal society acknowledging no authority but their own. They engaged in extortion by handing Black Hand notes to wealthy Sicilian businessmen and landowners, demanding money for protection. The protection, of course, was from themselves. If the victims didn't comply, they and their families could expect violence, kidnaps, bombings and murder. That's what began to happen in Sydney in the 1960s as the new wave of criminals sought to take over.

Police were certain O'Connor killed "Pretty Boy" Walker in Sydney's first machine gun murder at Randwick on 8 July 1963 and that soon after on 10 February 1964, he murdered greyhound trainer Charlie Bourke near his home at Randwick. But all potential witnesses suffered from lockjaw and nothing could be proved. He was likely to do anything and nobody felt safe from O'Connor, either the police or criminals.

As one crime reporter, Bill Archibald, said later: "It was as though a mad dog had been put down in the interests of public safety." The *Daily Mirror* said in an obituary: "What patch of decay in society or constituted authority allowed him and creatures like him to profit from terror?"

The first of the three criminals who had tried to kill Bristow had now parted this life violently. The other two would follow in the next few years. Ducky's passing prompted private eye Bristow to coin his cynical, often-used phrase: "You can't help bad luck."

The only sympathy Bristow had for O'Connor was that he was a victim of the new scourge, drugs, being addicted to morphine. Bristow hated drugs. For one thing, they offended his ideal of health and fitness and they were destroying young people, some of them close to him. As well, he'd seen the power of addiction at work as his mother lay dying from leukaemia. At night she craved for therapeutic morphine to ease the pain, tearing up the bed sheets in agony. Tim would never forget it.

He was already moving against drug cheats in a covert operation and in the next few years would be in the forefront of the fight against all forms of drugs.

11

Drug Crusader

TIM Bristow looked around cautiously as he led the small, thickly bespectacled man up the gangway of the freighter *Shan Si*, berthed at Sydney's No 9 Walsh Bay on the night of Saturday, 29 April 1967. The cheerful sounds of a party somewhere on board drifted down in the pale yellowish light. Bristow found his way to an officer's cabin where a drug pedlar was waiting.

Casually gesturing towards his slightly-built companion, Bristow said jocularly: "This fellow might look like a jockey but he's a chemist. He's okay. He'll check your stuff and if it's good quality, you're in business."

The pedlar was Robert Fraser, an American aged 25. Without any preamble Fraser reached in a drawer and handed over a packet of American sweets called Pez, laced with the mind-bending opiate, lysergic acid, or LSD. With no more than a quick glance at it, Bristow's small companion thrust the packet into one of his coat pockets. "I'll do the tests in the laboratory," he said. He didn't linger, nodding to Fraser and moving outside the cabin door. "With you in a minute," Tim said, staying briefly to exchange a few words with Fraser. Then he escorted the diminutive man in the rumpled suit off the ship, merging into the wharf shadows.

Fraser would have been shocked if he'd known the identity of the "chemist." So would the Customs officer on duty at the gate of No 9. He was none other than Harvey Bates, an Eliot Ness figure who was head of the narcotics branch of Sydney Customs. Keeping in the background, his photo had never appeared in the papers. His brilliance and dedication would soon make him director of the Federal Narcotics Bureau.

Bristow and Bates were just setting up Sydney's first big drug ring bust. Bates used the subterfuge because he had to identify the pedlar and know that the substance was an unlawful drug. Fraser and another American pedlar, who starred in the popular TV series *Surfside Six*, were totally unaware they were heading for a collision course with Bristow which would spell disaster for them.

Acting as an agent provocateur, Bristow would spend six weeks mixing with the drug distributors, pushers and numerous drug takers putting the evidence together before the authorities moved in to make arrests. It was the kind of undercover operation and covert betrayal that could easily get a man shot, but that didn't worry Bristow one bit. He was a driven man.

For several years he'd been coaching young football teams at Newport, but in this period he felt his heart was broken. Drug usage was then becoming rife among young surfies, footballers and other sportsmen on the Peninsula. Five of his under-18 football team had their minds destroyed by LSD and would probably end up as vegetables. A sixth stood in front of a jet as it landed at Sydney airport, screaming: "I'm Jesus Christ."

It was the beginning of a menace that would change the whole culture of Australian society, including the police force. Huge sums of unlawful money confiscated by poorly-paid police in drug raids would now be a real temptation.

Bristow began his crusade on April 20, a few days earlier than the *Shan Si* visit, when he received a call from an American calling himself Robert Fraser, asking if he could see him. Bristow told him he was busy in court all day, had to coach his football team that night but would see him at 9.45 p.m. in his office in Barrenjoey Road, Newport. When Fraser arrived that night he said: "I've called to discuss drugs with you, Tim." He showed Tim a Pez sweet impregnated with LSD, saying it was "perfectly harmless."

"Why did you choose me?" asked Tim. Fraser said: "I met a mate of yours in Hawaii who went to school with you. He said you'd know a lot of users. With all your contacts, the surfies, footballers and drinkers at the Newport Hotel, you could make millions."

Bristow knew about users, all right, after his young footballers who collapsed at training for no apparent reason told him when questioned they were using LSD. But he showed no emotion to Fraser, saying he knew nothing about drugs and couldn't give an answer until he'd made a few inquiries to check out the market.

As they walked outside, Fraser kept talking. He said LSD was odourless, colourless and tasteless and could be brought in undetected in the mail. He intended importing it in surfboards. He'd already brought a lot of it in through the post contained in gear for his yacht, moored at Mosman Bay, and nothing had been opened. They agreed to meet again.

That first meeting began an intense period of cloak and dagger tactics in which Bristow went back and forth between Fraser and other pushers, Drug Squad detectives and Customs officers until they could set up a raid. Before Harvey Bates and his men made the pinch, Bristow set out all the circumstances on his business letterhead, Newport Legal Services, that would make an exciting movie script.

Bristow liaised with another Customs man, Clive Bull, and with Det-Sgt Astill and Detective Kirkham from the Drug Squad, then with the OIC, Det-Sgt Cec Abbott. He began secretly taping Fraser from their next meeting. He brought in one of his agents, Clint Dawkins, as a witness and backup. The agent didn't create any suspicion because Bristow was always gregarious, liking people around him, even if only to have an audience.

More information came out in several more meetings. At their next in the Menzies Hotel, with two detectives observing them in the Trophy Bar, Fraser said he could bring in limitless supplies from his source in Hawaii and he already had the New Zealand market sewn up. "I'm certain people in Australia will go mad about it," he said, somewhat prophetically.

Bristow began mixing with the surfies and their suppliers on the Peninsula, talking about the drug and the scene. He still pretended to be sceptical to Fraser, saying the people pushing the drug were very dangerous and he would need to be certain of the quality before he could agree to distribute the LSD .

He insisted on a sample to test and nine days after their initial meeting, arranged the handover to his "chemist" on board the *Shan Si* freighter. He delayed giving Fraser a report as long as possible, eventually telling him it wasn't as strong as Fraser had suggested and he didn't think he could sell it for $10 a pill.

Meanwhile, Tim went to pains to meet the American TV actor, a major supplier whom he thought was getting his supplies from the same source as Fraser in Hawaii. He sought the meeting through one of the actor's pushers on the pretext that he wanted to know if the actor's acid was as good as Fraser's, or better. The pusher said: "It's just as good. I had a great trip which lasted roughly 12 hours. I didn't get any tightening of the neck at the commencement and it was a cool drift out. I'm going to introduce my mother to LSD if I can, because she knows I use pot and acid."

As an excuse for meeting the actor, who rented a house in Tim's own suburb of Newport, Bristow gave him two samples for comparison which he had left over from Fraser. The actor said he'd tell Tim the strength of his acid the following day, saying he'd been taking it for five years and could tell just by the taste how quickly it acted on the juices.

The actor boasted that he used to handle the scene in Hollywood and claimed he introduced the Beatles and numerous stars to acid. He said: "The acid I was bringing out here at first came from Mexico but the sample I'll get you comes from a buddy of mine called Tim Leary, from San Francisco. He's a well-known professor and a top man on the scene."

Bristow even went to a pot party at the actor's home, but didn't test a joint, saying with feigned naivete: "I wouldn't be game." He also kept up his contact with Robert Fraser, calling at his home in Paddington, learning the name of a doctor in Hawaii who was manufacturing LSD. While there an observant Tim noticed the sender's name and address on a parcel post, giving him a clue to Fraser's US supplier.

With that information and combining with postal officials, they were able to intercept Fraser's next shipment posted from America. Harvey Bates tested the LSD for identification and resealed the package.

The day the package was delivered to Fraser's house under a false name, Bristow and Bates led the raid on Fraser and arrested him. Several others were caught in the net. Fraser was sentenced to 18 months in jail, but later he appealed, had the sentence reduced to a $500 five-year bond and was deported.

A week or so later they raided the American TV actor and charged him but Customs could not prove the LSD they found in his possession had been imported. At the time NSW law did not cover mere possession of LSD and as they could not prove the actor had broken the law by importing it, he was freed. He left the country soon after and NSW laws were upgraded.

Bristow's investigation, however, had discovered the name of Dr Nasi in Hawaii who made Fraser's LSD and he was arrested. But more importantly, Bristow's combined operation with Harvey Bates led to the arrest and conviction of Dr Timothy Leary in the US, the counter-culture figure prominent in experimenting with psychedelic drugs, especially LSD. That was one of the biggest busts of the time in America.

Leary, sent down from Harvard for his use and promotion of consciousness-expanding drugs, was seen by many as one of the most dangerous men of the century. He escaped from a California prison in 1970 but after being extradited from Switzerland and locked up again, he turned informer.

After that success, Bristow co-operated with police and Customs on many other drug raids. The pushers hated him for ruining their rackets and tried to hit back. They sought to blame him for the murder of heroin addict and pusher Jan O'Truba, who was shot and dumped at Oxford Falls in Sydney's north. But it was a poor attempt - Bristow was abroad at the time attending an anti-drug congress.

Bristow's name was often the subject of rumours because of his interest in the drug scene. But the sneak who scrawled a message in the sand at Avalon beach, "Bristow is a

Pusher," would have needed hospital treatment if Tim had identified him.

Bristow hated pedlars with a vengeance but showed compassion for young people hooked on drugs. He took quite a few youths into his home to help sort them out. As the drug problem worsened in the late 60's, parents on the northern beaches became concerned and knowing Tim's interest, met at his home to suggest a discussion group be formed to consider it. They asked Tim to chair the meeting, held in the Newport RSL hall on 17 October 1969. Reporters were there and police attention was later drawn to a newspaper heading: "Vigilantes to Combat Growing Drug Menace."

A week or so later Tim was called to Neutral Bay police station to explain the vigilante aspect to the detective inspector in charge and to sign a statement. He said it had been misconstrued, that his intention was to pass on information to the police. Bristow thought questioning him was a bit of a joke. Not long before, the senior officer at Manly had asked for two extra detectives to counter the growing drug problem, but Commissioner Norm Allan said "don't worry about it - it's only a passing phase."

From the meeting of parents, a committee of Peninsula citizens and businessmen was set up to form the Anti Narcotics Trust (ANT), to expose the drug menace. Bristow called a public meeting for 10 November 1969, sending out invitations to various interested parties.

Among ANT's objectives were to awaken people to the problem, educate them to look for drug users in their families, create a body which parents could approach, to harass pushers and petition the Government for harsher penalties for drug sellers, possibly mandatory jail terms.

One of the persons Bristow had sent an invitation to was Dr Stella Dalton, famous for introducing methadone treatment in Australasia. A highly qualified doctor and psychiatrist, she had formed Wistaria House at Parramatta Psychiatric Centre to treat drug addicts and alcoholics. She was giving talks all over Australia. Dr Dalton, who had never heard of Tim, rang Det-Sgt Cec Abbott at the Drug Squad to see what the ANT meeting was all about. He said he wasn't sure but would be sending an officer along. On that basis she didn't go.

ANT folded after a few months because parents who had sons or daughters on the drug scene could see themselves getting unfavourable publicity from it, and they dropped out, shunning Tim to avoid his forthrightness. Having spent a lot of time on it, Tim was sour on the parents. But he kept up his anti-drug stance.

His dislike of pushers was so strong that he was even prepared to lose money in order to see them caught. Donald Tate was a drug trafficker who did business with distributors in the Golden Triangle, flying the stuff in with his own plane and landing on one of the many convenient isolated Northern Territory strips built in the Second World War.

Bristow was asked by several Sydney bookmakers to collect gambling debts from Tate. Learning that Tate was flying into Sydney airport on a commercial plane, he confronted him about the debts. But he also tipped off the cops about Tate's arrival and they moved in, grabbed and charged him over drug matters. Tate, who worked in with a well-known young Australian, died later when his plane crashed.

Solicitor Bruce Miles, another man who liked to help the underdog, was defending a hopeless drug addict in the Darlinghurst Criminal Courts one day and asked Dr Dalton if she would come to court to see if she could help. She gave evidence saying she would treat him, and as a result he got off a serious charge. When she approached him outside the court to arrange his treatment, he laughed at her and said: "Not on your life, I'm not going for treatment."

As she was getting into her car, Bruce walked over to thank her and he had a chap with him. It was Tim, whom Bruce introduced to Dr Dalton. Tim took it from there. She then became aware he was looking after some of the young kids and footballers in his area and trying to do anti-drug work. But as Stella explained to this writer: "He was very 'old type.' Very much of the view of take them and hit them over the head and hope they do well. Lock them up for a while and that will do them some good."

Stella was doing quite a lot of television work on the drug debate and took a leading role with another doctor in a Channel 7 programme called *No Roses for Michael*, about a young addict Tim had coached at football. Some of Stella's patients were there to recount their experiences. Tim exchanged his strong views on the programme with the other doctor, advocating punishment for pedlars.

Tim then began regularly attending Wistaria House at night to check on patients he was personally interested in. Stella said that although he was trying to help a lot of young people on drugs in the Newport area, he didn't quite know how to do so in a positive way. She then understood why he'd called the meeting to form ANT.

"But," she said, "little by little he changed his views on drug addiction and treatment and became therapeutic in his approach. So he really became very keen to do anything he could to help solve the problem. I'm sure he was always keen, but didn't know how to go about it."

Tim could not have had a better guide on the problem than Dr Dalton, who held an impressive array of degrees to her credit. In all she had ten degrees (or was it 11?),

Bristow ready for action. The tough private eye was never known to back off from a challenge or dangerous situation. Yet there was a soft side to the big man . . . a hero to many.

ABOVE LEFT: Charles Bristow, Tim's wealthy woolbroker father of German background. Gentleman, sportsman and pianist.
ABOVE RIGHT: Josie Bristow, Tim's convent-educated socialite mother. Of Irish descent, she spoiled her "beautiful boy."

ABOVE: Georgian homestead at historic Hobartville Stud near Sydney. Tim's grandfather built it into the world's biggest. Several Melbourne Cup winners were sired there.

Two-fisted investigator and phone user. How waiting clients saw him *(John Fairfax Group)*.

ABOVE: Successful young man about town as a sales rep and packaging consultant.

LEFT: Fresh from Shore private school, Bristow values wool with his father. His wool career was short - he kept thumping bosses.

LEFT: Bristow in the his early 20's was a leading Sydney fashion and photographic model for companies like Coca Cola, Akubra, Jantzen, Holeproof. One of the first Chesty Bonds.

ABOVE: Tim in the 1940s showing off a surfboard at Collaroy in the manner he preferred - with girls.
LEFT: Riding a wave at Newport. Was world ski and board champion and Australia's first sponsored surfer.

ABOVE: Tim Bristow's first wife, glamorous model Judy Pointing, with their son Stephen. *LEFT:* She shows off a perfect figure. *BELOW:* Bristow the fisherman. Caught sharks and lobsters, too.

Glamorous Glenda Roberts, a New Zealand blue-eyed blonde model who was Bristow's second wife. She divorced him after he went to jail the first time.

ABOVE: After being barred from playing rugby (and rugby league), Tim formed and coached this rugby team known as the "Newport Nasties." He's fourth from left in the top row.

RIGHT: Oh oh, here's trouble Tearaway Tim, the wild terrifying forward from Gordon, closes in on an opponent in the Sydney rugby competition. He was in the 1960 Gordon premiership winning side.

SYDNEY RUGBY FOOTBALL UNION

RUGBY UNION HOUSE, CRANE PLACE, SYDNEY, N.S.W. 2000.

CABLE & TELEGRAPHIC ADDRESS "RUGUNION" SYDNEY

PHONE 27-2004

15th July, 1969.

Mr. C. J. Bristow,
73 Crescent Road,
NEWPORT.   2106.

Your application for reinstatement to Rugby Union was thoroughly investigated by the Judicial Committee at its meeting on 14th July at which you were in attendance and interviewed at length by the Committee.

However, I regret to advise that your application has been refused and you are ineligible to participate in Rugby matches or become a member of any affiliated Rugby Club.

However this does not preclude you coaching Rugby sides and you are eligible to continue to coach Newport Club.

The decision of the Committee is in no way connected with any action taken by the Metropolitan Sub-District Rugby Union concerning alleged incidents at a recent match involving the team that you coach.

Yours faithfully,

J.B. SUHAN
SECRETARY.

Official letter refusing Tim's application to ever play Rugby Union again after he was barred for "over vigorous play." So he turned to coaching junior teams.

ABOVE: Playgirl bunny
Baroness Rita Boronyi . . .
found in bed with Tim.
TOP RIGHT: Hollywood star
Jean Simmons . . . seduced by
Tim in Mosman Bay Park.
BELOW: Ava Gardner . . . one
night stand with Tim.
RIGHT: Lady Sonia McMahon .
. . former girlfriend of Tim's.

ABOVE: Max Bristow, Tim's younger brother and wife Ann.
BOTTOM LEFT: Renate, another of Tim's pretty mistresses.
BOTTOM RIGHT: Averil Trenerry, beautiful fashion consultant . . .
Tim had a fling with her. She later married Sir Percy Spender.

ABOVE: Tim and pals Ward "Pally" Austin and Abe Saffron.
BOTTOM LEFT: With daughter Isis.
BOTTOM RIGHT: Son Stephen.

ABOVE: Tim and crew, diving for King's gold from the historic *Port Au Prince* wreck in Tonga.
RIGHT: Tim the diver. A legend on Sydney's northern beaches for his rescues. Could free dive to incredible depths. *(John Fairfax Group).*

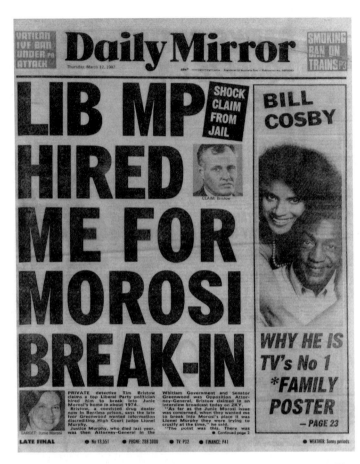

ABOVE: Even from inside prison, the outrageous private eye still made headlines.
BELOW: How the newspapers saw him.

ABOVE: Action! Lights! Camera! Bristow drops in uninvited on a divorce raid. He did all the celebrity divorce raids on TV stars, actors, millionaires. Was shot and stabbed by angry lovers caught in the act.

BELOW: Bristow lost his detective's licence when things went wrong on one of his divorce raids.

ABOVE: Former Broadway showgirl, Folies Begere dancer and English actress Denise "Big Red" McGlaglen, gave Bristow evidence that TWO gunmen took part in the assassination of JFK. *LEFT:* American John Meier, former Howard Hughes aide on the run in Australia from the FBI and CIA. Bristow helped him escape.

Bristow's son, Stephen, third on the oars from right, twice rowed in the Head of the River for the Kings School, Parramatta. A champion swimmer, too.

NEWPORT S L.S.C.

All communications
to be addressed to
Hon. Secretary,
Post Office Box 57, Newport.

NEWPORT SURF
LIFE SAVING CLUB

NEWPORT BEACH

(Affiliated with S.L.S.A. of Australia)

Phone 99 5116

.........23/3/.69.................196

Mr.T. BRISTOW.,
71 Crescent Rd.,
NEWPORT.

Dear Tim

     I have been instructed by the committee of the Newport
Surf Life Saving Club to convey to you their unanimous vote
of commendation for your actions on the evening of Wed.5th
of February.

     Although Newport beach was closed due to the huge seas
two young boys entered the water,and were promptly carried out
to sea.Without hesitation you donned the belt and proceeded to
battle your way through the surf to them.You were forced to
drop the belt and then continued to swim out with Greg.Owen to
the boys.The two of you together with Tony Anderson,who had
managed to make the break with a paddle board,then supported
them for approximately one hour untill such time that the
motorised surf boat from Newport picked you up,and assisted you
to shore.

     A fine example of determined immediate action averting
a probable tradgety.

Yours faithfully

Hon. Secretary.

Letter of commendation to Tim from Newport Surf Life Saving
Club for swimming a mile out in mountainous seas with Greg
Owen in 1969 and rescuing two drowning boys. One of the
longest and most difficult rescues in Australian surf history. He
received the Merit Award from the Royal Humane Society.

TOP: Tim giving a kerbside news conference on crime at Kings Cross.

ABOVE: Tim's last and longest partner Sue Ellis and friend, former Revlon Girl model Di Parkinson-Maddox.

RIGHT: Man, a keen animal lover and his friends.

ABOVE: In the style of New York gangsters, Tim had a shoeshine every day.
BELOW LEFT: Scandalous banker Frank Nugan. Bristow believed he was murdered.
BOTTOM LEFT: Kings Cross identity "Morals" Martin in his Knight's regalia.
BOTTOM RIGHT: Tim and agent "Tropical John" Petford. Collected election donations for NSW Premier Sir Robert Askin.

ABOVE: Tim's famous speed boat, "The See You Off Club."
LEFT: Tim's friend, Michael "Tarzan" Fomenko, whom he brought back to civilisation from the jungle.
BELOW: Bristow's friend Lennie "Mr Big" McPherson.

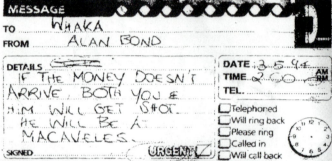

MESSAGE

TO WHAKA

FROM ALAN BOND

DATE: 3.5.94
TIME 2.00 AM

TEL.

DETAILS
IF THE MONEY DOESN'T
ARRIVE, BOTH YOU &
HIM WILL GET SHOT.
HE WILL BE AT
MACAVELES.

SIGNED URGENT

☐ Telephoned
☐ Will ring back
☐ Please ring
☐ Called in
☐ Will call back

TOP: Tim's horse Bilgola Boy gives 'em a fright leading first time round in the 1978 Melbourne Cup.

ABOVE: Bristow was caught removing documents from tycoon fraudster Alan Bond, including this murder threat from Bond to his secret partner, Whaka Kele.

LEFT: Bond the anti hero.

ABOVE: Author Kevin Perkins at Bristow's 70th birthday, posing the question everyone was asking: How the hell did Tim survive for so long?

BELOW: Bristow's birthday cake with a difference. Where else would the party be except in a surf club? At Bilgola.

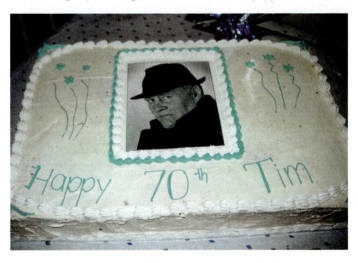

TOP: Tim and his long-lasting partner, Sue Ellis, enjoy a night out on the town.

ABOVE: End of an era and colourful career as family and friends carry Tim Bristow's casket from St Thomas' Anglican Church, North Sydney, on 19 February, 2003. Mourners wept without restraint. *(News Ltd)*

LEFT: As friends and clients remember him.

including a degree in psychology from the Sorbonne, Paris; a PCB or diploma in physics, chemistry and biology from the Faculty of Science at the University of Paris; an MA or master of arts also from the University of Paris. From the Institute of Psychology in Paris, she had a diploma of psycho physiology.

Stella had an MD or doctorate in medicine from Switzerland and a degree in psychiatry (FRANCP) as a Fellow of the Royal Australian and New Zealand College of Psychiatry; she also had the DPM, a diploma of psychological medicine from the Royal College of Physicians and Surgeons in London; another as a hypnotherapist, and yet another one, a Certificate of the Educational Council for Foreign Medical Graduates (USA). As if that wasn't enough to make any student reel, she had recently been accorded, as a Fellow of the Royal College of Physicians in Sydney, a degree for work of renown in the field of addiction. Phew!

Her mother, a French diplomat, wanted her to go into the diplomatic corps but she had to be 21. So having obtained her first degree at 18 and with time to fill in, she joined Unesco on the Australian list, doing education. She also spoke two languages apart from English.

Stella realised she couldn't stand life in the diplomatic corps because it was repetitive with the same superficial round of parties. So she decided to be a doctor and do psychiatry. While working as a psychiatrist in a London hospital, she was asked to show a new doctor around and recognised him as a former patient who had been an alcoholic and on drugs - and that's how she came to specialise in rehabilitation.

Tim, with Dr Dalton as the psychiatrist and medical director, then formed the Way Back Committee in July 1971 as an after-care organisation with community houses for patients after they had been in Wistaria House. Instead of going out into the hard cruel world after an addiction illness, they could stay there in a sheltered environment.

The organisation's constitution contained a long list of noble objectives. Tim was the first president. He had some solid and worthwhile people on the committee to help, including three judges - Justices Goran, Hicks and Healey. Margaret Whitlam was one of the social workers.

From his friendship with Judge Alf Goran, he managed to get bonds for a few people instead of them being sentenced - he didn't have to pay, simply putting it down to the judge agreeing to help his fellow man. He'd known Goran from previous days when Goran and Judge Amsberg went to the illegal casinos, including Thommos. He took Judge Goran to the Newport Arms and introduced him to the knockabouts there.

The need for the Way Back's kind of community aid was so great they were simply overwhelmed and could not cope with the demands, but it still functions today. Dr Dalton told me: "I know from that experience that Tim's interest in helping people on drugs was genuine."

As part of his contribution on the subject, Tim arranged a submission by Bruce Miles to the Senate Select Committee inquiring into Drug Trafficking and Drug Abuse. Also, Dr Dalton and Tim, with a small group, attended an international World Health Organisation drug conference in Amsterdam, going on to Stockholm, London, Toronto and Los Angeles to study drug rehabilitation centres.

He would form a close relationship with Dr Dalton.

12

ME TARZAN, YOU TIM

WHEN old boys from Shore reminisce at reunions or parties going back to the mid 1940s, they always mention one event - the fight between Bristow and Fomenko. Tim couldn't even remember what started it, but it was an epic stoush. In reality it seemed just a case of two tough, strong young fellows refusing to give way to the other. Two bulls in a paddock.

Bristow recalled that Michael Fomenko started it and they went into the dressing sheds after school to have it out. It lasted two or three hours. Fomenko would not stay down and kept wanting to fight on, even when obviously beaten. His blood would leave stains on the floor and wall seats. He stopped only when physically exhausted. Tim felt sorry because the fellow could not admit defeat. It was a fair fight, no kicking or gouging, only punches as sportsmanship required then.

Tim was amazed when Michael came to school next morning looking like a mummy, his face swathed in bandages, wanting to continue with the support of his father, who was a teacher at the posh school and also a coach in sport there. "We are Cossacks, we never give up," said his father. Here was a scholarly master wanting to referee a fight between his son and another student. Tim had nothing to prove, he'd won, and to avoid more bloodshed he said, "I'd rather shake hands." After some hesitation, Fomenko shook hands with him. And they became friends.

Tim regarded Fomenko as arrogant but an athletic freak. He led the school's pentathlon event, later holding seven club records with the Northern Suburbs Athletics Club and running third in a national decathlon title. The family had fled from persecution in native Georgia in the Soviet Union, where Michael was born in 1930, the same year as Tim. His mother was a former Russian aristocrat, Princess Elizabeth Macciabelli.

Michael was an even worse student than Tim, but shared his interest in sport. That's where the similarity ended. Fomenko would make world headlines as the modern Tarzan, living like an animal in the jungle. And it would be hilarious whenever the two old Shore boys met again. At one stage Tim went into the wild scrub of Northern Australia to bring him back to civilisation, but at the first chance he fled back to the bush.

In Sydney Tim took the toothless, wild-looking "escapee" to smart parties at Palm Beach where he terrorised the women. Tim found pleasure and fun in the wild man's company. With his animal-like existence in the Cape York wilderness, Michael "Tarzan" Fomenko would have made the original Tarzan creation by master story teller Edgar Rice Burroughs look like a palsied wimp.

Stripping to his jocks and thumbing his nose at society, Fomenko left his Sydney family in 1955 and vanished into the lush tropical jungle of North Queensland looking for adventure. He was inspired by stories of the wild white man of Borneo, of dugout canoes, native peoples and their primitive lifestyles.

But what stimulated his interest most were the stirring tales Tim told him of the freedom and beauty and amazing wildlife he encountered in his own adventurous days in North Queensland when he left the police force. Next thing Tim knew, his friend had become "Tarzan."

Snippets of his bizarre lifestyle surfaced from time to time as he pitted himself against nature. He became known as the Wild White Man of Wujal Wujal but roamed the Cape York area generally, one of the world's most hostile terrains for "al fresco" living. He fought off sharks with his bare hands, killed crocodiles with a bowie knife, lived amid deadly snakes like the taipan, was bitten by scorpions and gored by a wild boar.

Fomenko lived on snake and dugong, wild pork, coconuts, mangoes, cane sugar, fish, wild vegetables and even birds. He slept on the open bush ground, warding off mosquitoes by rubbing the powdery ash of his cooking fire on his body.

After four years of that rugged life he came to the world's notice as the elusive "Tarzan of the North" by hacking out a dugout canoe from a huge cedar log and setting off on a 640 km voyage from Cooktown north into the reef-strewn Torres Strait to Thursday Island. Against the advice of the local islanders he continued his perilous escapade north.

Nothing was heard of him for weeks and he was feared lost at sea. He battled storms and constant thirst and eventually turned up on the southern shore of Irian Jaya, formerly Dutch New Guinea, at a place called Merauke which almost two years later would be the search centre for Michael Rockefeller. Headhunters still existed in the hinterland of that wild green hell where the Sepik River surges 1200 km from the mountains to the sea.

"Tarzan" suffered dysentery for two months, needing blood transfusions. Finally the Indonesians deported him. Flown back to Sydney, he was admitted to the Royal North

Shore Hospital and received a blast of international publicity. He told Tim he'd fallen in love with quite a few of the Aboriginal women. But as soon as he came out of hospital, he headed for the Queensland jungle again.

He occasionally appeared near the rainforest community of Ayton on the Bloomfield River, wearing only old leopard skin bikini briefs and battered sandals, a frightful sight with matted hair tumbling down his forehead and tufts of hair sticking out of his nose and ears.

Women complained to police of being "terrorised" by the sight of this weird-looking man who at times came to steal or beg for food. Police from Cooktown took a week to find him and arrested him after a struggle in a lagoon. He was sentenced to six months' prison for vagrancy, indecent exposure and stealing.

A Townsville doctor then judged him to be insane. He was locked in a special wagon behind a goods train and transported to Ipswich where he was interned at the Sandy Gallop Mental Hospital for 18 months. He received electric shock "therapy" to treat a condition that seemed little more than an aversion to modern society where every Russian was thought to be a Communist.

"Tarzan's" father contacted Tim in 1969 and asked him if he would go to Queensland and bring his son back. Tim did it as a love job, driving there, finding him and heading back to Sydney. But once more the cops soon grabbed Fomenko, transferring him to the Morisset mental institution near Newcastle.

Tim several times obtained permission to have Michael released from Sydney's Callan Park Mental Institution for the weekend, taking him to his home, going diving from his boat or to parties. Tim took it on the chin when his friend Di Parkinson cracked a joke: "That's interesting - a lunatic in charge of a lunatic."

Michael wanted to sleep roughly, not in a bed, so Tim put him under his house with the dog. There was a terrific commotion and yelping when the dog tried to steal Michael's tucker.

Tim insisted on taking "Tarzan" to parties on the Peninsula. He looked like a wild beast with his straggly flowing hair, teeth missing and hollow cheeks. At one swish party at Eddie Bergin's Whale Beach home, he was right out of his element. With Tim's encouragement, he pawed the women who drew back in horror from this apparition looking like a cousin of King Kong. "Get him away, get him away." they called, locking themselves in rooms. Tim thought it was great, laughing hugely.

Eventually Michael Fomenko obtained a certificate declaring he was not insane and never had been. He returned to the north, emerging only once more to find his aged mother before she died. But the tale showed that Tim would not let a friend down, no matter how odd the circumstances. Once a friend, always a friend. "You only kiss your friends," he would say.

Licensed clubs in New South Wales were a social phenomenon that didn't exist anywhere else in the world. Working class men and women enjoyed privileges such as entertainment, food and sporting facilities - not to mention social equality - that could not be matched in any other country.

The growth of RSL, rugby league and other sporting clubs from the 1950s reflected the community's growing prosperity and social expansion. Many wives were being taken out to dinner and a show at the clubs for the first time in their married lives, all due to the wealth spawned by one-armed bandits.

It wasn't long, as Federal police would find in 1971, before organised criminals began penetrating the clubs to cash in on the lucrative entertainment, food and liquor services and the booming poker machine market. Pilfering from the pokies by dishonest employees and professional cheats was widespread, as this writer recorded many times in the newspapers. The year 1969 was important to observers of the Sydney scene because that's when a Chicago businessman named Joseph Dan Testa came to town and met the local hoods.

He was entertained by such criminal luminaries as McPherson, race fixer, casino and SP racketeer George Freeman and standover merchant Milan "Iron Bar Miller" Petricevic. McPherson then went to Chicago and Las Vegas as the guest of Testa, who picked up the tab. Federal police knew Testa to be at least a financial adviser to a Chicago organised crime syndicate. Testa would be back in Sydney, trying to bust into the club poker machine business, holding a summit meeting with McPherson, Freeman and co at Double Bay in 1972.

But before all that blew up in the papers and the Moffitt Royal Commission, Tim did a big favour for McPherson by organising a pig and kangaroo shooting expedition for McPherson and his Chicago cohorts on the property of a friend. It was always described as taking place at Bourke in western New South Wales. In fact, the shooting occurred on the property of John Cobcroft at Willow Tree in the NSW north. Tim, a friend of John, asked him if he could bring a few chaps up without mentioning their names and in the casual, friendly way of Australian country folk, it was arranged without any fuss.

Tim stayed inside a blitz wagon while the others blasted away with rifles, not machine guns as reported. McPherson was a crack pistol shot, practising in a special sandbagged target area at the rear of his home in the Sydney suburb of Gladesville. Nobody knew about McPhersons's expedition for several years until crime crusader Bob Bottom published pictures of the gun-toting McPherson, Testa and fellow Chicagoan Nick Giordano on the shoot in his book *The Godfather in Australia*. The shooters flew up by helicopter, but Tim drove there and took the pictures.

He secretly gave them to an old News Limited reporter, Joe Morris, who in earlier days was chauffeur to crime queen Kate Leigh, and Morris gave them to Bottom. The shooting spree was portrayed by Bryan Brown in the film *Dirty Deeds*.

Bristow was called in to investigate many licensed club rorts, setting traps by hiding agents under the stages after clubs closed for the night, catching thieves such as cleaners who emptied poker machines in the early hours. Money was being milked from probably half the clubs in the State.

One with a difference occurred when the Associated Motor Club had its licence suspended after something like $750,000 went missing. Two groups were fighting for control, one from a rival club. Bristow was brought in to see what he could do about the licence. He saw a NSW State Cabinet Minister and obtained a provisional licence so the club could keep trading.

Evidence of the missing money was confirmed when a reform group opened the safe, finding tapes of conversations detailing payments to a senior cop at the CIB - no small amount, either - and implicating others in rorts from the club's coffers. Things grew tense between the two groups. Then two heavy criminals walked into the club on a Sunday night and sat quietly at a table, saying nothing. Everyone got the message - they were representing the former management and the reform staff fled. Who should it be but Big Lennie and George Freeman.

Next morning the reformists called in Bristow again, asking him to come the heavy. But for once in his hard career he felt obliged to go on the soft pedal, agreeing to help but only as a diplomat trying to make peace. As a result progress was made without him crossing swords with Big Lennie. And public relations and security men were even engaged on both sides.

I wrote a two-column byline piece on this amusing situation, with acknowledgments to Damon Runyon, which appeared in the *Sunday Telegraph* on 21 December 1969. It didn't please Lennie, saying in part:-

"Well, there is this licensed club in Sydney which is very popular but is never more popular than now. Indeed, it is so popular they are fighting to get in, in more ways than one.

"It is so popular that Christmas comes early to this club and already it is the merriest Christmas in Australia. But it seems for one reason and another that things are not always as merry...

"Anyhow, there are some cop raids on this popular club and one of the big noises gets the heave-ho. Now, if there's anything that upsets this guy it's the old heave-ho. Some tough guys are introduced to straighten things out. One is known in this man's town as the Big Fella, and indeed, it's said he is so tough he makes Harry the Horse look like blancmange.

"Anyway, the new Charlie in this popular club doesn't take too kindly to unfriendliness. It is stated he is not too delighted at being threatened with death, his noggin beaten or his house bombed, so he tries to get a tough guy, a private eye, to look after his interests.

"But this private eye, perhaps because he has so much respect for the Big Fella and knows how critical he is of guys who do not mind their own business, declines the generous offer...

"And with all this talk of getting the old equaliser out, there are sometimes more security men than customers in this popular club. Also it seems the previous boss misplaces the key of the safe. And it is one of the funniest sights of the year to see the new team legally blow open the same - Big Butch would have loved this bust.

"About 12 guys are crouched around the safe with sledge hammers and oxy torches and the like and it takes them about five hours to get inside the tank and even then they have to go through a brick wall at the back to get at it.

"These guys take possession of various tape-recorded conversations and letters and Christmas cards from certain politicians and cops, and it is being widely stated, rightly or wrongly, that if these certain cops and politicians knew about this they would reach for the aspirin...

"Well, things have settled down quite a deal and everyone in the club is now giving you big castor-oil grins when you show up. And because the previous Charlie is trying to make his comeback all nice and legal, he gets himself signed into this club every day as a visitor and bends over backwards buying drinks for all and sundry, no doubt hoping to win supporters.

"And no sooner does he shell out than the guys on the other side show up and buy you a heart starter. More free drinks are being dispensed in this club at the moment than anywhere else in town. It's the merriest Christmas in Australia."

I received a terse telephone call from McPherson the following Tuesday. "You're sailing close to the wind, you red-headed bastard," he said:

Shortly afterwards I again wrote something that didn't delight Lennie. In those days newspaper offices didn't have security guards and people could just walk in. Suddenly this big brutish-looking fellow appeared and sat opposite me at my news editor's desk in the Packer-owned *Sunday Telegraph*, and started yelling and ranting. He thumped my desk and bellowed. Four-letter words flew. The thin partitions of the adjoining news room rattled and shook.

It was 12.30 and the editor, Johnny Moyes, decided it was an excellent time to go to lunch. So did the reporters, sub-editors and secretaries, leaving me alone with a roaring Lennie. He was quite a frightening sight when stirred. I talked to him for about an hour and after he'd quietened down, I said to him: "Would you like a beer, Lennie?" He said: "Yes, all right."

I took him downstairs into Park Street and around the corner in Elizabeth Street to the journalists' watering hole, the *Kings Head*. It was crowded. We moved to the saloon bar trying to get a drink and when they saw it was Big Lennie, they parted magically to make room, leaving bar space for about 10 drinkers. Such was the effect McPherson had on people.

From that "interview," I wrote a front-page story on McPherson and was the first person to name him as Mr Big. The name would stick, used in royal commissions, inquiries and the press. Bristow even named one of his racehorses Mr Big after him.

Following that incident, I received a call on the office intercom from the *Telegraph's* editor-in-chief David McNicoll who said in his droll way: "Kevin, would you mind not inviting your friend into the office? - he makes us rather nervous."

"He's not my friend and I didn't invite him," I said. "Nonetheless," said McNicoll, "would you mind asking him to desist from coming in." I didn't do so, hoping Lennie would prefer to use the phone next time. I had a few other threats from him over the years and in one unusual incident he screamed on the phone: "I'm going to hire a plane and rain f——g pamphlets all over Sydney about you."

"That doesn't sound too bad, Lennie," I said. "What do you mean?" he demanded, shrewdly. "Well," I said, "at least you're not going to shoot me." He hung up, cursing. After that, I bumped into him several times and he was always courteous and, for some reason, friendly - perhaps because I was a friend of Tim's. I had occasion to call at his home once. We sat upstairs in his study where he could observe the scene through bullet-proof windows. The heavy front door was bullet proof. A buzzer sounded inside from electronic beams if anyone came on to his property.

Bristow's relationship with McPherson was strange.

Tim had an amazing capacity to get on with people from all spheres of life. Criminals generally hated him, knowing he had cops on side and knowing, or at least suspecting, he was informing to them. But he talked to everyone and all types. Compared to McPherson, he dressed like a toff, came from a completely different background, dropped names of people who were anti-crime, was always talking to the newspapers and people in authority, which naturally made McPherson sceptical of him. Yet McPherson was friendly towards him and stuck by him when things were tough, although he made fun of him privately.

For his part, instead of trying to hide his association with Mr Big, Bristow flaunted it. He even took him to football matches and introduced him all around. One night Tim dropped half a bucket of fresh lobsters on my porch with a note: "Sorry, but I had to give Lennie some on the way home."

Tim was also friendly with Chief Stipendiary Magistrate Murray Farquhar who would run into trouble later being photographed at Randwick races with criminal George Freeman, and was then in 1985 sentenced to four years jail on a charge of perverting the course of justice over the Kevin Humphreys affair. Football executive Humphreys was convicted of fraudulently appropriating money from Balmain Leagues Club following a highly publicised Royal Commission forced by the ABC's *Four Corners*.

Tim had met Farquhar after driving him home one night with race tipster Jack Armstrong - Tim was always happy to drive people home at night. After that he would ring Farquhar and discuss cases in which he had an interest, asking the magistrate to do him a favour. He liked Farquhar, respecting his war record and never paid him any money.

Bristow also knew George Freeman, meeting him through McPherson.

He saw how Freeman maintained his enormous power in the underworld. Freeman always kept about $100,000 in his house and whenever he spoke to criminals about a "job," he always had $5,000 or $10,000 on the table. Even if they couldn't succeed, he'd say: "Take this for your trouble." McPherson was tight with money and ruled more by fear, but as his one-time lawyer Andrew Leary pointed out, he always paid his bills on time and never asked him to do anything that was wrong.

Freeman boasted to Bristow and one of Tim's lieutenants one day how he had set up Robbie and Bill Waterhouse over the Fine Cotton racing ring-in, saying he made sure it was exposed so they got the blame. He claimed he had his money on the eventual winner of the race, Harbour Gold, knowing the substitute running as Fine Cotton would be ruled out by stewards.

Freeman and McPherson were killers and psychopaths. But Tim played the dangerous game of staying on side with them because of their strength in the underworld, believing it could save his life.

Bristow said of McPherson when looking back on the years when he was Mr Big: "He was probably the strongest man I've ever met in my life, physically and on the enforcement side. He wasn't huge in stature, but he could fight exceptionally well. If he said he'd do something, he'd do it. In other words, if he said you were to die, you'd die.

"There was no man more frightening than Len McPherson, no man with more knowledge of killings than him. There was no greater enforcer than McPherson. Many blokes challenged him but none are around to tell the tale. In Sydney he was the Godfather."

Perversely, Tim liked to give the impression he was a gangster like McPherson and other big names. It padded his ego, helped build his reputation by making self-promotion a lot easier and it enhanced his business. But it left a doubt in many people's minds that there was an element of criminality in him.

He might have capitalised on or taken advantage of a criminal situation to satisfy his own ends, but he would not create it in any major way. Break the rules, yes. He might have operated on the shady side and mixed with criminals as if he were one of them, but to those who knew him, his pretensions to gangsterism were mostly fanciful.

But as a professional gumshoe, walking both sides of the street helped him survive.

13

DIVING FOR KING'S GOLD

THE surf was mountainous, breakers 15-feet high crashing onto the beach below Newport's lifesaving clubhouse.

For almost a mile out, the Newport reef was a seething maelstrom of white water - the kind of wild day seen only a few times a year. The beach had been closed all day and only a few foolhardy youngsters were skylarking near the water's edge, unaware of a powerful rip sweeping south toward the line of rocks.

It was late in the day, about 4.30 on Wednesday, 5 February 1969 and one of the few people on the beach was Tim Bristow, training the Newport Nippers' march-past team. Then Greg Owen, 17, a strong swimmer from Mona Vale and captain of Pittwater High, arrived with a mate, Dennis Miller, son of famous cricketer Keith Miller, and decided to risk it for a quick dip.

The waves were dumping hard, the rip was too strong and they decided to take one last shoot into the beach. Then Greg heard someone cry: "Help, save me." A boy was in trouble about 30 metres out, drifting south in the rip. He dropped off his wave and swam towards him.

Tim, then a member of Bilgola lifesaving club aged 39 and weighing 18 stone, saw the trouble developing. Renowned on the northern beaches as a master of heavy surf, he donned the belt and ran into the water, with Nippers and a few bystanders manning the line.

By now Owen had reached the boy, Graham Roberts, 11, of Bungan Head who was crying in panic and scratching his rescuer. To his surprise Owen saw another boy further out. Then he spotted two men swimming not far away but they headed for the beach, one calling out: "We're going for the surf boat."

Tim was dragged south as he swam across the rip, using the full 400 yards of line. It was dragging him down and backwards. He was forced to climb out of the belt and dump it. He swam to Owen to find young Roberts still crying and panicking. "Look at the other fellow, he's not crying," said Tim, but when that didn't work he said to the boy: "If you don't behave, I'll have to knock you out."

Bristow told Owen to drift out with him so he could grab the other kid. They reached him, Gary Kearaus, 13, of Newport, and they all lay on their backs, holding hands and kicking. Then Tim and Greg tried angling across the rip with the boys clinging to their shoulders, but they couldn't stop drifting towards the breakers which marked Newport reef, where many years before Tim had speared a record 9ft 7in shark.

Tim was worried about sharks. He'd seen stacks of them on the reef at this time of year when fish were around and mullet were starting to move, And it was real shark weather, raining and growing dark. Tim being the tallest, with his feet below the others, would be the first one attacked.

But even more worrying, the drift was taking them south-east towards a bombora where waves 20 feet high were breaking on rocks. Nobody could survive there. One boy complained of a stomach ache, the other of leg stiffness. Bristow forced them to move their limbs to fight off cramp, bullying them into being calm by repeating: "We'll be all right."

But in fact, both Bristow and Owen were feeling desperate. The flying spray of the bombora was only about 100 metres off. As it crashed and boomed behind them, they grimly breast stroked to the north, holding on to the boys. It seemed they were facing certain death.

Tim and Greg were exhausted, swimming only by reflex action now, and feared they would have to give up. In the gathering dusk they could not see the shoreline and were about a mile offshore. But it never entered their heads to leave the boys. Suddenly a remarkable thing happened - the drag of the water eased. They were out of the rip.

Still no rescue attempt, and they'd been in the water for more than two hours. Slowly they began swimming towards the distant surf club, stopping often to rest. To their great relief, they saw a lone surfboard rider approaching. Lifesaver Tony Anderson had gone out from the quieter northern end of the beach. He met them about 500 metres from the beach. They eased the boys onto the board and with Anderson kicking from behind with his flippers and Bristow and Owen holding the boys with one hand and side stroking with the other, they moved slowly towards the beach.

Once more they were caught in the rip, turning them towards the reef, threatening to repeat the earlier grim struggle. But when 150 metres off the beach, the club power boat turned up, slowed because its drive-shaft had been bent by the heavy waves. "Don't lose 'em now," said Tim, joking grimly. Finally they made it back to the beach, where they were astonished to find that throughout the ordeal, young Roberts had grasped a 20-cent coin his mother had given him to buy boot polish.

Journalist Keith Willey, who wrote up the heroic rescue in the Sydney *Sun*, quoted experts as saying Bristow and

Owen had travelled at least three miles in seas so rough that nobody could swim out to help them. Lifesaving officials described the effort as magnificent, regarding it as one of the longest and most difficult rescues in Australian surf history. Tim and Greg were awarded the Royal Humane Society's Merit Award - 50 years after Tim's father received his award in 1919 for rescuing the woman in the Collaroy shark attack.

Publicity from that brave effort led to Tim being offered a contract to dive for gold bullion and coin for the King of Tonga, a treasure trove from one of the greatest pirate enterprises in history. The treasure was aboard the English privateer, *Port Au Prince,* which was burned and sunk in 1806 off the Tongan island of Lifuka in the Ha'apai group after islanders massacred most of the crew. The *Port Au Prince* dropped anchor at the very spot where Captain Cook had stopped 30 years before in his globe-encircling *Endeavour* to be greeted by the natives of the Friendly Isles.

The story of that pirate adventure and its tragic aftermath, one of the classic tales of the South Pacific, was told only through the courage and sharp mindedness of Will Mariner, a boy clerk on the *Port Au Prince.* He survived the massacre and became the adopted son of the Tongan warrior king Finau, who made him a chief. The Tongans, who practised cannibalism then, were engaged in tribal warfare.

After four years in Tonga young Will managed to get on a ship and return to England where a London doctor, John Martin, heard about his story in 1811, corroborated it with three other survivors, and encouraged him to make notes of all he could remember about the life and culture of Tonga and the details of his remarkable escapade.

His story appeared in 1816 in a book entitled "*An Account of the Natives of the Tonga Islands in the South Pacific Ocean*," published by Constable. A second edition was sold the following year and various editions have appeared in the last 190-odd years in several languages. James Michener wrote about it with Professor A. Grove Day in his book *"Rascals in Paradise,"* saying: "Today it is treasured as a work of first importance in Pacific ethnology as well as a stirring narrative of world adventure."

Tim didn't know too much about the science of the Tongans but the prospect of adventure and diving for hidden treasure appealed to him. He was approached by Mike Adare, a former mate from Long Reef surf club, who recommended him for the job to the King of Tonga and the Harrison Shipping Company, which was putting up the funds.

Bristow's invitation was to lead and organise the expedition in 1970 with all expenses paid and, to match the risks involved, he was offered the inducement of 10 per cent of what he recovered. He set to, persuading two expert police divers, CIB Detective Sergeants Jim Rope and Ollie Knight, to take their holidays and accompany him.

But first, he checked on the loot. From Will Mariner's account and the Harrison Shipping Company, he learned that the *Port Au Prince*, a private ship of war owned by a London merchant named Robert Bent, left London in 1805 - the year of Trafalgar - to loot Spanish ships and settlements in the Atlantic and Pacific and to catch whales.

The vessel was a 500 tonner with a crew of 96 and 32 guns - nine and twelve pounders. They were nothing short of thieves on the high seas, sometimes entering Spanish ports under the American flag, looting madly ashore and kidnapping Spanish grandees until ransom was paid.

At one undefended Peruvian town, Ilo, these acquisitive English chaps burnt the town down and knocked off all the silver candlesticks, chalices, incense holders and crucifixes from the churches. And so on as their voyage of pillaging continued.

The ship sprang a leak in the Pacific and headed for the Hawaiian Islands for repairs. In Honolulu Will Mariner, then 15, learned some rudimentary language which would soon save his life. The leak persisted and missing the Society Islands due to an adverse current, they sailed to the Friendly Islands, reaching the island of Lifuka a month later.

As the crew pumped to keep the vessel afloat and moved all the bigger guns aft on the deck so carpenters could get at the leaky spots, Tongan visitors kept coming on board but the fool of a captain could not see a treacherous situation developing. About 20 crewmen virtually mutinied by going ashore against orders, hoping to get among the Tongan girls.

When the massacre began, Mariner was below writing up the log and when the shrieks of the maimed and dying filled the air, he led the ship's cooper to the powder magazine preparing to blow up the ship, but then decided to join the fight. But seeing the carnage he went to a chief, held out his hands to show he wasn't armed and uttered the Hawaiian word aloa, meaning friendliness or love which was similar to the Tongan word alofa, and was spared.

The Tongans could not sail the ship and High Chief Finau consulted young Will, who directed the crew members who had been ashore at the time of the massacre to steer and work the sails and they navigated the *Port Au Prince* through the reefs to close in shore. In the next few days the Tongans dismantled the ship, bringing ashore the cannons, eight barrels of gunpowder and all the cannon balls. Every scrap of metal was hacked off, even the hoops on the barrels of whale and sea-elephant oil which floated away. The *Port Au Prince* was then set alight.

Will Mariner spent most of his four years on the isle of Vava'u, except when helping Chief Finau introduce the terror of his newly-acquired cannons to blast hell out of his enemies. Some of these cannons still stand today in the Royal Palace grounds of the Tongan capital, Nuku'alofa.

After gaining a remarkable insight into the little-known Tongan way of life and the power of the Chief representing the divine right of the gods, Mariner finally departed on the visiting brig *Favourite*, taking some of the remaining crew with him and reaching England more than six months later.

He managed to save his precious log book, which recorded details of the pirated booty, Spanish currency, silver and so on. Mariner's story made no mention of the treasure's fate but Michener in his book said of the charred, sinking *Port Au Prince* hulk: "Mingled therein was a mass of fused silver, where coins and church plate had been stowed in the strong box."

To finish the tale, Will married and became a successful London stockbroker but after his narrow escapes and surviving the perils of the world's oceans, he drowned on the Thames when a skiff capsized.

Bristow needed a shallow-drawing boat for the voyage to suit Tonga's coral reefs, shallows and deeps, where monsoonal winds could reach hurricane force. He helped choose the *Maraenui*, a motor sailer which had previously run between Port Stephens and Middleton Reef off the Australian east coast.

He knew the area he had to dive in was remote, without airstrips or hospitals, and if anyone was injured or hurt it could take days to reach help. So he put together an extensive first aid kit to meet any emergency, including penicillin and even the old-fashioned Condy's Crystals for snake bite, one of his worst fears being from deadly sea snakes. Sharks were expected to be numerous too.

Tim supervised the equipment, which had to be kept to a minimum because of the *Maraenui's* modest size, but it included radar. The plan was for the boat to sail from Sydney via Fiji to Nuku'alofa, the Tongan capital in the main Tongitapu group, to where Tim and his diving companions would fly. The boat duly arrived but was late after being blown off course by strong winds.

The diving site had been pinpointed by several New Zealanders who had visited there and convinced the expedition financiers that they had found the wreck of the *Port Au Prince* which legend insisted was the resting place of a king's ransom - said to be nine tonnes of gold bullion and coin, enough to make the eyes of any modern adventure seeker roll back. Much mythology surrounded this legend in the minds of the 100,000 or so Tongans in their far-flung islands sprinkled over 700,000 square kilometres of the South Pacific.

In Nuku'alofa Tim and his mates were treated as VIPs, meeting two young princes, the sons of King Taufa'ahau Tupou 1V. They stayed at the King's Dateline Hotel before checking their gear and taking a Tongan crew aboard the *Maraenui*. The King put two policemen on board, presumably to make sure nobody absconded with the kingdom's treasure.

They cruised for more than 30 hours to reach their destination, Ha'apai, an island in one of the three main groups, about 300 kilometres from Nuku'alofa. When they went ashore after taking refuge on the leeward side of the island, they were mobbed by Tongan children and even adults. Word of their mission had somehow reached this remote outpost.

Tim was struck by the sense of timelessness and natural beauty of the place, the colour and cleanliness of the water. The people were poor by Western standards but happy, without electricity, living mostly in primitive thatch-roofed dwellings and eating fish, yams and fruit.

The diving team quickly went to work. Although it was summer, the wind was surprisingly strong, whipping up abnormal waves of about three metres and making diving conditions difficult off the reef as the waves thundered over it. Only divers of exceptional skill could handle the situation.

Consulting their maps and studying the scene, they noted that the spot where the wreck was supposed to be was on the Tongan Deep side of the island, where it didn't take much to blow up strong winds. As Tim was aware, the Tongan Deep was a trench of water renowned as the second deepest in the world, reaching a depth of 10,000 metres.

The coral island sloped down to a flat reef on the seaward side, then dropped sheer into fairly deep water of about 30 metres at the next level. The wreck was somewhere in there. Wherever Tim, Jim Rope or Ollie Knight dived, they each saw a different underwater scene.

The Tongan Deep continually replenished the Tongan reefs with nutrients from its abyss, making them the richest and most diverse in the South Pacific. And this coral reef area where the *Port Au Prince* was supposed to lie with its pirate secrets intact, was another fertile ground for marine life, nestling in a setting of azure blue water.

Getting down there in the windy, choppy conditions was the problem but once down, the underwater visibility was superb. Diving was still difficult, though, because of the strong movement of the water running around the island

and surging through fissures, or huge cracks in the coral. Tim had never seen such a variety and abundance of fish. The reef was teeming with all types of fish and the coral was the prettiest he'd ever seen.

But there were dangers, apart from surging water. Sea snakes lurked everywhere and he was staggered to see their size. He carried a spear gun to prod them away if necessary because a bite there from an unknown species of sea snake, so far away from medical help, could have been fatal.

He saw many moray eels, some up to three or four metres long and surprisingly thick, regarding them as dangerous. They mostly hid in cracks and crevices and were likely to attack if they felt their domain was being invaded. Several times he saw schools of deadly barracuda and was relieved to see they were on a mission heading somewhere else. If they had taken an interest in him, it would have been goodnight. He'd seen the waters of north Australia silver with them.

Sharks were as numerous as he'd ever seen, but they gave no trouble. Quite a few were whalers, normally harmless to humans. Fortunately the others, fast moving types most of which he couldn't identify, were well fed on the ample stocks of commercially untouched fish. It was nothing to have four or five sharks swimming underneath him. He also saw turtles and giant clams.

When Tim first broke the water, with curious Tongans watching from the shore, he wore only a costume, snorkel and mask but realising the depth, turbulence and risks, he and the other divers donned suits and used self-contained scuba gear. The boat could not be anchored on the seaward side of the island because of the deep water and the divers had to wade at low tide or swim across the coral reef to get to the diving site. As strong as he was, Tim was knocked over by a wave and washed across the coral, cutting his wet suit.

They dived for four days, careful not to get caught in any of the fissures in the coral. The water surge was so strong they probably could not have swum backwards to safety if trapped in a narrow cave-like crevice. Tim found the atmosphere quite eerie.

He felt a great responsibility in the operation, was excited and wanted to find the gold for the Tongans, who were poor and the kingdom could make good use of the wealth. A lot of money had been invested in the expedition and he wanted to succeed on that account, too. And, somewhat obliquely, he said to his companions: "Wouldn't it be nice, because this is the bicentenary of Captain Cook discovering Australia."

On the third day they struck what they believed to be paydirt. They found the remnants of a wreck. The ship had been smashed to pieces and bits were scattered about. Most of the wreckage was trapped in a kind of crevice. They guessed it had gone in broad on at first, then twisted around, finishing up aft to the shore, broken up over the years by the waves.

Was this the ill-fated *Port Au Prince*, proof of a legendary tale of the white man's invasion of the South Seas, of greed and plunder and stirring adventure? Tim didn't know. Neither did his two friends. But in the limited time still available, they searched hard, recovering a few artefacts like a rudder pin - Jim Rope found it in a three-metre deep gutter in the coral - and a few other things like bricks and screws, hoping it might enable them to identify the wreckage. The Tongan police on board promptly took possession of the items.

But no gold. Had someone already beaten them to it? Had the King already claimed it? Had some modern pirate already recovered it? Was it still there? That night on the *Maraenui* Tim gave his views on the situation.

"I think this is the wrong spot," he said. "It's possible the bullion might have moved with the ferocity of the current into deeper water, but I doubt it. If the Tongans had got hold of it early in the piece, there would have been some evidence of it. If anyone produced something pretty like shiny gold coins 170 years ago, the villagers would have grabbed them."

The others agreed. He went on: "This isn't the site where Mariner said the *Port Au Prince* burned. It's about 60 kilometres away on the island of Lifuka. That's where we should be looking. I'm glad it wasn't us who picked this spot. We've run out of time now, but I suggest if our backers are game, we all come back again and look at Lifuka where young Mariner said it all happened."

Bristow had cast a new twist to the violent history of the *Port Au Prince* and he wanted to return to solve the mystery that the sea would not give up. They steamed back to Nuku'alofa and flew to Sydney.

A year later almost the same team, with the addition of Mike Adare, returned on the *Maraenui* and moored in the same spot as Captain Cook and Captain Brown of the *Port Au Prince*. Using hooker gear this time with a machine on top supplying the air, they dived, including on a reef called Mariner's Reef. There was even a cannon on the island from the English privateer.

All in the party, including their New Zealand navigator who was doing a thesis on Mariner's tale, agreed it was the right spot. Jim Rope found a few pieces of brass, some screws and other items, but no gold. Neither did Ollie Knight. Over the edge of the reef where the *Port Au Prince* wreckage had obviously been washed, the pieces just disappeared into a great deep blue where no ordinary diver could survive.

If the bullion had been found nearly 200 years previously - and Will Mariner made no mention of that in his narrative - the villagers would have retrieved it excitedly as trinkets. They didn't use money for yams then. Or perhaps it floated silently into the Tongan Deep.

Tim didn't make it for the second expedition. He had too many other commitments going on.

14

Jimmy The Weasel and other Celebs

SYDNEY developer Gary Dent suddenly heard a rumpus in the back garden of a North Shore home where he'd taken his friend Tim Bristow to a party one evening in 1970. He went outside to see Tim in action mode with several fellows laid out on the lawn. He moved in to stop him and Tim wheeled around, right fist ready.

"For God's sake," said Gary, "I'm your friend. And stop this fighting." Tim reluctantly lowered his fists and said: "But isn't it fun!"

Tim was still taking life full on, his own man, unavoidably making enemies. Parties aside, he was like a cop working in the dark, always in the shadows, making enemies simply by doing the work he was paid to do. Friends said that if you didn't know him, it was easy to take offence, but those who did know him just accepted him for who he was. He had offended people at all levels, from bank chiefs, to top businessmen and multi millionaires.

Even in minor ways, Tim had the knack of putting people offside. At his 40th birthday party, black-tied guests were arriving at the big marquee set up on his tennis court, singer Delilah was ready to entertain when it was found the hired grand piano was out of tune. "Come with me," said Tim to three or four mates.

Borrowing a neighbour's truck, he went to the Newport Arms, walked into the dining room where the pianist was tinkling away for the benefit of diners and had his boys lift it from under the pianist's fingertips and carry it to the truck. All Tim said was: "Borrowing this." Then, as an afterthought, while the pianist still sat stunned on the stool, Tim reached down to it and said: "Taking this too." The diners couldn't believe it.

Tim's father was a foundation member of the Elanora Golf Club on the northern beaches but when Max Bristow joined, the committee asked him not to take Tim there. Max joined some clubs, like the exclusive Cabbage Tree Club at Palm Beach next to Kerry Packer's holiday home, just to prove that he could, expecting to be blackballed because of Tim's loudness and colourful reputation. Naturally Max never mentioned it to Tim.

But when it came to the crunch, Bristow had what it took. He sued a tight-fisted Sir Reg Ansett who reneged on paying him for work he did when Ansett had a fight with TNT over the carrying of mail, and payment was arranged on the court steps. Admiring his pluck, TNT boss Sir Peter Abeles hired him as a trouble-shooter on a $40,000 annual retainer.

Bristow took on the triads in his area. When a gang began standing over shopkeepers for protection money, he went in on his own and simply threw them out into the street, belting them for good measure. As a result Tim was a loved figure by businessmen in the Newport area.

After the Whisky Au Go Go's boom nightclub days in William Street, Sydney, it was physically taken over by a team of bouncers, led by "Iron Bar" Miller. The owners gave Tim the job of clearing them out. He went in with Tropical John, Iron Bar Freddy Coote and Graham Stolz, nicknamed The Kraut, and after a willing encounter, threw the bruised infiltrators into the street. "They didn't like chairs," said Tim, in a laconic understatement.

A fire then destroyed the club. Tim believed it was that blaze which motivated two moronic Sydney criminals, in attempting to extend their rackets, to ignite two drums of petrol at the foot of a stairwell leading from the street of the Whisky Au Go Go nightclub in Brisbane in the early hours of 8 March 1973, causing a fireball which killed 15 people. Another 20 survived the inferno by smashing windows and escaping. They had tried to stand over the club for protection money.

The criminals, cockney James Richard Finch and John Andrew Stuart, were arrested and charged, found guilty of the murder of one of the victims and jailed for life. After serving 15 years, Finch was deported to England, where he freely admitted his guilt. Stuart was one of the men who had tried to kill Bristow at the Newport Arms. In Tim's vocabulary, he suffered bad luck, dying mysteriously in his cell. But before he departed, Tim's other attempted murderer, Stewart John Regan, also ran into bad luck.

Regan, only 29, wanted to be a gangster and set a hot pace, standing over casinos, prostitutes and massage parlours for protection, making increasing inroads. McPherson told Bristow that Regan used to boast to him how he would "control this whole country." Big Lennie would laugh and ask: "And what would I be doing? The same as your other friends?"

Detectives believed that Regan was responsible for eight murders. People associated with him disappeared, including a six-year-old boy whom police thought Regan had killed in a fit of temper. McPherson told Bristow that two of Regan's associates, William Donnelly and Kevin Victor Gore, were murdered by Regan and dumped at sea.

While crossing Chapel Street, Marrickville one night in September 1974, Regan was hit by at least one gunman. Eight .38 bullets were pumped into him, one for each suspected murder he committed. Bristow had no doubt that McPherson arranged it, as he did the shooting a month earlier of John Edward "Chocka" Clark. Both were encroaching on his casino protection territory and he considered Regan out of control.

Regan's shooting was of passing interest to me. Bob Bottom, the plucky crime fighter, writing in the *Courier Mail* later on 31 October 2002, referred to threats made to investigative journalists. He said in part:-

"An early lesson for me - that you never allow anyone to think they may frighten you out of pursuing a story - occurred in 1969, when the *Sunday Telegraph* ran a front-page story on a killing spree by up-and-coming gangster John Regan. An editor who took a call from him went white as a ghost when Regan threatened to shoot him and other journalists as they left the building.

"A mentor of mine, Kevin Perkins, an astute and fearless writer on criminal goings-on, took over the phone, listened to a continuing tirade of threats for 30 seconds, then said: "Listen, dear boy, get f——" and slammed down the phone. No more was heard from Regan and more stories followed."

Even when doing good deeds, Bristow was apt to upset somebody, as when a young Sydney mother hired him at the last minute in 1973 to prevent her Yugoslav husband from taking their two-year-old son out of the country without her permission. The drama made front page headlines.

Learning that the husband was booked that morning on a flight to Athens, Tim took the mother, Mrs Theresa Urlich, to the Family Law Division of the Supreme Court where Mr Justice Jenkyn granted her temporary custody of her son, Vladimir. Then they dashed to Sydney airport.

Fearing the police would not turn up in time, and with the final call due, Bristow brushed past officials without even waving the court documents stuck in his back pocket. And with Customs men chasing him he ran aboard the plane, grabbed the boy and held a pistol to the man's head until police detained him. In those Iron Curtain days there would have been no legal way of recovering a child from Yugoslavia. The mother then received death threats from Yugoslavs, so did Bristow. But the boy stayed by court order.

In between his private eye jobs, most of which were difficult to pull off, requiring aggression and skill, Bristow continued his community work, including coaching his youthful rugby teams and the Newport Breakers Rugby team, aka the "Newport Nasties," and doing active anti-drug work.

As always he would turn a negative into a positive if he could, a side of his character not always understood. A perfect example of that occurred when a son of businessman Walter McGrath died after a heroin dealer sold him a strong fix, causing him to overdose. His distraught father called Bristow before he called the police.

Tim went to their home in the eastern suburbs and saw the dead son in the bath. The father wanted Bristow to retaliate, offering him $50,000 to find the criminal drug dealer and kill him. Tim said: "I wouldn't do that, there are better things you can do." He suggested forming a charity to help people addicted to drugs. From that was formed the James McGrath Foundation which became Odyssey House, a rehabilitation organisation. Tim knew the benefits that would flow, already having a similar organisation in his Way Back group.

Life changed pace quickly in Bristow's world and was never without fast-moving variation. Right after that, three killers called on him for breakfast in the early hours one morning. They were tow truck men, desperadoes, who had escaped from Central police station cells. One had murdered a department store night watchman who was a friend of his. At least one was armed and they wanted money and help while on the run.

He didn't give them money. But he lent a sympathetic ear, took out the silver tea service, fussed over the pot and made them tea and toast. When they left on motor bikes about 5 a.m. he rang his main police contact at home and told him about his interesting visitors. They were arrested as they crossed the Spit Bridge on Middle Harbour.

Other developments in this period that took Bristow's close attention included the mysterious deaths of Det-Supt Don Fergusson and Juanita Nielsen. Fergusson was found shot dead seated in a toilet cubicle at the CIB, and Juanita went missing, obviously murdered.

Fergusson's death caused widespread suspicion, first because he was shot in the head on the opposite side of the hand he normally used. As a protege of Ray Kelly and another corrupt cop, Fred Krahe, Fergusson had been in the rackets, mainly abortion. He'd done some good work too, like solving Sydney's first thallium murders. He also persuaded Commissioner Norman Allan to introduce phone tapping to counter crime, leading to the Age Tapes on police and "big shot" corruption.

But then Fergusson learned Allan intended retiring early due to recurring thrombosis, and he saw himself getting the top job. Suddenly his old colleagues felt vulnerable, seeing themselves threatened by a born-again puritan. Although Fergusson suffered from depression and his death was officially suicide, Bristow talked to various police about it including the one who found him and he had no doubt Fred Krahe murdered him to prevent an embarrassing situation if Fergusson became Commissioner.

Nielsen, 36, generally referred to as heiress to the Mark Foy retail fortune, had been stirring the pot on Frank Theeman's major redevelopment of Victoria Street, Potts Point, in her fortnightly Kings Cross journal, *NOW*. Although two people were convicted later for conspiracy to abduct her, Bristow was convinced Fred Krahe was also behind her disappearance and murder in 1975 to silence her objections to the Victoria Street projects.

Krahe, who retired on medical grounds in 1972, ending his career in disgrace after being accused of all sorts of underworld activities, was employed by Theeman to evict squatters from the Victoria Street buildings.

Jimmy "The Weasel" Fratianno, hit man for the Mafia, wasn't the kind of man you just dropped in on, but Bristow wanted to see him. Tim went to London first to collect a wad of money for Warren Anderson, the Sydney property developer who had a passion for collecting guns. Warren had sold a rare shotgun to a London collector who was a little slow on the draw. Then Tim headed for Chicago.

Bristow had a mission to complete for newly-knighted Sir Peter Abeles, the poor Hungarian immigrant made good who was extending TNT's transport interests abroad. He'd bought a transport company in the US and it turned out to be a dud. Mafia types were involved, including Fratianno. Abeles wanted Bristow to see if he could turn it around.

Tim used his old networking skills to get through. Fratianno was the Mafia's executioner, having killed about 15 men, later turning informer and becoming a protected Government witness. Tim was aware from "Morals" Martin that Hungarian Ivan Markovics, the abortion figure he knew who fled Sydney to avoid possible arrest when the heat went on through reformist Dr Bertram Wainer, was friendly with Fratianno and Sinatra.

Markovics, with Fratianno's help, and claiming to be a high ranking Knight of Malta, had donned red silk robes in a dubious private ceremony and presented Sinatra with scroll, medals, ceremonial passport and a red flag with a white Maltese cross to induct him into the ultra-exclusive social order. Bristow contacted Markovics who lined up a meeting through Sinatra.

The Weasel warmly welcomed Tim, the pair of them forming the physical long and short of it. Tim couldn't help telling friends later what a runt Fratianno was, how all the trigger men he'd known were little squirts, whereas big blokes tended to use muscle only. After Tim explained his problem politely, Jimmy said he'd see what could be done. Tim put him in direct contact with Sir Peter, and friendly discussions were held.

While in Chicago Tim made contact with Joe Testa, who remembered him fondly as the guy who arranged his kangaroo shooting trip with Big Lennie. But Tim didn't hang around long in Chicago. Neither did Testa for that matter, because it wasn't too long afterwards that he ran into the Bristow bad luck syndrome with his house bombed, moving to Florida where he died in 1981 after another bomb attack.

With Federal Attorney-General Lionel Murphy about to introduce his controversial libertarian *Family Law Act* in late

1974 to do away with adultery as a ground for divorce, legal raids on copulating couples would soon become a thing of the past. Bristow and his keyhole operators would do the last celebrity raids of the era. But other jobs had to be done first.

One of Tim's clients was advertising man John Singleton, whom Tim had introduced to Clyde Packer. Tim would pop around to Singo's regular Friday night office drinks session and casually put his shooting iron on the table. "Mate, can you put the gun away?" Singo would ask, respectfully.

Just before the 1974 NSW State election, Singleton and Premier Askin gave Tim the task of collecting funds from many of the well-heeled families and socialites from the eastern suburbs for the NSW Liberal Party, presumably to finance Askin's expensive advertising campaign run by Singo's agency. Tim took Tropical John with him to collect "bread" from the Packers and Fairfaxes and other big names, joking about how much easier it was not having to threaten or "touch up" anyone. They also provided a courier service delivering documents between Singo, Askin and the Liberal Party organisers in the Boulevard Hotel.

Then the chief executive officer of one of Australia's largest companies gave Tim a brief to find his missing wife and ensure her safety. He tracked her to a motel and went in. Screaming, she climbed out the fourth floor window to jump, but Tim grabbed her by a leg and Tropical gripped one foot. She was popping pills from 50 bottles in the bathroom.

Tropical stayed with her for two days, Tim coming back to check several times a day. The situation was hopeless and after discussing it with her husband, Tim had her committed to the Parramatta Psychiatric Hospital. He and Tropical wore white coats to look like staff as they delivered the struggling woman.

The last big divorce sorties followed.

Bristow received instructions from Sydney solicitor Paul McGrath in early 1974 to raid TV commentator and top current affairs man Mike Willesee, on behalf of his estranged wife, the former Joan Stanbury, who was the first Miss Australia to come from Western Australia.

His team did a week's surveillance on a Sydney model, Caroline Brent, noting when she left Balmain and visited the Cremorne home where Mike was living with his brother, Terry. Tim took along his reliable team of Tropical John and Iron Bar Freddy.

They went in just before midnight after the lights went out, removing a fuse from the junction box so the lights could not be switched on in the house. They carried torches. The first person they met was Terry at the end of a corridor. He wasn't too happy about the intrusion, wanting to fight a four rounder but Iron Bar Freddy suggested he be quiet like a good fellow, giving him a gentle tap with his persuader.

Mike, wearing pyjamas, met Tim at the bedroom door. Tim took a flashlight shot. Mike said: "Oh Tim, I guess I know why you're here," indicating they already knew each other. They went into the bedroom and Tim quickly suggested Mike and Caroline hop into bed and pull the sheets up for the photo shoot.

That done, Tim and his boys sat on the bed and all except Tim and Caroline drank cans of beer until about 3 a.m., with Mike and Tim talking racehorses. It was all very civilised. Mike had a stud at Cootamundra and Tim owned about a dozen racehorses at the time. He tried to pick Mike's brains for Saturday's races. Tim was a keen punter and much of the money he made was played on the horses.

Next day Channel 9 boss Clyde Packer appropriately enough sent his current affairs man Peter Meakin to Tim's home to see if the photos could be lost. But Tim had given the shots to a chemist to develop and next day supplied them and his invoice to the solicitor who engaged him, with strict instructions that no information was to be leaked out. He had given Willesee his word.

A couple of days later the *Daily Mirror* splashed the exclusive story on page one in the boldest type: "WILLESEE $250,000 DIVORCE!" Next thing Bristow was on to Tropical, angrily demanding: "Jack, what have you done?"

Tropical protested his innocence. Like Tim, he always kept faith, and he too was upset by the incident. Tim was so disturbed by this breach of his undertaking that he insisted on an inquiry. A clerk in the solicitor's office was found to have sold the story for $400. She was sacked. But it meant Mike could not have a quiet divorce. The proceedings did become close-up and personal, but not because of Tim, and the tabloids made a feast of it. The divorce went through and Mike married Caroline Brent.

The last dramatic divorce raid in Australia was done by Tim for the future wife of John Laws in, of all places, the remote highlands of New Guinea.

John, keeping in the background, wanted Tim to obtain divorce evidence for a lady he'd known in earlier years who was married to Dick Hagon, an old boy of The Kings School and a respected pioneer of the Highlands coffee industry. Dick was said to be having an affair with a European school teacher in the local Mount Hagen area. The job was simply to get in and get the pictures.

But was it so simple? The problem was how to get into the well-lit residence of an isolated jungle plantation with a huge staff of natives when news of strangers in the area would travel like wildfire? And to do it without creating a minor WW3 situation?

An interesting love story lay behind the proposed raid. Caroline Waller, a young North Shore beauty, had taken the eye of John Laws, the former Barker College-educated son of New Guinea expatriates, when he was a young radio announcer. Dick Hagon was also attracted to her.

Caroline chose the older man and a life of lingering colonial splendour on a coffee plantation, even if they did have kerosene lamps in their first home. They raised four daughters. Now Caroline was temporarily back in Sydney for a dental appointment, unhappy about her situation. She bumped into the new king of radio at Luna Park and the future became clear.

Through an advertising agency to keep things at arm's length, Tim met Caroline Hagon who told him she wanted to petition for divorce. He then had a covert meeting at the Chevron Hotel with Caroline Hagon and John Laws, who indicated his support. Caroline completed legal formalities and drew up a map of the plantation. Tim was glad to have Tropical John on this one because he'd once had his own coconut plantation in New Guinea, a land of about 3,000 dialects, and he could speak pidgin, a form of English devised in German occupation times. Tim also took Graham Stolz, and all carried pistols.

They flew by Ansett to Port Moresby, checking their guns in with the Royal Papuan Constabulary for the internal DC3 flight to Mount Hagen via Lae and Goroka, and obtaining a receipt. But Goroka was clouded in and they were diverted to Madang for an unscheduled overnight stay. Several expatriates from Australia were also on the flight.

Tim didn't like flying at the best of times and the conditions worried him. New Guinea is one of the world's most hazardous places for flying because of the wild mountainous terrain and turbulence. Pilots taking off from Moresby on a perfect day can run into cloud a few minutes out from mountain peaks jutting to 13,000 feet in the Owen Stanley Ranges. Often they fly into valleys and can't find a way out through clouds, which they say are "filled with bricks." Many American pilots taking off in the Second World War were never seen again, their planes sticking out from mountains like darts.

They were billeted at the Smugglers Inn and two of the ex-pats asked to change their accommodation from the Madang Hotel to theirs. At dinner that night, ordering their meals by numbers as was the custom, they were asked persistent questions by one ex-pat on the reason for their visit. He antagonised one of Tim's agents so much he told the man to mind his own business.

Next morning Tim looked somewhat terrorised on arrival at Mount Hagen to see dozens of squat Kukukuku tribesman waiting at the aerodrome's unfenced tin shed which served as a waiting room. They wore only short grass skirts but looked menacing, carrying spears and bows and arrows. "What's this, Tropical? Tim bellowed.

Tropical made light of it. "Don't worry about it mate. All they'll do is give you a dark look." Which they did. After having a bit of fun with Tim about their fighting qualities, he explained that the cargo cult had originated in this area. These fellows met every plane, believing they would deliver goods from ex-patriates that were rightfully theirs according to their gods.

They booked into the Hagen Park Hotel and checked their guns in at the police station. After hiring a vehicle, they made some inquiries, including talking to a woman friend of Caroline's. Tropical took photos of vehicles at the home of the woman named as co-respondent, one of which belonged to the nosey fellow who had questioned them the previous night.

But everywhere they went they were followed by Kukukukus, on foot and in vehicles, making no attempt to hide. These fellows had been the last of the highland cannibals and still loved fighting. It indicated that Dick Hagon was aware of their presence and mission.

Tim might not have thought much of the pigmy-type tribesmen but he liked what he saw of the indigenous girls. They went around topless, their breasts jutting straight out, enough to make any European male visitor's eyes pop. He also liked the Territory's richly-coloured bougainvillea, hibiscus and orchids.

Tropical took Tim to the local markets and had a bit of fun with him by suggesting these natives chewing red betel nut and spitting it out were very dangerous. Then he tried his pidgin. "Me know new fella come half along," he said, pointing south. "Me come half along Rabaul," meaning he was a longtime Territorian, and they warmed to him quickly.

Tim was keen to get down to business. "Do a survey, Tropical," he ordered. So Tropical, trying to look like a tourist, hired a taxi, telling the driver: "Me like lookum big fella coffee plantation."

He knew Hagon's *Gumanch* plantation was four or five kilometres out of town and wanted to reconnoitre the place in case they had to go there at night, dodging behind trees to get to the bungalow. It would be nice to know where they were putting their feet.

He picked up two natives on the way and chatted. As a result he didn't go right to the plantation. They told him that the workers there had set up some kind of a trap or ambush for somebody at a bridge near the plantation. Returning to the hotel he told Tim the news. It was now clear that Dick Hagon was ready for them and this made their task difficult. It was no use trying to put up a cock and bull story as a way in. They would have to confront the situation head on.

Tim, Tropical and Graham Stolz were sitting in Tim's motel room, unit 9, at 6 p.m. studying maps and discussing how they might go about it now, when in walked Dick Hagon and said: "G'day Tim. I believe you're up here for a job on me. What's the story?"

As surprised as he was, Tim appeared calm and relaxed and shook hands warmly. He'd known Dick at school sports between Shore and Kings, and had met him again about twenty years previously. Dick again came to the point: "This surprises me because I was talking to Caroline on the phone just a couple of hours ago, and she denies you're working under her instructions."

Tim said: "I intended calling to see you as I've been hired by a solicitor to act on your wife's behalf. I couldn't knock back the job, even though I was reluctant to do it. But I feel this can be settled in an amicable way."

The conversation showed Bristow's cleverness and ability to quickly change his approach. Taken completely by surprise, while planning to burst in on his quarry, he was now talking diplomatically, feeling his way for a solution. This flexibility was one of the reasons for his success.

They talked and at 6.15 the phone rang. It was passed to Tim. The caller was Frank Dockery, a friend in Sydney, who said: "Caroline had a call from Dick Hagon today. He knows you're up there looking for him. I'm concerned for your safety as I think you're walking into a trap."

Without saying anything to give a hint of who had called or what it was about, Tim put down the phone and continued where he'd left off, applying the pressure now: "We have sufficient evidence of your adultery with this girl, but to save you adverse publicity and embarrassment I decided to come to Mount Hagen to see if I could get an admission of your adultery. I assure you that in this matter your wife is only looking for her rights and security for the children."

According to written evidence which Bristow later prepared for the solicitor representing Caroline, Dick Hagon then allegedly admitted the adultery. He too wanted a divorce. They then discussed the most delicate settlement details arising out of the proposed divorce, matters Bristow was familiar with due to his vast experience. But Bristow was also angling for the photos. At the psychological moment when Dick was about to leave, he said: "I'll follow you to where the girl is hiding out and photograph you in a bedroom with her."

Dick suggested he could supply a picture of them together but Tim said: "That's not good enough. We want to take the photographs ourselves and at the same time speak to the co-respondent."

Dick didn't want anyone to go to the plantation or the girl's home but made arrangements to bring her back to the motel that night. He rang later and put her on the phone. She said she admitted the adultery but didn't think the pictures were necessary. They didn't show up that night. But they turned up at the motel next day. In Tim's suite he told them: "Get into bed and pull the sheets up around your neck."

It was a technique they'd often used, even throwing people into bed at times, telling them "we only want the photos, we don't want any blood." Dick and the girl complied, and three pictures of them were taken while they lay in bed fully dressed under the sheets. Divorce, Australian style!

But Dick must have had a change of heart overnight. Just before Bristow and his boys were about to board the Air

Niugini flight out of Mount Hagen next morning, he was served with a "summons to a person upon complaint," in which Dick alleged that Bristow, Petford and Stolz had unlawfully detained certain of his property, namely, three photographs.

Tim had removed the 35mm roll of film from the camera and carefully hidden it on his person, just in case. The summons, returnable to the Mount Hagen District Court the following Monday, meant that technically they could not leave Papua New Guinea without appearing in court.

Arriving in Port Moresby, he rang Sydney executives of Ansett to make sure he was not stopped from getting on the flight to Australia. There was some trouble in Moresby getting their guns back but they made it aboard. As they left the plane on arrival in Sydney they were surrounded by cops with guns drawn, handcuffed and taken to a room for questioning. Incredibly, they were suspected of being plane hijackers. Tim soon cleared up that allegation but the cops kept their pistols, although they had documentation to show they'd surrendered them at every point. Tim had to ring his Customs friend, Harvey Bates, to get them back.

Tim arranged for the New Guinea office of Sydney solicitors Gaden, Bowen & Stewart to represent them in Mount Hagen on the summons complaint, which was eventually withdrawn.

The Hagon divorce went through uncontested and later John Laws married Caroline, whom on air he constantly called The Princess. Dick Hagon was awarded the OBE for his services in developing the coffee industry in a country that unfortunately would degenerate into lawlessness.

For Tim Bristow too it was a good result in what was probably the world's most unusual divorce "raid."

15

BEHIND THE JUNIE MOROSI AFFAIR

AFFAIRS of the heart are usually considered out of bounds by politicians in Australia's otherwise parochial capital city when they dig the dirt. It's a kind of self-interest mechanism. Who knows where it would end if politicians in Canberra started throwing that kind of stuff around? There's enough "tooling" going on in that town to destroy the moral pretences of both main political parties for good if the truth were known.

But the "Morosi Affair" was different. The Whitlam Government was looking decidedly shaky in late 1974 and the Liberals smelled blood. They saw an opportunity to rip the boot in and nakedly, grubby politics shot to the surface - all in the public interest of course, not to mention decency and morality.

Yes, there was "tooling" going on with a beautiful woman at the centre, there was innuendo and heavy sexuality in the air. But that was just a sideshow. The real substance in this heady era of Whitlam politics was that the Federal Liberal Opposition saw a chance to get back into power if they could make enough mud stick. As an example of all-round political hypocrisy, it would be hard to beat.

It all blew up when Deputy Prime Minister and Treasurer Dr Jim Cairns appointed the slashingly beautiful Shanghai-born Junie Morosi to his staff in December 1974 as his principal private secretary. Junie, 41, had migrated from the Philippines and was married to David Ditchburn, the local boss of Ethiopian Airlines. Junie was already known as a lobbyist, having begun with some members of the Liberal Party.

After the Cairns appointment, questions were raised in Federal Parliament, tentatively at first against Attorney-General Lionel Murphy - had Murphy and his wife received concessional air tickets from Ethiopian Airlines, had Junie Morosi applied for a job at Qantas and had the result of an investigation into her suitability been supplied to Murphy and Cairns for whom she worked?

It soon became highly personalised and whipped into a scandal with flaring headlines, focusing on her looks, calling for her removal or sacking, questioning her qualifications, high salary and government accommodation - also her relationship with Dr Cairns.

He stubbornly refused to yield any ground and would not accept her resignation, even after a Cabinet reshuffle in which he lost the Treasury portfolio. He kept her on in spite of some members of his staff resigning in protest. Asked publicly if he was in love with her, Dr Cairns expressed "a kind of love for Junie," keeping the controversy on the boil.

The affair was further fuelled when Dr Cairns and Junie were photographed together on a swing at a motel in Terrigal in New South Wales during the ALP's federal conference. She called her own press conference to say there was nothing improper in their relationship.

Junie took a high moral stance throughout, claiming the furore wasn't about sexuality, but sexism and - tossing in the old standby - racism, because she was a migrant. Golly, if that race card had been true, Australia compared with most other countries where racism is rife would have been an innocent cherub at a booze-up of bearded, rum-soaked pirates.

Then the bombshell hit. Somebody raided her Sydney flat, causing more headlines. Bristow was right in the thick of it.

After the story of Junie's appointment broke in the *Mirror* on 2 December 1974, Bristow was approached by a bosomy blonde wanting to hire a private detective to "dig up all the dirt" on Morosi. The blonde, from Bellevue Hill, came with Sydney ABC television presenter, Ian Finlay. They met Tim and Tropical John in a crowded pub in Sussex Street, City, obviously to steer it away from the Liberal Party. Without mentioning names she surprised Tim by saying "we" had $250,000 to spend to ruin Morosi's credibility, damage the Whitlam Labor Government and Cairns too.

The blonde handed Bristow an envelope containing money as a deposit. He slipped it inside his coat pocket but said he wanted to think about it. He talked it over with a friend, Federal MP Billy Wentworth, who took him to a Liberal Party office in Sydney. An official there dialled a Canberra number and said: "Senator Greenwood would like to speak to you about it."

He was certain the man he spoke to was Senator Ivor Greenwood, the Opposition Attorney-General. He had a long talk to the Senator who said "we" wanted a total bugging and background search on Morosi and her husband. The job would entail searching Morosi's residence in Batemans Road, Gladesville, bugging it with a hidden electronic microphone or FM transmitter and having all sounds from the flat monitored on a nearby receiver for two or three months until the necessary "dirt" was obtained.

The Senator wanted the same thing done to Morosi's Canberra residence, concentrating on her bedroom, and to

Ditchburn's airline office in suite 803 of Australia Square Tower in Sydney. Also, two people would be sent overseas, one to Hong Kong and Bangkok, returning via Manila, to check on business activities and personal backgrounds, and another person would go to London, returning to Sydney via Ethiopia.

Answering a question by Bristow, the Senator said "We have a lot of money to spend on this, we now have a quarter of a million dollars."

Bristow told him he thought all the money would be spent on airfares and accommodation and he couldn't see anything left for him. He asked for $250 a day to take the job. The Senator said "we" would think about it. The bosomy blonde came back to him, said $250 was too much, they had already arranged to send people to Hong Kong, Bangkok and Manila, and would he do it for $100 a day. Bristow said no.

But then Alan Felton, a NSW Liberal Party official, approached him and said he'd be well paid on completion if he took it on, and he agreed. Felton said the person they were trying to get at was not Cairns but Lionel Murphy, whom they were sure was having an affair with Morosi before Cairns. Any evidence on Murphy was a priority. It was just after this conversation that questions about Murphy were raised in the Parliament by Senator Greenwood, a Victorian Liberal, although he left out any direct references to an alleged affair.

Just before Christmas 1974 Tim took Tropical and "Fingers" Wigglesworth with him to Gladesville, joking that it was "just behind Lennie's place." The locksmith picked the tilt door lock, then sat in Tim's car. Tim looked around in the garage where some documents were kept but didn't find anything of interest - except one letter.

The letter had nothing to do with Labor politicians but came from a high-flying Liberal MP with aspirations to become prime minister. It was amorous too, described as "lovey dovey," suggesting he too might have had an affair with Junie. Tim pocketed it and left. He told Alan Felton he hadn't found anything on Murphy. Felton was angry, didn't believe he'd tried hard enough and refused to pay him. What's more, he insisted on another raid and said he'd come along to see for himself.

Bristow then did one of his occasional "double enders," compounding the issue further and taking advantage of a private eye's position to earn "bread" on the side. If Felton wouldn't pay him, he'd go the other way and be paid by the Labor Party. After all, he had to pay his agents for the raid anyway. So he somersaulted, took the Liberal MP's letter to a solicitor with Labor Party links and negotiated a payment, without saying where he obtained it.

Apart from resenting not being paid, Bristow didn't have much heart for the job anyway. He was the wrong man to expect to get excited about moral issues involving a bit of sex on the side being played up solely for political purposes. Besides, his own personal life was very complicated in that area, a fact that would soon bubble to the surface.

On the second raid Felton didn't want to hang about outside at the scene while someone fiddled around to open the door. So to explain the situation, Tim took Felton to meet his locksmith in the shop he managed at Ashfield. "Okay," said Rick Wigglesworth, "I'll go and eyeball the joint, see if there are any code numbers on the lock, take a note of them, come back here to the shop and cut a key and we can do the business any time after tomorrow."

"Fingers" cut a key and next day they arranged the meeting time on the phone for the following morning. That was about three weeks after the first raid. Tim and Felton arrived to pick up Wigglesworth, Tim in his conspicuous white Mercedes with Tropical beside him, Felton looking casual in an old Kombi van. They drove to near Morosi's townhouse in Batemans Road, Gladesville.

Bristow parked in a back street well away from the townhouse, leaving Tropical in the car and he travelled to the address in the van with Felton and the locksmith. Felton parked in a lane fairly close to the townhouse, in sight of the garage.

Everything looked normal for a suburban street. A few cars were parked there, tradesmen were working on houses, painting, a TV set was being delivered. Wigglesworth handed the key to Felton and stayed in the van, saying he'd come and fix it if there was trouble with the door. Tim and Felton walked to the garage.

Watching from the van, Rick saw the door go up, Tim and Felton go in and the door close. They were in there about 10 minutes, then they came out and closed the door. Felton, carrying what looked like a lady's vanity case, walked towards the van. Tim hung back. Rick leaned over to open the driver's door for Felton and the next time he looked up, Tim had disappeared. There one moment, gone the next. Must have walked back to the Merc, he thought. Felton started the van and moved off to go left out of Batemans Road before turning into the main thoroughfare.

Suddenly a car came flying around the corner, almost on two wheels, and screamed to a halt in front of them, blokes leaping out with guns drawn, *Homicide* style. Another car screamed up the laneway behind them. The "workmen" were cops. Felton turned white as Wigglesworth said: "Just remember what I told you, I'm just a locksmith and I was opening your garage for you. That's the story."

The Kombi's doors were reefed open, both men were thrown to the ground and handcuffed, Rick face down in the gutter yelling: "What the hell's going on?" They said they were Commonwealth police. "I was just called out to open this man's garage," he protested. They were taken to HQ in Commonwealth Street in the city and questioned in separate rooms.

"Who was the third man?" they asked Wigglesworth. "I don't know, never seen him in my life before," he said. "Come on," a cop said, "Don't bullshit to us, you must know." But he refused to say.

Bristow had not "disappeared." He'd told Felton he would walk back to his own car and meet him a few streets away. But with his sixth sense he had smelled a rat after seeing a "painter" look around and suddenly stiffen. When he heard cars start up he knew, but it was too late to warn Felton.

He jumped over several residential fences, beating cops who covered both ends of the lane and sprinted for his car with a turn of speed that would have amazed his old Gordon rugby club mates. While the cops zoomed in on the scene he escaped and headed for the office of the lawyer whom he thought must have leaked the information.

Tim knew he'd talked too freely. That was one of his faults - talking too much about some of his clients' business. But he hadn't done it deliberately. He'd spoken about it in a conversational way to two lawyer friends who both had strong Labor connections and one was a personal friend of Murphy's. The lawyer had mentioned Senator Greenwood to him after Greenwood's name appeared in the papers, saying he had a bee in his bonnet about Lionel Murphy and was causing him a lot of trouble.

Bristow remembered saying to him: "Yes, he's one of a group anxious to get information on Murphy. I've been hired to do a raid on Junie Morosi's house to find some documents relating to Murphy. I did one raid but didn't find anything and they won't pay me. Now they want me to go to the place again."

He found the lawyer in his office. "I've just come from Morosi's place at Batemans Road, There were police everywhere. I think they've arrested my man Wigglesworth. You must have tipped off Lionel." The lawyer laughed and said: "I'm sorry Tim. But I'll look after it for you." He lifted the phone and spoke to a person whom Bristow took to be the lawyer Morgan Ryan, another friend of Murphy's.

"Tim's here," he said. "The big fellow is upset." He briefly described what happened and Tim butted in loudly: "This fellow Wigglesworth is a good friend of mine and a good fellow. It's an embarrassment to me and I'm sure he's been taken into custody."

The lawyer then rang Lionel Murphy and told him of Tim's predicament, asking him to see what could be done. He handed the phone to Tim and a polite and friendly Lionel said to him: "I'm sorry about this Tim, but it will be attended to." When the lawyer got off the phone he said: "Yes, we're sorry about this Tim, but it will be attended to. I'll ring Murray Farquhar."

Tim had nobody to blame but himself. The lawyers in this group were all mates who dined and wined together, he'd opened his mouth and naturally one of them had tipped off Lionel.

He now realised that Murphy had simply told the Federal Police of the impending raid and they had tapped Bristow's telephones, knowing exactly when it would take place. That would have occurred naturally to Murphy who as Attorney-General, with a few drinks aboard, had personally led a dawn raid of 30 cops on ASIO in Melbourne in 1973 to obtain information they had refused to give him.

Meanwhile, back in Commonwealth Street, the cops were still grilling Wigglesworth and Felton. The keen young cops eventually left Rick and, playing good cops bad cops, sent in a big fat senior officer. With a hand on Rick's left shoulder he said: "Look, Mr Wigglesworth. We know the score. Just tell 'em something you feel you can to shut 'em up and we'll get you out of here." He still refused to betray the third man.

Bristow's approach to Lionel Murphy and his mates obviously paid off because some time later solicitor Bruce Miles, also a friend of Murphy, turned up. "OK Rick, you're free to go now," he said, "no charges." Rick was never charged. Neither was Bristow, although the cops knew he was connected. Neither of their names appeared in media reports of the incident, only references to "a locksmith" and "a private eye."

As soon as he left the cops, Wigglesworth rang Bristow from a public phone: "You bastard, you left me to it," he accused. They sorted it out, Bristow explaining he had already rung his parents to advise them of what happened. Felton was not so lucky. He was charged with possessing goods stolen from Morosi and possessing a false set of number plates, and was fined. He then went on TV and in the newspapers and said he did it all "in the national interest."

But it wasn't the end for Wigglesworth. One of the Labor lawyers, annoyed over the raid for Murphy's sake, dobbed him in to the Federal Police, falsely alleging he'd sent a letter bomb to Queensland Premier Joh Bjelke-Petersen. They came to the shop which he managed, flourishing a warrant for his arrest, turned the place inside out looking for bomb making equipment, then turned his home inside out. Finding nothing, they said: "We're prepared to admit we made a mistake." He said: "You're not wrong."

Lionel Murphy resigned from Federal Parliament soon after and went on the High Court Bench, destined to see out his career amid controversy. In one incident he was accused of trying to influence the outcome of a court case to help his "little mate," Morgan Ryan. But he was a man with a heart prepared to help others, with many genuine friends who later mourned his passing.

After several years, following the dramatic sacking of the Whitlam Government on 11 November 1975, the Morosi Affair quietened down. Then, nearly 30 years after all those headlines, on 15 September 2002, an 87-year-old Dr Cairns finally admitted, to ABC radio interviewer John Cleary, what everyone had long believed - yes, he had gone to bed with Junie Morosi.

And, boasting that he'd reached his highest popularity in opinion polls all those years ago after six months of "Morosi publicity," he added: "I don't think the ordinary person thought I was wrong or a fool in going to bed with Junie Morosi. They thought it was a pretty good thing."

In a followup, Cairns told *Herald* journalist Tony Stephens he hadn't admitted it before because "nobody had asked if I'd been to bed with her." Well, he had been asked, telling a jury he'd never had an adulterous relationship and claiming a *National Times* article which referred to Cairns's "girlfriend Morosi" was defamatory because it imputed he was "improperly involved with his assistant, Junie Morosi, in a romantic or sexual association contrary to the obligations of his marriage and to that of Miss Morosi."

But get a load of what Junie told the jury: "I felt insulted, angry, upset and hurt. It was very demeaning to me as a woman. I saw myself as a professional, as a competent person doing her job. It was cheap. It was as though it had nothing to do with business but everything to do with sex."

The good Dr Cairns wasn't so smart opening his trap like that by admitting, in effect, that what was published at the time was true. Junie had benefited from defamation claims against the *Mirror* in which Gough Whitlam gave evidence for her, and against 2GB. They could have asked for their money back on the ground of, ah, breathtaking hypocrisy.

Tim's own affairs of the heart were about to cause him much more trouble than had Jim's fling with Junie.

16

GUEST OF HER MAJESTY

RENATE was beautiful, she was German and the private investigator found her irresistible.

Bristow was hired by her successful businessman husband to obtain evidence of her alleged adultery when divorce raids were still legal back in the early '70s. Due to the high octane emotion involved in divorce jobs, Tim had been reluctant to accept this brief because he knew the parties.

Renate was a young mother living apart from her husband in a Darling Point townhouse with Harbour views. Even other women described her as pretty. Tim was slow in producing evidence and the husband asked him to speed it up. At that point Tim told him he was no longer representing him but was now acting for the wife. That caused anger and resentment. It also led to some solicitors calling him 007 for sleeping with the enemy.

The story Tim told friends was that he found Renate to be a good mother who needed help in her divorce situation. No doubt that was true, but the compelling reason for the switch was that Tim had fallen for her. He didn't stop to think that his habit of somersaulting in divorce matters where a beautiful woman was involved would soon mar his private and professional life. As a married man he'd always pleased himself. And he was stunningly open about it.

He wanted not just the best girls but for each one to see him with another, creating drama around his relationships. Often in his casual conversations, after being introduced to someone, he would raise the subject of sex by saying something like "they were saying I was having an affair with his wife," bringing himself and his sexual prowess to the fore. Boasting about his affairs became a theme song of his conversations.

Life had been difficult since his first wife Judy walked out when their son Stephen was two. As a single parent Tim genuinely tried to do his best for Stephen, but the unpredictable nature of his work with its crazy hours made the task mountainous. In between the help from Max and sister-in-law Ann, he often took Stephen to the Newport Arms for meals. But it wasn't the same as a child having a normal stable home life. Neighbours remembered often seeing a young boy at home on his own.

The worst aspect from Stephen's point of view was the emotional tug of war over him between his parents. Although Tim had custody, his mother loved and wanted him also and although he sometimes went to his mother in Queensland, there was constant drama over the situation.

That settled down a good deal when Glenda came on the scene. A New Zealand school teacher, Glenda reversed local folklore by leaving a place at the bottom of the North Island called Lower Hutt (where they used to say "come to the Hutt to get out of the rut"), and met Tim while modelling in Sydney. She lived with Tim for some time at his Newport home before they were married on 6 September 1968.

Glenda, a tall blonde with bright blue eyes, became a real mother to Stephen, looking after him superbly in all ways. He looked upon her as his soulmate. By contrast, his relations with his father were often marked by tensions and argument. As a kid, he was terrified of Tim because he was so tough on him. Tim wanted to mould his son into what he was, and that didn't suit Stephen.

Tim introduced Stephen to surfing at an early age and freely admitted he was tough on the boy, embarrassing him in front of his peers if he didn't win a surf race by making him go around the buoys again on the spot, forcing him to train to agonising lengths, even to running up and down the beach late at night.

Stephen could never please his father, no matter what he did. If he won a race, Tim would be aggressive and say, well, you could have done it in half the time. Some close observers believed that Tim wasn't happy with himself, and he therefore wasn't happy with Stephen because he was trying to live his life again through Stephen.

Tim's justification was that he regretted a lot of silly things he did as a youth and although he didn't want Stephen to be a clone of himself, he wanted him to be a good physical specimen and to excel at sport which in Tim's view was a good foundation for life, in fact, the only foundation. "I wanted him to arm himself as I did in later life, and not be over gullible when a youth as I was," he said.

As a result he wanted him to become a lawyer, as Tim's father had wanted of Tim. With that in mind he sent Stephen to the exclusive Kings School at Parramatta as a boarder.

Stephen certainly fulfilled his father's expectations in sport. He was a champion surfer, a State swimmer and an outstanding sportsman at Kings, where he held records as a swimmer, played in the rugby XV and rowed in the eights two years running. He was big, strong, tall and good looking.

Stephen couldn't understand how Tim could get down to the personal level with kids in the Peninsula area and help them in their problems with such patience and care, yet be so difficult with him. "Those who had to live with him saw him in a different light," said Stephen. "He seemed to take out the stresses and strains of his occupation on those nearest and dearest to him."

Glenda often found it that way too. Naturally she objected to his philandering with female clients, but there was little she could do about it. Tim was a law unto himself. He would often take his mistress Renate to the house while Glenda was there.

Nobody seemed to know what it was that sometimes annoyed Tim about Glenda. It could not have been that she was always conscious of her appearance, because he liked her looking glamorous. She was beautiful. He made lame excuses to friends for sometimes treating her harshly, saying she had social inclinations "and got off on being on the mother's committee."

She was late one day to do a city fashion parade and apologised to the other models, explaining to one who looked at her wet hair and asked what happened: "Tim tried to stop me coming. He threw a bucket of water over me when I was dressed and just getting into the car." It seemed that Tim would just suddenly snap emotionally with those close to him.

Once Tim had won a woman, and she was living in the house, the chase was over and his attitude changed. That happened with Glenda. But Glenda, an Aries woman, tried to give as good as she got. She stood up to Tim and, although a refined person, spoke back to Tim as he spoke to her.

The night he found Renate with a King's Cross bouncer named Louis Vaja from the *33 Club* gambling joint, was an occasion when his emotions were raw. Tim, then having a strong affair with Renate, had just spent three or four days with her at her Darling Point townhouse and, as court evidence would show, told her late on a Friday that he'd have to leave for a few hours to have dinner with his wife and some of her friends.

Renate had booked a babysitter for the night, believing they were going out. He said he'd be back later and they could go somewhere then. Obviously piqued, she rang Louis Vaja after Tim left and they went to dinner at the French Tavern, calling at the Hofbrau Haus for more drinks.

Meanwhile, Tim returned and spoke to the babysitter, who told him Renate had gone out. He asked her to let Renate know he'd called and left, vainly looking for Renate in several night spots. He returned two or three hours later, let himself in with his key and sat waiting, without disturbing the babysitter asleep upstairs.

Tim knew Vaja and believed he also was having an affair with Renate. Time dragged and about 2 a.m. Tim went into the laundry area to get a glass of water and at that moment Renate came in with Vaja. She asked him to stay for coffee. Tim remained in the laundry, claiming later he was embarrassed in the circumstances to do anything else. He heard Renate ask the babysitter if anyone had called and she said yes, Mr Bristow had been and said he'd be back.

Tim said he heard Renate tell Vaja it would be better if he left. He didn't move and Bristow suddenly emerged and said: "Best you leave." Vaja replied: "You don't tell me to leave."

Things quickly deteriorated. Versions differed but the evidence indicated that Vaja, a big man but not as big as Bristow, struck the first blow. They fought and wrestled on the floor, with Renate screaming "stop this," and Tim put Vaja out the door. Vaja came back and hit Bristow on the back of the head with a chair and there were more fisticuffs. Vaja finished up getting the worst of it, suffering shocking facial injuries.

He came back with five policemen from Rose Bay and when they went inside the townhouse he screamed at Bristow: "I'll kill you." An ambulance was called and he was taken to St Vincent's Hospital where he remained for two weeks and was operated on for severe facial injuries.

Tim phoned Louis Vaja's flatmate next day and apologised, saying, "he brought this on himself because he came back into the house after he was put out and hit me with a chair, and that's why I lost my temper."

No police action was taken but Bristow and Vaja summonsed each other for assault. Then a friend of Louis Vaja's, Max Werner, phoned Bristow and said Louis didn't really want to go to court and all he wanted was his expenses as compensation. Although he believed it had been a fair fight which Vaja had started, Tim thought it best all round to settle it out of court to avoid publicity and also preserve his agent's licence.

A meeting was arranged at the Grape Escape wine bar at North Sydney between Louis, Max Werner and Tim, who took along Tropical John and another agent. Louis wanted $4,000 for medical and legal expenses and $3,000 for his loss of wages.

Tim said to them: "It cuts against my grain having to pay anything but my son and wife mean so much to me I don't wish to have any further adverse publicity." He gave Louis $4,000 in cash on the spot, went to the Royal Exchange branch of the (then) Bank of NSW in Pitt Street, drew out $3,000 and gave it to Vaja, who wrote out an indemnity on the back of a bank deposit slip saying he would drop all charges and make no further claims.

Bristow shook hands with Louis who said: "I'm satisfied now. I'll pay my lawyers and medical expenses and as far as I'm concerned, the matter is settled." They both withdrew the summonses. Vaja went mining at Coober Pedy and about two months later visited Bristow's house, said he was running short of money, and Tim bought some opal chips from him.

That should have been the end of the matter. But someone was kicking it along behind the scenes, insisting that Bristow be charged by police. Tim always believed it was the Minister of Justice, John Maddison, whom he had made an enemy of over a divorce raid on Maddison's developer friend and by inquiring into cases involving solicitors who were friends of Maddison.

Bristow was eventually charged by police that on 25 November 1972 he had assaulted, beaten and otherwise ill treated Louis Vaja, occasioning him actual bodily harm. Tim was committed to stand trial. Trying to counter the situation, he asked legal friends and MPs to make legitimate representations on his behalf. George Neilly, the member for Cessnock, made a written approach to the Attorney-General Ken McCaw, and Keith Doyle, the member for Wentworth, approached Maddison.

Tim was assured these efforts had been well received, but feared otherwise, especially when Maddison told a journalist off the record that as far as he was concerned, Bristow could "rot in jail." It seemed clear some power players wanted Bristow off the scene.

Realising he could be jailed due to the influence of powerful forces opposed to him, Bristow sought a way out by using the backdoor system which he knew to have worked for others - he attempted to pay a bribe to Attorney-General McCaw to obtain a no-bill and have the charges withdrawn by Ministerial discretion. He knew that McCaw, well-known for issuing no bills, was "open to suggestion." Bristow gave $10,000 to a carwash business friend who knew McCaw, asking him to pass it on. Later he learned the "friend" kept the money and did nothing.

Adding to his worries just before the trial came on, his private life went into reverse gear - a burden which he kept to himself.

Travelling abroad at the time with Dr Stella Dalton on their anti-drug studies in 1974, including a World Health Organisation conference in Amsterdam, they had been in close contact every day for several weeks. Attraction quickly developed and they became lovers.

They continued their relationship in Sydney with Tim pursuing Stella. Her academic standing and intelligence appealed enormously to that side of him from his family background which influenced him to always put his best foot forward. Stella believed that Tim wanted her to have his child.

Stella confided to a friend that Tim had told her he wasn't married, that the lady in his house, Glenda, was only his housekeeper. This fragile situation was put to the test when Stella fell pregnant. In a tense discussion on their future, Tim admitted he was already married and wished to remain so. Stella decided to have the baby and then married a friend before the birth.

Tim loved children and had also wanted Glenda to have a baby. They had not been able to achieve it but suddenly Glenda too became pregnant. In the one crucial week, Tim would visit both Stella and Glenda in different hospitals. Stella was giving birth and Glenda, sadly, was suffering a miscarriage. At the same time, he was continuing his affair with Renate, demonstrating still that while he had permanent ladies, he always had mistresses and lovers.

Without knowing that background, Tim's friend Di Parkinson popped in by co-incidence to see Stella soon after the birth and was surprised to see her with a baby girl. She was shocked when Stella said: "Tim's baby." Tim swore Di to silence, threatening reprisals if she said anything to Glenda.

Stella would raise her daughter, Isis, to be a beautiful young woman, outstanding in sport and graduating from university as a bachelor of science. But Isis would not know her father until she reached her teens. When Isis was a child, Tim would call late at night and leave a Christmas present on the doorstep.

The Vaja trial, set down for 12 August 1975, would last four days in the District Court. Vaja, a Czech migrant, admitted in evidence that he'd had plenty of fights and could handle himself, but lied by denying he'd been a bouncer at a Kings Cross club and a casino in Chinatown. He said that on the night he took Renate out she told him she was having an affair with Bristow, who was helping her obtain a lump sum settlement from her divorce, but she wanted to be free of him.

The Crown case alleged that Bristow had attacked Vaja and struck the first blow, there was a fight during which Bristow evicted him and Vaja suffered serious injuries. Vaja admitted that on returning with police he told Bristow he would kill him.

Bristow pleaded that Vaja had first attacked him and he acted in self defence. He had to put strength into his blows because he feared for his life, and he too suffered injuries although Vaja's were far worse. In cross examination, he said he often saw Renate, sometimes seven times a week. Renate in her evidence confirmed Tim's story that Vaja had thrown the first punch but she said it was Bristow, not her, who told

Vaja to leave. She said that when she returned to the townhouse that night, Bristow was extremely angry after waiting nearly five hours.

I was then news editor of the *Sunday Telegraph* and was one of those who gave character evidence for Bristow.

An extraordinary aspect of the trial occurred when the Crown raised the question of compensation. Vaja got in the witness box and perjured himself by saying he wanted compensation for expenses incurred, knowing but not disclosing he'd already been paid and had signed an indemnity.

Tim was mystified why his earlier payment wasn't pointed out to the court, thinking it would have helped him with the jury. But Tim's legal team thought that might have looked like a sign of guilt, or it could have been seized upon by the Crown as an alleged attempt to pervert the course of justice. In any case, they told the court Tim was prepared to pay compensation. Tim was critical later of other aspects of his defence, such as no medical evidence being called to show that he, too, had been injured and that Vaja had changed his lower court evidence.

In his summing up to the jury of 12 men, Judge Muir said it was for them to decide whether the blows were excessive in the circumstances. If so, self defence must fail. After a two-hour adjournment, the jury found Tim guilty.

In passing sentence, Judge Muir said he was very greatly impressed by the evidence before him as to what Bristow had done for others. His Honour said: "When a person has evidence tendered that you have done great good for many people, young people and others, you are entitled to all that has been said about you and must be given full value, in my opinion, for what you have done." But he added that the violence was "very severe, quite extreme."

He ordered that Tim pay $4,000 compensation for the injury sustained by Vaja and, expressing regret, sentenced him to 18 months imprisonment. But he made a point of specifying the minimum non-parole period of six months. Tim's family was grateful that his parents were not alive to see it.

Ironically, Tim had lost his licence over a raid at Port Macquarie a few months before when he and three agents seized two children in a custody case. A man was injured when he had to be restrained and Tim insisted he had been mistaken for one of his agents, and he appealed. But now, with the Vaja conviction, that was merely academic. He wanted to appeal in the Vaja case too but his legal advisers said he was unlikely to get bail due to the political hostility from Maddison. Also, an appeal would take at least six months to come on and he'd be out then anyway.

He went to Long Bay jail, known as The Puzzle because it puzzled most people as to why they were there. He was summoned to the office of the acting governor and told by a prison official that he was "a political prisoner" and if he caused any trouble he would never be released. Rightly or wrongly, he took that to mean he would meet his end in jail.

Tim told friends who visited him that he was heavily dosed up with drugs - valium and mogadon - and had been subjected to psychiatric tests. He was certain the tests were politically motivated. Speaking through a wire grill, he also told friends that while repairing his shoes one day near the bathroom in his wing, he was suddenly attacked by two other prisoners who tried to kill him. One had a hammer, the other a screwdriver.

Tim belted them both. A warder who accompanied them annoyed him by standing by and watching, so he thumped him too. That was a big mistake. They put him into solitary confinement for 20 days in The Hole. The only time he came out was to shower. He went close to being sent to notorious Grafton Jail.

He was repeatedly given latrine-cleaning duties but he copped it and apart from the fight, abided by the rules. Among friends who visited and wrote was former Test cricket great Keith Miller. He sent a Christmas card with a mischievous little *Reader's Digest* article headed "Why Husbands Cheat on Their Wives."

Former drug addicts whom he'd helped wrote with uplifting messages. Stella wrote regularly as his friend and psychiatrist, reminding him of her family motto, "triumph through adversity," and imploring him to follow the Serenity Prayer: "Accept the things you cannot change, change the things you can and have the wisdom to know the difference." He took to reading the Bible for long periods and thinking about his Christian upbringing.

Stella sent pictures and news of Isis. In between the good advice in her letters, her words showed the trauma of their romantic past. In one note she said: "You will be out and about before you realise it. Please don't tear me emotionally apart as you have done in the past. Please do not spoil my relationship with Isis. I am too fragile for such things."

While inside a rumour went around that Bristow had been raped in his cell. That was the joke of the year. But it was no joke that Stephen had to leave Kings School because of the embarrassment and taunts he suffered from his father being behind bars. Glenda, too, found it difficult personally and among her friends trying to come to grips with his jailbird status. Tim wanted her to leave a picture of herself with him, but not knowing where or with whom it might end up in the prison, she declined to do so.

Tim lost registration of his racehorses because of his conviction, signing ownership over to Glenda. It would be embarrassing with his family's splendid Hobartville stud background having to go cap in hand later to the AJC with old schoolmate, Alec Shand QC, to get his registration back. Glenda sold his family racing colours and he would have trouble getting them back, too. She also sold some of his horses, including Lightning Bend for $1,000. It would go on to earn nearly $1 million for another owner. Glenda sold his red Mercedes sports, too.

As the time for his release neared, Stella wrote that she believed he should return to his home and family to make the best of what he had and that they cease contacting each other in any form. Glenda, on one of her last visits to see him, delivered a severe emotional blow by telling him she no longer had any love for him and wanted a divorce.

He felt extremely frustrated. Locked up, allowed to write six letters a month and receive only two half-hour visits a month, he was powerless to take any remedial steps. All he could do was write a pleading, heart-rending letter to his son, asking him to write and keep writing and to tell him everything that was happening, especially anything that was worrying him.

"I have saved all your letters and read them over and over," Tim said. He begged his son to "be very careful about everything you do as there are very few people you can trust...Please Stephen, do everything I ask of you, keep out of fights and say your prayers. Please help me son, I need your help. Keep in touch with all the people I told you to..."

Glenda looked after Stephen as her own son until the day Tim came out after six months. Then she moved out and went to live close by, supporting herself. She still could not accept his jailing. Stephen left too, going to Queensland to live with his mother, Judy. He explained: "I love him as my father, but we are better friends if we remain apart."

Tim found it difficult to accept Glenda and Stephen's departure. He unashamedly stalked Glenda. Once at a party in Bilgola Plateau, she was swirling around in a sarong with a tropical flower in her hair, drinking champagne, enjoying her new freedom and there was Tim up in a nearby tree, watching her. He tried hard to arrange a reconciliation, taking her on a cruise to Singapore and buying her expensive jewellery there. But they fought most of the time. Then Glenda gave Tim a bit of his own back by having an affair with a surfing friend of his, a younger man.

But he didn't remain forlorn too long. Soon after coming out of jail Tim met a lovely young woman in a restaurant at Avalon, Sue Ellis, a professional tennis coach. She was only 21, fresh and natural who came from a strong family background at Weemelah near Goondiwindi on the Queensland border. Her father, a lieutenant commander in the Australian Navy during the war, was born in Nottingham. Her mother was of Danish background.

Sue went to school on Sydney's northern beaches at Beacon Hill and Pittwater Highs and took up tennis when very young. At 17 she went abroad and played in professional tournaments. After knowing Tim for a while he asked her if she would become his housekeeper and she agreed. Being remarkably neat and tidy for a man, he told her how everything should be done in the house. Fluffy white towels had to be folded and placed in the bathroom a certain way, bedrooms kept immaculate like a first-class hotel room.

A relationship gradually developed but Sue grew weary of waiting around for Tim to make up his mind about Glenda and she left and took a Club Med tennis coaching job at Quantan on the east coast of Malaysia.

Meanwhile Glenda returned to New Zealand and while on holiday at the scenically beautiful Tongariro Chateau ski resort she met Dunbar Sloane, a wealthy New Zealand art dealer. He was so smitten by her that he took her to Sydney for a week, telling his wife he was buying art. Tim found out about it and just missed out on meeting up with them at several places. But he rang Dunbar's wife and when she said he was away buying works of art in Sydney, Tim said: "No, he's over here with my wife."

Tim then went to New Zealand, spreading fear and loathing, and called on Dunbar at his office. Friends said Dunbar was so terrified he could hardly speak. While Tim was talking to him, he heard a creak in the cupboard. "What's that?" Tim asked. "There's a man in there to mind me in case you try to kill me," said Dunbar.

Tim opened the cupboard door and standing in there was Pat Rippin, a tough rugby forward, six foot six and more than 20 stone on the old scale, who made Tim look small. "What the ——are you doing?" asked Tim. "Mate," said Pat, "I'm just here in case something happens to him." "

Tim and Pat saw the humour of it and made Dunbar take them to the most expensive restaurant in Wellington to smooth things out. But Dunbar remained nervous. Next day Dunbar called at Pat's retail car yard and was sipping a cup of tea when he learned Tim had arrived too. Dunbar took off up the street, still holding the tea. The NZ Police Commissioner rang Pat wanting to know what Bristow was doing in town.

The funny thing is Tim and Pat, who was also a property developer, became the best of friends - typical of Tim with people whom he met in tense situations. Pat and a mate travelled to Sydney soon after and stayed at Tim's Newport home. Tim took them out in his boat, *The See You Off Club*, joking to cops who pulled alongside in Pittwater: "You won't see these boys again - they're joining the see you off club."

Pat said they had a lot of fun but they missed the plane back three times. "By the time Tim called here and there and chatted to this one and that, it took three days to get to the bloody airport," he laughed.

On that trip, finally accepting that Glenda was gone, Tim sentimentally retrieved his mother's sapphire and diamond engagement ring which he had given to Glenda at the time of their wedding. On Glenda's application on 21 October 1976 she and Tim were divorced under the new *Family Law Act,* the ground being irretrievable breakdown of the marriage. Later Glenda and Dunbar were married. Tim would never have left Glenda, no matter what. He certainly would have continued his multiple infidelities, but he believed in and needed the stability of a marriage and in a strangely loyal way would never have left his wife.

With Glenda gone, he then went to Malaysia to persuade Sue to return. But when he arrived at Club Med, the gates were locked and they refused to let him in. Not surprising, seeing it was about 3 a.m. He'd missed an early plane because he had a horse running at Randwick, had given away football tickets in a box sitting one seat away from the Premier in order to catch another plane and arriving late, had caught a taxi from Singapore.

Locked gates? No problem. Tim just walked around on the beach and got in that way. The receptionist was a little worried when he asked forthrightly to see Sue Ellis, but she gave him a room number. Tim found the room and went in without knocking. Two figures were under the sheets. One, a male, sprang out, speaking volubly in French. Ignoring him, Tim went straight to the other reclining figure, pulled back the sheets with a vigorous flourish - and it was another bloke! Sue wasn't anywhere to be seen.

They all stood there yelling at one another, the two guys in French, Tim in his best Aussie knockabout phrasing telling them what he thought they should go and do. One of them was the manager, which was why the receptionist gave Tim his room number. Tim caused such a scene that Sue, who was alone in her own bedroom when he burst in on the manager and his boyfriend, had to grab some things and leave right away to return to Australia with Tim. She flew back to Malaysia soon after to complete her contract to avoid a financial penalty.

After his sojourn at The Bay, Tim was back in town.

17

HUGHES, MARCOS, MEIER AND JFK

BRISTOW had always spoken out boldly, telling it as he saw it. When giving evidence connected with his work, he made indelible enemies.

But prison, where he had time to think, made him realise how easy he'd made it for his enemies to snipe at him because of his forthright manner. He was staggered to see how seriously he could be affected by people, in this case some Liberal politicians, using their influence.

So he became more cautious and circumspect. He now realised there was always a reason for things that happened and he looked more closely at situations than before. He could see there were times when he should walk on eggshells, to look behind the scenes and consider what his enemies were up to before taking on a job.

Tim could now understand why so many people settled out of court rather than face the publicity and risk of damage. He saw more clearly the role of the media and decided to make more friends there. He also set about making more friends in the Labor Party to counter Liberal enemies. He was now more aware of the true worth of people. For instance, he hadn't been sure about Sir Peter Abeles but now he saw him in a different light, and he really liked the man. In short, Bristow was now a more perceptive person and a better investigator as a result of adversity.

Being in prison had not changed his opinion that there were more people in the world engaged in wrongdoing, dishonesty, cheating, indecency and improper behaviour than there were people doing the right thing. Self preservation was a strong motivation with most people. If he stopped to think about it too much he could easily have become disillusioned by the evil sides of people exposed to him when he discussed a job. Fortunately he still had so much work that he could move on quickly to another job without dwelling on a bad one. Often he had to swim along with it to survive.

From his family background he was fully aware that the socialites, businessmen and others from a full range of society who asked him to do unlawful things to save them from guilt or embarrassment, were not too good morally. By comparison, he thought he wasn't such a bad guy after all. A boy scout, in fact.

However, it occurred to him that by doing these things, it also put him in the same moral camp. That certainly left him open to blackmail if enemies wanted to get at him. But Tim believed his dubious deeds were far outweighed by the genuinely oppressed people he helped who could not achieve results without his intervention. Since coming out of prison he was amazed to see that the two things he placed at the lowest end of human life, drug dealing and prostitution, had become popular and condoned in a way he'd never known before.

Among other observations he realised that by being inside he'd also gained a heavy reputation, causing a new problem. Some people were now using his name to frighten and gain advantages over others. He had to be sure clients weren't just wanting to use his reputation for the sake of it, especially as he no longer had a licence. He solved the licence problem by becoming a "consultant," still advising clients although officially passing jobs on to reliable offsiders with licences. But Tim was still in charge.

One interesting job was helping save the day when Lennie McPherson and a couple of friends were locked up in death row in the dreaded Fort Benefacio military prison just outside Manila, threatened with facing one of President Marcos's firing squads. They were arrested at gunpoint in their Manila hotel by Marcos's military police and accused of entering the Philippines to assassinate the President. Questioned in prison, they said they were just on a holiday but the security men didn't believe them.

The Australians were worried stiff because the prospect of execution was real. Thousands of political prisoners were executed there when the corrupt, despotic Marcos was in power and several executions took place while Lennie and co were in the prison. They could hear the cheers of a rabble of onlookers as prisoners were tied to a pole, blindfolded and shot down by the firing squad.

The Australians imprisoned with Lennie were Trevor Christian, a former boxing champion and a fine Australian and George Kawani, a Greek-Australian who owned a fruit market in Sydney. Several other Sydneyites were loosely in the party, including Eric Jury and Jimmy Nolan, all taking a holiday. Eric was exploring the possibility of opening a casino in Manila.

Trevor Christian, a friend of Tim's from the old Kings Cross days, taught a lot of kids to box including McPherson's sons. He would not accept money for his tuition and young people showed their appreciation by contributing to a fund to send him on the Manila trip. That's how he was innocently in the hotel with Lennie when the military police swooped.

Eric Jury returned to the hotel from shopping to see armoured cars all around the place and uniformed goons bristling with pointed guns hustling a handcuffed Lennie, Trevor and George into the cars. "What's going on?" he asked and was told: "Get away or we'll take you too." He didn't know what was behind it or where they were being taken.

Inside Fort Benefacio the "political prisoners" were grilled relentlessly about any military training or experience they might have had, and finally were given the charge - they had come to Manila to assassinate President Marcos. The interrogators didn't believe a word of their denials.

Lennie talked to other prisoners. One said he'd been in there 16 years. "What for?" Lennie asked and he replied: "They haven't told me yet." McPherson was worried and angry. "I'll bet that bloody Ysmael is behind this," he told his perplexed friends. McPherson had met Ysmael through Bristow, who was hired by several bookmakers to retrieve gambling debts from him.

Felipe "The Babe" Ysmael was a Filipino billionaire who had put Marcos in power, supporting him with a torchlight parade of thousands in Quezon City. They had been mates, working corrupt deals together and Ysmael built his fortune in manufacturing, forestry and mining leases with the help of Marcos. But they fell out, Marcos robbed Ysmael of his wealth and The Babe was sitting in Sydney fuming and frittering away the last of his ready cash by gambling on the horses. The last straw which broke their friendship occurred when the grossly extravagant Imelda Marcos found out that The Babe was flying in two new European girls for the President every three weeks as a kind of kinky sex thrill for an Asian man.

The full story of Marcos and Ysmael was told in my best-selling book *The Gambling Man*, in which I described how a scornful Marcos had ignored his friend's plight and robbed him of assets, treating his pleas for help from Australia with contempt. The fiery Babe was ringing Marcos's palace and making death threats, even putting threats in writing.

As disclosed in *The Gambling Man* I tipped off Ysmael that the Federal police were tapping his phones and knew of his threats. They were also obviously tapping McPherson's phones. When McPherson travelled to Manila at the height of this drama, they drew the wrong conclusion that he intended carrying out Ysmael's threats and informed security services there.

A former private eye living in Manila phoned Tim and told him of McPherson's plight. To save Lennie's hide would be a feather in Tim's cap. It was late in the piece when he came into it but he managed to get through to Lionel Murphy, the former Attorney-General then on the High Court Bench, and explained the problem. As Australian citizens were involved, Lionel said he would speak to the right authorities.

He apparently did so and no doubt their lives would have been saved as a result of that late appeal. After the ordeal Tim convinced himself and quite a few others that he'd saved Lennie's life, giving the story an extra boost, but in fact another man was responsible for the break through.

Eric Jury, a successful Sydney businessman who had run four entertainment clubs including the Motor Club in its heyday, wasted no time in Manila after witnessing the arrests. He rang around, spoke to expatriates and diplomatic sources and finally struck oil on the third day through a contact named Frankie who knew General Fidel Ramos, the Philippine Army commander.

Frankie took Eric to the general's HQ where armed guards stood every few metres on both sides of his long driveway. He introduced Eric and the general said: "What can I do for you, Mr Eric? He was an impressive man who had won a scholarship to West Point Military Academy in New York, had fought communist insurgents and was "father" of the Philippine Army Special Forces. Later, in 1992, he would become the 12th President of the Philippines, restoring democracy after the disastrous 20-year dictatorship of the crooked Marcos.

Eric told General Ramos the men were just on a holiday and the whole thing was ridiculous. "What would you like me to do, Mr Eric?" the general asked. Told they should be released, he said he couldn't do that.

But asked if they could be deported or just sent back to Australia, he said, "Yes, how about tomorrow morning?" They shook hands and as Eric and Frankie left, the general said with a smile: "You might do something for me. Send me back a nice blonde." And a grateful Lennie McPherson, after being returned to Australia next morning, did just that.

The three men had lost considerable weight as they sweated it out in the prison for four days. Back in Sydney an angry Lennie, with Trevor Christian, confronted Babe Ysmael but he was able to convince Lennie that he hadn't set him up and the Federal police had caused the problem.

John Meier, the high-flying Howard Hughes aide, brought a fascinating touch of international intrigue into Tim Bristow's environment at quiet Newport when he desperately sought his help in 1977.

Meier's qualifications as an environmentalist were impressive. Scientific adviser and general courtier to Hughes from 1966 to 1970, he reported to Hughes on radiation effects of the Nevada bomb blasts and led the charge against the Atomic Energy Commission and Government to stop the tests. Backed by the Hughes influence and bankroll, the energetic Meier moved comfortably in the highest circles of power as a lobbyist and front man.

He was a President Nixon adviser on the environment, a personal friend of Senator Robert Kennedy, travelling with him in his presidential bid in 1967 and was the recipient of numerous awards including Aerospace Man of the Year. Meier often visited Washington on Hughes business. The Hughes empire generated billions of dollars in strategic weapons for the nuclear age, yet Hughes strenuously fought underground atomic testing in his own desert backyard, buying Washington politicians, even trying to install his own man in the Oval Office.

Hughes at that stage was ensconced in a darkened penthouse of the Desert Inn hotel casino in Las Vegas, secluded from the outside world and conducting his mega business by remote control, mainly through detailed instructions to trusted aides like Meier, usually written on yellow legal paper.

I had met Meier in 1968 in Las Vegas through a friend, Charlie Kandel, the respected credit manager of the Hughes-owned Sands hotel casino there. Kandel liked Australians from the days when he fought alongside them in France in the First World War. I was trying my luck to do a biography of the reclusive Hughes and Charlie was helping by introducing me to Meier and other people.

Meier was extremely helpful, we corresponded on the subject, but after some encouraging signs the project eventually lapsed. (Later American reporter Michael Drosnin wrote a great book based on stolen Hughes documents written on yellow legal paper).

Meier's reputation at that stage was unassailable. But there was also about him a whiff of James Bond espionage, linking him to the CIA, FBI, Secret Service and the White House. When he left the Hughes organisation in 1970 to form a research foundation, the Hughes chief executive Robert A. Maheu gave him a big rap in the *Las Vegas Sun* for his contribution to the Hughes organisation.

But behind the scenes Meier had made enemies, riling the CIA by trying to stop the underground nuclear tests and claiming the CIA had tried to take over the Hughes organisation. He upset the Secret Service because of his close association with Nixon's indiscreet, wheeler-dealing brother, Donald.

Meier was involved in the payment of a $US100,000 cash bribe from Hughes to President Nixon, channelled through Nixon's confidant and slush fund operator, Bebe Rebozo, as part of a $US250,000 Hughes "campaign contribution." The $100,000 cash was intended to go directly to Nixon. Meier also knew about an aborted attempt by Hughes to pay Nixon $1 million to stop the bomb tests.

He was suspected of passing on this information to Larry O'Brien whom Hughes hired as a Washington lobbyist after O'Brien finished working for the powerful Kennedys. When he joined Hughes, O'Brien was chairman of the Democratic Party with an office in the Watergate building.

Nixon was obsessed with the fear that O'Brien knew of the bribes. As a Republican he was still haunted by having lost the 1960 election to Democrat Jack Kennedy, blaming the scandal of an earlier Hughes "loan" of $205,000 to his brother Donald for that result.

After leaving Hughes, Meier continued to meddle in the big league of American politics, including running as a Democrat Senator for New Mexico. After boasting that he intended to tell all he knew about Nixon, things began to fall apart for him. The CIA tapped his phones, burgled his campaign office and kept him under surveillance.

Then the Hughes Tool Company sued him for swindling $8 million from Hughes in bogus mining leases. The Inland Revenue Service targeted him. Nixon secretly ordered the Watergate break-in of Larry O'Brien's office to see what O'Brien really knew of his affairs and whether Meier had told him about the bribes. The burglars were arrested and Nixon was finished.

Meier had moved to Canada with his family and began a running fight with US authorities over his knowledge of Nixon's corruption and his relationship with Hughes. He was declared a fugitive from justice for failing to turn up in Reno to face trial over his mining leases.

Meier then bobbed up in Sydney in May 1977 after visiting Tonga where he gave undertakings to build an international airport to promote tourism, obtaining a diplomatic passport from Tonga's King Taufa'ahau. A few years earlier, Sydney bookmaker Bill Waterhouse had independently met Meier in Canada. Meier was impressed with Waterhouse's diplomatic passport as Consul-General of Tonga. He also discussed the possibility of starting a bank in Tonga, which had off-shore banking legislation.

Meier looked me up when he arrived in Sydney with his family, reviving interest in the Hughes biography by telling me he had a trunk load of confidential Hughes documents. He showed me some in Hughes's handwriting on yellow legal paper which looked the real McCoy. He promised to call me again after taking his family to Japan.

He also called on Consul-General Waterhouse, but apparently only because he needed a visa for Japan. Waterhouse felt Meier had not contacted him earlier because he was embarrassed for not telling him about his business dealings in Tonga or that he had been appointed a roving economic envoy for Tonga.

Waterhouse arranged for him to visit Japan's wealthiest man, Ryochi Sasagawa, who greeted Meier with open arms. After Japan, Meier called in to Tonga on his way back to Sydney, hoping to obtain Australian citizenship status. In Tonga he had told the King he'd seen the Japanese foreign minister, claiming the minister would be delighted to arrange a State visit for His Majesty to Tokyo.

The King, normally laid back, was excited by the news. He couldn't really go anywhere unless on a State visit. As soon as Meier left to fly to Australia, the King lifted the phone to his Prime Minister, Baron Vaea, told him he'd be getting an official Japan invitation and to go straight to Wellington to see the Japanese ambassador there to make the necessary arrangements.

When Baron Vaea went to New Zealand the ambassador said to him: "Ah, I'm so embarrassed. This is typical of those fools in Japan. They have not informed me of the pending visit. Please don't tell the King of my embarrassment. I'll ring Tokyo and get the full details. Come back tomorrow and it will be arranged." But when the Prime Minister went back, the ambassador was a different man. He said, in effect, the Japanese Government would be glad to invite him but nobody had seen the foreign minister and nothing had happened.

The King was embarrassed, and angry. In the background, Meier's situation was degenerating rapidly. By now the King knew the Americans were after him and he told them he would cancel Meier's diplomatic passport. Back in Sydney, Meier somehow got wind of his imminent arrest. He rang Waterhouse who told him there must be something wrong because he had immunity as a Tongan diplomat, and to say nothing until he could check with Foreign Affairs. Waterhouse did so and was told it was an American diplomatic problem and they didn't wish to be involved.

Meier then rang me as news editor of the *Sunday Telegraph* and repeated what the Consul-General had told him in confidence. Unknown to Waterhouse, I began making inquiries for a newspaper story.

The Americans panicked and asked the Federal Police to arrest him for alleged obstruction of justice. CIA operators were in town and the US State Department and the FBI wanted him extradited. Federal police arrested him at the Boulevard Hotel on a Friday afternoon and put him in the cockroach-ridden cells at Phillip Street station- where Bristow was a cop back in 1949.

Meier rang Waterhouse who again contacted Foreign Affairs. The Consul-General pointed out that Meier's passport was still valid. The police had no choice but to release him on the Saturday morning, although the Americans hoped to hold him until the courts opened on Monday morning when they would have had all the documentation in place to extradite him.

Sending his wife and children back to Canada out of harm's way, Meier then went on the toe, skipping his hotel without a trace. He left behind a $2,000 hotel bill and a $10,000 bill in fees for legal work which Waterhouse had arranged for him. Waterhouse felt he was personally obligated and later paid both accounts.

Meanwhile, the King cancelled his diplomatic status and he was *persona non grata*. Where Waterhouse at first was obliged to help Meier, he now wanted to see him arrested, even asking me to tell police if Meier contacted me and he sent the police to see me.

Meier had been shown up as a consummate liar and con artist. Waterhouse doubted if he ever obtained a bank in Tonga. He'd impressed the King by offering to build the airport to international standard to promote tourism - there was a ceremony, some equipment moved in, but there it stayed. Just window dressing. His trouble seemed not so much to do with the mining leases as with his Hughes-Nixon connection.

Soon after all this frantic activity, Meier contacted Bristow, who had a number in the phone book. Bristow told Meier to call and see him at his Newport home, where he listened to his story. He doubted that Meier was the lily white he professed to be, but he knew the law enforcement agencies were capable of treachery. He could see the fellow was desperate with police searching for him and decided to help him.

He took Meier to a plastic surgeon who made some facial changes, had his photo taken showing his latest appearance and arranged a new passport. "That's good enough to beat the immigration checks," he told Meier. Then he planned his route to Canada which he reached safely. Later Meier spent some time in prison.

In their meetings before skipping town, Meier talked at length about behind-the-scenes Washington, of his days with Hughes, Nixon in the White House, the CIA plot with the Mafia to murder Fidel Castro and Kennedy's assassination.

The JFK shooting fascinated Bristow. Even before seeing the later Oliver Stone *JFK* film, Tim knew there had been a massive cover-up of Kennedy's killing by the CIA and FBI. He never did believe the official lone gunman theory that the shot that killed Kennedy was fired only by Lee Harvey Oswald from the sixth floor window of the Texas School Book Depository.

Meier told him he was certain the killing was arranged by FBI director J. Edgar Hoover in complicity with the Mob. Certainly, Hoover hated Kennedy's left-wing politics and although homosexual himself, deplored President Kennedy's indiscreet White House sex affairs with girlfriends of Chicago mobster Sam Giancana, bringing one affair with Giancana mistress Judith Campbell to an end by personally taking a report on her to the President. That sex evidence was given to the Senate Select Committee on Assassinations.

Meier's contrary view to the official version encouraged Bristow to make his own inquiries. He found strong evidence that there were two gunmen that day in Dallas on November 22, 1963, not one as the Warren Commission influenced by the CIA and FBI would have us all believe. The two gunmen belief was the firm view of Texas Governor John Connally, who was wounded in the car with the President.

The view was another nail in the coffin of the "lone nut" pushers, and supported the conspiracy theory which the majority of Americans believed. It raised questions of who really wielded the power in America and whether its democracy was a sham. Governor Connally had tried to get his view across to the Warren Commission but it was brushed aside.

Tim revived this evidence by locating a witness nicknamed Big Red, who was associated with Connally. She is Denise McLaglen, an English-born actress and showgirl whose uncle was Victor McLaglen, star of *The Quiet Man*. Her cousin Andrew McLaglen made westerns like *Gunsmoke* and *Have Gun Will Travel*. Denise started off in the *Folies Begere* and played Broadway in many big shows including the original *Gypsy* with Ethel Merman.

She was in Texas just before the shooting and later represented Governor Connally after he recovered from his wounds. Jack Ruby, the man who shot Oswald, wanted her to perform in his Dallas nightclub.

In giving the information to Tim she recalled how unpopular President Kennedy was in Texas mainly because of his left-wing politics and the corrupt legacy of his father, old Joe. President Kennedy was warned not to go there. After Texas was blamed for the shooting, she was asked by Connally to represent him and Texas in a mammoth World Fair show in New York called *To Broadway with Love*, the idea being to show Texas wasn't so bad after all. Representing Connally, Denise had to go around all the eastern State governors, including Rockefeller, to sweeten them up over Texas.

Connally freely discussed the shooting with her and he was emphatic there wasn't just one but two gunmen. He had tried to convince the Warren Commission of that but the CIA and FBI had too much influence and hosed down the idea.

Governor Connally also had the advantage of inside knowledge from Dallas police and other officials to add to his own experience. He explained in detail to Denise the directions and angles of the shots and was certain there were two gunmen, the second firing from in front of the President's car. He proved to her by logic that it was impossible for only one gunman, Oswald, to have fired the fatal shot. He was also convinced there were six shots, not three as the official version indicated.

Denise, who married Australian land owner John Cobcroft of "Parraweena" at Willow Tree in New South Wales, told me: "Connally didn't offer any positive suggestion to me as to who he thought was behind it. But he was certain it was a conspiracy that involved far more than

Lee Harvey Oswald. That being the case, other people must have clues and probably in the years ahead, the truth of it will all come out."

The Governor died before he could convince the world of his views. Tim did nothing to carry Connally's evidence further, except to put it on video and mention it to a few people to ensure it did not die on the vine and be lost forever in the assassination cover-up.

Tim shared the great Aussie love of racehorses with a passion, although to him it was casual and personal pleasure rather than hard tough business. But for all that, he gave 'em a fright in the Melbourne Cup one day.

He had moderate success as an owner with his string of 20-odd horses. The best was probably Bilgola Boy, which won more than a dozen races including several feature events like the McKell Cup. The gelding ate banana leaves and was usually trained either by Tim riding him up and down the beach bareback or by one-horse hobby trainer Harold Lacey.

After Bilgola Boy landed his first metropolitan win, the Thompson's Bay Handicap at Randwick, Tim was quoted on the *Telegraph* back page: "Everyone at the Newport Arms backs my horses and I've been embarrassed lately - now I'll be on good terms with all my mates."

Bilgola Boy was what you might call a backyard horse who stayed out in the paddock - no posh stable boxes - and was trained on the sandhills at Bayview on the northern beaches. Getting a thoroughbred fit there on the north side of the harbour was akin to racing greyhounds at Royal Randwick. But it worked.

After one big win when Bilgola Boy outclassed the opposition in the Chester Hill Handicap at Warwick Farm, trainer Lacey dumbfounded rival trainers by saying he'd given the horse only one gallop over 500m on the beach during the week as his "final preparation."

Tim demonstrated his rapport with animals by calling out George, his nickname for Bilgola Boy, who would whinny and gallop to him. Even at the races out on the track the horse whinnied when Tim called "George." He often rode him bareback to football, tethering him near the sideline.

Master trainer Bart Cummings took over the horse's preparation at one stage but the association didn't last long. Tim ruffled Bart's feathers by putting battling jockey Harold Light on Bilgola Boy in the Brisbane Cup soon after he returned to racing after fourteen years as a taxi driver. Said Tim in the papers: "I know Harold's only a battler but the horse is a battler too and I don't care if Bart Cummings doesn't like it."

Bart, by way of reply, simply notified the Queensland Turf Club that another jockey, Doug Messingham, would ride Bilgola in the Cup. Fancy Tim, just because he owned and paid for the upkeep of the horse, thinking he had any say in where it raced or who rode it!

Bilgola Boy frightened the life out of the Cummings stable in his very next race after Bart handed the horse back, saying he didn't have the ability to win a feature race. Bilgola Boy was unlucky in pushing Cummings' mare and favourite Lady Upstage to a neck in the Christmas Cup at Rosehill, causing Bart to eat his words.

Among Tim's other horses was Irish Belle and Mr Big, winner of several races. He also had a horse called Pickwick, a full brother to Winston on which the Queen used to troop the colours in Horse Guards Parade. Sir Frank Packer had paid a fortune for it but gave it to his mate, polo hero Sinclair Hill. Somehow Tim acquired Pickwick through friendship but didn't race it, keeping it at Warren Anderson's showplace Fern Hill estate at Mulgoa on Sydney's western outskirts.

Tim had no illusions about the racing game, believing it to be less than honest but he never complained about any of his horses being pulled. He enjoyed the atmosphere of meeting and greeting old friends like Hollywood George as much as punting and seeing his horses run around.

Came the 1978 Melbourne Cup and Bilgola Boy had earned his candidature as one of the nation's good stayers. Tim was between serious ladies at the time and needed a woman to take him to the Cup - do all those little things for him. So he asked brother Max if he could take his wife Ann. She paid her own fares and expenses and off they went.

Ann found on arrival that Tim had booked only one suite. "Tim, are we sharing the same suite?" she asked. A somewhat offended Tim replied: "You're my sister-in-law aren't you?" She said: "Well, okay, I guess you'd better have the big bed."

They had a fine dinner, with AFL legend Ron Barassi at their table. When it came up that Ann was Tim's sister-in-law, one or two looked as if they thought it peculiar. But as Ann said later to a female friend: "I would probably be the only woman whose husband would know she was completely safe with Tim because of his strong sense of family honour."

But where was Bilgola Boy? Ann wanted to go to sleep but she spent almost the entire night before the Cup waiting at the airport for Bilgola Boy to be flown in, because Tim always liked a woman to be in attendance. The horse was due to be flown in earlier that night on Ansett but there was a problem back in Sydney - straps holding the horse box had snapped and they couldn't secure the horse box until another one was flown in.

So, instead of resting and being pampered like the other runners, Bilgola Boy spent the night standing up, flying and being messed about generally. When Ann finally got to bed after 4 a.m., she was so over-tired she couldn't sleep. Tim slept like a baby, ordering himself a hearty breakfast on waking, leaving Ann to order hers. Then they went out and had a great day.

A hush fell on the big Flemington crowd as the field settled for the start. Bilgola Boy went like a rocket, leading the field the first time around from Massuk, Rain Circle and Drumshambo. Tim's hopes went wild as "George" led into the famous straight but then petered out, with heavily-backed Arwon racing to the lead 200m from the winning post and narrowly taking out the Cup from New Zealanders Dandaleith and Karu.

Tim savoured the moment by breaking out for once and having quite a few drinks. In common parlance, Tim was pissed. Ann had never seen him like that but was delighted that instead of being aggressive, he was sweet and rosy. Too late to fly back to Sydney, they had to find a motel in the crowded city where she slept on a little couch, having to shepherd Tim into the shower and get him to bed. But she refused to do all the little things his normal lady would have done for him, like putting drops in his eyes and un-knotting his tie.

It left a question hanging in the air: If Tim had been properly organised, where might Bilgola Boy have run with a good night's rest?

18

THE NUGAN HAND BANK SCANDAL

IT began as a routine police matter and looked like an apparent suicide.

About 4 a.m. on Sunday 27 January 1980, Sergeant Neville Brown and Constable Les Cross from the Lithgow police station were patrolling the Great Western Highway at South Bowenfels in the Blue Mountains west of Sydney when they noticed something unusual. A car was parked in the old adjacent highway known as Forty Bends with its lights burning.

They drove to the scene and saw it was a 1977 gold-coloured Mercedes Benz sedan. Inside on the driver's side, slumped over the centre console towards the passenger's side, was a man dressed in light bone-coloured slacks, dark blue short sleeved shirt and casual slip-on shoes. His left hand held the barrel of a .30 semi-automatic carbine rifle, its muzzle close to the right side of his head, and his right hand rested on the butt near the trigger. The man had a severe wound to the right temple and the left ear where a bullet exited, and dried blood covered the console and front seats. A spent cartridge case lay on the floor, one live bullet remained in the magazine and a box of 47 bullets was found on the back seat. The police removed the man's property from his pockets, called an ambulance and took the body to Lithgow Hospital where Dr Derek Li pronounced him dead.

A scientific officer, Detective Jeff Devine, of Orange, examined the car and the body at Lithgow. He noted in his report that a fingerprint examination of the firearm proved negative and he was satisfied the evidence was consistent with the deceased having inflicted the fatal wound on himself.

From initial inquiries the deceased appeared to be Francis John Nugan, 37, of 29 Coolong Road, Vaucluse, confirmed a few hours later by his brother, Kenneth Nugan. Later that Sunday, Det-Sgt William McDonnell went to the dead man's home and, in the company of relatives and two solicitors, let himself in with keys found on the body and searched the premises "but without success in finding any document that may throw some light on the death of Frank Nugan."

Other inquiries showed that Nugan had bought the rifle and ammunition and an axe about three weeks before his death at Shooters Supplies in George Street, Sydney. He had been invited to lunch with an unnamed person at Penrith at the foot of the Blue Mountains on the Sunday, the day he died. Obviously he had not made it to the luncheon.

That was basically the official police version presented later to the inquest. The death made the newspapers, lifted above the mundane by the fact that Frank Nugan was a busy man about town in Sydney as co-director of a little-known merchant bank, the Nugan Hand Bank Ltd.

But behind the scenes his death caused trepidation. Investors had laid out big money on short term loans for handsome profits and they were worried about where they stood. However, none of that surfaced publicly at that stage. There were a few rumours, but nothing solid.

Some details of Nugan's background, a migrant success story, were published in the following weeks. His Spanish parents came to Australia in 1938 with one son, Alf, to escape fascism and the threat of war. After a year in

Melbourne they moved to Griffith in New South Wales where they formed a citrus fruit distributing company.

The family worked hard and built up a big business, Frank working there only in school holidays. He got his law degree at Sydney University in 1963, went to California to get a master's degree in law, then studied for a doctorate in Canada. He travelled, joined a Sydney law firm and later he and a partner floated a mineral company, Meekatharra Minerals, making his first financial coup of $2 million or so. He joined up with Michael Hand, a New Yorker and one of the most highly decorated Americans from the Vietnam war. After doing some land development they formed the merchant bank in 1973.

Right after Nugan's death, Tim Bristow suddenly turned up on the scene, as he usually did when a big story broke or bad news was imminent.

Tim had met Frank Nugan a few years before in the company of lawyers and politicians and knew some of the bank's executives through his work as an investigator. Now, a creditor named John Lindenburg, who was owed a substantial amount of money by the bank, hired Tim to accompany him to the Nugan Hand office to clarify the position. Other investors were ringing Bristow too.

He met Hand in the presence of his solicitor Michael Moloney and general manager Graham Edelston. Hand agreed to some arrangement. Apparently deciding it was best to have Bristow on side rather than against him, Hand asked him to work for him in recovering money owed to the bank, and Tim agreed.

Hand asked Bristow if he would help the company to obtain an open verdict at the coming coroner's inquest into Nugan's death, claiming this would assist the bank's liquidity - suicide would frighten their investors. Tim brought in two of his licensed agents to assist with direct inquiries.

Tim quickly sniffed that the bank's operation was crooked, sensing drugs in the background. With his hatred of drugs, he began feeding information to me on the quiet. I had just joined *The Sun-Herald* and began writing about the bank, throwing up suspicion based on Tim's inside material and from other inquiries.

Through Tim, I was the only journalist to get an interview with Michael Hand. Tim took me into the bank's office on the 8th floor of 55 Macquarie Street, enabling me to get past office staff unchallenged. He walked around corridors and pointing to an office door, said: "He's in there," and kept walking.

Without knocking I walked in and sat down opposite a man I took to be Hand. "Who the ——are you?" he demanded, leaping to his feet. He looked huge. I told him, and went on talking, trying to look casual as he continued opening and shutting clenched fists as if he wanted to smash me. After a while he sat down and talked cautiously about the bank, and I wrote it. But no reporter got to him after that.

I wrote about the bank every Sunday for about 10 weeks, hinting at drug and arms dealing, missing money and CIA connections. Nobody else picked up on it. The editor, Chris Anderson, said to me: "This is becoming a boring story, Kev." I said: "If you're bored by a good story, so be it."

What he really meant was that nobody else was taking it up, so was it true? We were vindicated when others in the media began running with it and suddenly it became a major international story with American politicians and papers like the *Wall Street Journal* and *New York Times* focusing on it, although the CIA involvement remained shadowy.

I take credit for breaking the Nugan Hand story of spies, intrigue and drug dealing, but Tim Bristow was responsible. Without his sleuthing and courage to leak the details when working for a tough guy like Hand, I doubt if the lid would have been lifted enough to grab the attention of royal commissions and drug agencies, although the bank's accounts were under suspicion with the Corporate Affairs Commission. But official inquiries didn't get to the bottom of it, producing voluminous reports that did little to clear up the mystery of a shady financial operation described as "a giant theft machine."

Official inquiries did manage to show that the bank engaged in a continuous and calculated fraud on an international scale, at least by the partners Nugan and Hand, and that the concealment and destruction of the bank's records began the very day after Nugan's death. Also, the Corporate Affairs Commission report to Parliament on the bank found that after Nugan's death, Messrs Hand and Moloney "experienced little difficulty in perjuring themselves and generally seeking to frustrate official interest in the affairs of the bank with contemptible and probably criminal behaviour."

The Coroner found Nugan's death was suicide. Bristow didn't believe that. Neither did a QC, Mr B Mahoney, who suggested to the inquest that Nugan could not have shot himself, that he would have had to be a contortionist to inflict the fatal wound.

Insiders connected with the bank didn't believe he took his own life either. Even if he said it only for appearance sake, Michael Hand told the inquest: "I believe, in my very humble opinion, that he would not have taken his own life." Hand also said in an affidavit that Nugan had "fraudulently misappropriated a vast amount of money" from the company and other companies in his group and he was advised it would be a long and involved process to recover these moneys, if at all.

What of the fingerprints? It appeared from police evidence - "a fingerprint examination of the firearm proved negative" - that there weren't any at all on the rifle, not even Nugan's. That added greatly to the mystery. Nugan would have had to be mighty quick to wipe the rifle clean of fingerprints after potting himself. It put suicide out of the question. Elementary, my dear Watson!

Only local police investigated, whereas CIB Homicide experts from Sydney should have been called in. And what was he doing supposedly due to have lunch in out-of-the-way Penrith?

Bristow was convinced Nugan was murdered. Initially he thought an American living on Sydney's northern beaches could have been responsible rather than international conspirators connected with drug running or money laundering. Tim learned that before Nugan's death, the American complained to his wife that Nugan wasn't sharing the profits of business dealings he had with the banker, and he spoke about Nugan in threatening terms.

The wife then left the American and asked Tim to obtain divorce evidence by bugging his house and boat. That's when she told Tim about his association with Nugan. She said the business dealings somehow involved Aussie Bob Trimboli, so Tim assumed it had to do with drugs. The wife believed her husband had either pulled the trigger or arranged Nugan's murder. The husband later returned to America.

She is believed to be the same woman who figured in an earlier incident in which Tim was brought in to save her life. Ron Dickerson, of Newport, who lived on a boat moored at the Princess Street marina in Newport, was having a quiet drink aboard one evening in 1980 when a woman suddenly ran along the wharf and jumped down on the back of his boat, screaming: "They're going to kill me, they're going to kill me. They've got guns."

Ron told me: "I said to her, 'just stay here.' I had a phone line to my boat but I thought it was no use ringing the police. So I rang Tim, who was a friend of mine, and got him at once. I could see the four fellows waiting on the wharf nearby and the woman stayed with me. Tim came in three or four minutes. He spoke to the woman, then confronted the four fellows.

"I could hear his voice but couldn't hear what he said. He must have said something pretty severe to them because they left. He was casually dressed in shorts and tee shirt, wasn't armed and I thought what a game bloke Tim was. He took the terrified woman with him in his car. After that he looked after her, escorting her around for months to ensure her safety. I never knew her name. But later Tim said to me it was to do with the Nugan Hand Bank."

That was a fascinating incident, but probably just a sidelight to the main event. Others associated with Bristow and close to the action remained convinced that Nugan was murdered in an international plot and the cover-up which followed was one of the biggest that had ever been seen in this country. The most likely theory centred on the fact that much of the millions of dollars that went missing finished up in Nugan's personal account in Melbourne - enough to qualify him for the see-you-off club.

After the bank went into provisional liquidation, owing untold millions to investors, Michael Hand fled Australia on 14 June 1980 using a false passport after a man called Thomas Clines, a former CIA chief in Laos, flew to Sydney allegedly to help him leave. Clines wasn't the only mysterious figure to pop up at that time. A fellow called Charlie, believed to be a hit man from Las Vegas, came to Sydney in the week Nugan was shot. He turned up again when Hand disappeared, helping him arrange his false passport and return to the US via Brisbane.

Hand hasn't been seen since, although he was later believed to be living in Washington not far from the White House. He remains Australia's most wanted fugitive, investigators wanting to talk to him about fraud, drugs money and the obscure operations of the bank.

A former US Green Beret soldier hero, Hand almost single-handedly held off a 14-hour Vietcong attack on his Special Forces compound in Vietnam, then became a contract agent for the CIA in Vietnam and Laos. He was a pilot with Air America, the CIA's private airline which was used to provide supplies to the secret wars in Laos and Burma, flying opium out of the Golden Triangle to fund its activities there.

When Nugan's death was accepted as suicide, the sighs of relief could be heard almost on the other side of the globe, especially after the business card of William Colby, the former head of the CIA, was found in Nugan's wallet. Colby, who earlier had headed the CIA's "Department of Dirty Tricks" as it was called, was legal counsel for Nugan Hand.

The bank, officially based in the Cayman Islands to maintain secrecy, had a board composed almost entirely of retired US intelligence officials from the CIA or other services. One known to Australians was Bernie Houghton, a Texan who arrived in Sydney in 1967, establishing the Bourbon and Beefsteak in Kings Cross, Harpoon Harry's and the Texas Tavern where, incidentally, Tim Bristow celebrated his 50th birthday with a rousing party.

Houghton had spent three years in Vietnam as a "construction material expediter," but according to American journalist Jonathan Kwitny who wrote a book on the bank, he transported contraband like drugs and gambling devices in South-East Asia along with surplus military equipment. After meeting up with Hand, Houghton found himself running the bank's operations in Saudi Arabia, returning to Sydney after Nugan's death. Until his own death in 2000, Houghton was a vague but popular figure and generous to local charities.

Although the CIA would always remain in the background due to difficulty in proving the bank to be a direct CIA offshoot, a picture emerged of Nugan Hand's activities, including being involved in drug trafficking, international arms dealing, links to organised crime, laundering money and assisting the Shah to move his fortune out of Iran.

The Shah's funds were shifted by Bernie Houghton when he was in Saudi Arabia. Hand helped him move the money to Beirut, then to a private merchant bank in Hamburg, in which Nugan Hand had a controlling interest. Frank Nugan visited that bank immediately before returning to Sydney from an overseas trip on the Friday, two days before his death.

The role of banking in the heroin trade and CIA money transfer activities surfaced well before the Nugan Hand bank was formed. A bank in Nassau called the Castle Bank was set up by a retired CIA operative and quickly grew into a Latin American network of banks. Professor Alfred McCoy, the respected researcher and professor of South-East Asian history at the University of Wisconsin, has said the Castle Bank was used by the CIA to launder money.

After it was uncovered, an Internal Revenue Service investigation into it was blocked by the CIA, and the bank collapsed. That's when the small Nugan Hand Bank suddenly developed into a global network of banks, acquiring the Castle Bank's Latin American and European structures. How else could the small Nugan Hand outfit with a gross turnover of only $26 million jump to $1,000 million in its various branches around the world?

Professor McCoy said in a 1991 interview that Nugan Hand was a pioneer in smuggling heroin between South-East Asia and Australia, helping Australian organised crime figures transfer their money overseas so they could buy heroin and ship it back to Australia.

Tim Bristow, in an interview with investigators of the Joint Task Force on Drug Trafficking in 1981, said that within the bank a rift had been developing between Nugan and Hand over the influence of Bernie Houghton and his activities in the Middle East. That was caused by Houghton's interest in Eastern money - apparently the Shah's - and his manner and "standover tactics" which were frightening Nugan. Houghton and Hand were giving Nugan a hard time.

Bristow also told the investigators that one of his agents, who had lunch with Hand every Friday in a seafood restaurant at Sydney's Birkenhead Point, had helped Hand's solicitor move documents to premises at Picton south of Sydney. One of the documents the agent browsed through was a green covered book called the Third Journal which recorded the true financial affairs of the bank. In discussing that with Tim later, the agent agreed he'd been stupid not to have taken it. That was apparently one of the many important documents found by Corporate Affairs investigators to have been deliberately destroyed by Hand.

Tim said in his signed interview that Hand had spoken to him of his CIA connections, mentioning a lot of names and saying how he had the protection of the CIA. Tim laughed about it because he didn't believe it at the time.

But then he realised something he'd always known. Truth was stranger than fiction.

19

THE SEE YOU OFF CLUB

MANY people still walked the streets as a result of negotiations or action by Bristow to spare their lives.

For all his braggadocio and exaggeration in turning stories about himself into amusing Damon Runyon tales, it was no joke with Tim when it came to saving lives. That was a strange irony in his character. Like a pyromaniac drawn to fires, Tim was attracted to violence. If he saw a fight, he'd want to be in it. Yet when he was approached to kill people or he knew of someone about to be "put off," unless they were worthless crims or sworn enemies of his, he would want to save them.

It happened many times, a situation confirmed by his close associates. He was more effective than the police in that regard. The police normally don't save a threatened person because they tend to come in *after* the damage has been done. Tim acted *before* the deed because people came to him wanting him to belt or kill someone and he would turn them around, put them on the right path and make peace.

That was one of Tim's good qualities. Even if offered money to do it he would say no, we'll go a different way. And in helping the people threatened, he did it for nothing. A criminal would have taken the money and someone would have been shot.

But one life he couldn't save was that of an attractive young Yugoslav mother, Mrs Milena Kruscic, of Woollahra. Tim received a telephone call from a man with a foreign accent in November, 1980 saying only that he wanted to see him. Two men came to his house and walked confidently to the downstairs door, with his three Alsatian dogs barking furiously.

One said they had a job. What kind of a job? "A knock job," he said. Tim excused himself for a moment, went up the stairs and asked his new partner, Sue Ellis, to wander down to the front gate and get the number of their vehicle. Then he told the men he wasn't interested. Having had a falling out with a Yugoslav family, he thought it might be a trap anyway. "Are you sure you haven't been sent here by the police?" he asked, trying to draw them out. They gave nothing away, no names, refusing even to say who had recommended him to them. Tim repeated he couldn't help them, giving the excuse the police were watching his every move.

They left and he immediately rang a detective sergeant at Mona Vale, describing the men and giving their car registration number. Several days later the same Yugoslav man rang again, but Tim said he didn't want him to come to his house, arranging to meet him at Bondi. At the time he was playing tennis with three friends on his court at the rear of the house and asked them to accompany him, intending to tell the man to drop off.

They met the surrogate killers at Bondi and this time the men gave Tim a photo of a woman, saying they wanted revenge. Once again Tim told them he wasn't interested, but tried to find out what they were doing. One of his friends said to Tim: "Fancy those wogs wanting you to kill a woman." He rang the same detective and filled him in. Bumping into the detective a few weeks later, he was told: "You've mucked me about with a lot of inquiries over nothing."

Then on 10 June 1981 the *Telegraph* front page headline read: "GUNMAN SLAYS TRAGIC WIDOW. Revenge theory in anniversary killing. " Mrs Kruscic, described as a loving mother of two, was gunned down in the carpark of her Woollahra flat while her children played nearby. She was the woman whose photo had been shown to Tim.

Mrs Kruscic had been acquitted of murdering her husband in their Point Piper home four years before and sentenced to three years for manslaughter. Her killing took place four years to the day on which she was jailed. Tim and Sue both signed records of interview with Homicide detectives and gave evidence after two men were charged. But they were not convicted. Tim believed the killing could have been averted with more effort by the police. The incident distressed him and he determined to try harder in future, although he had done everything possible.

It didn't thrill him to be approached in that way but he knew it was due to his bad reputation, high profile and notoriety for being in jail. Many of the cases that came to him were genuine but some were bizarre, with unbelievable twists and turns. He attracted more than his fair share of nuts due to the publicity he received in the media but couldn't complain because he'd deliberately courted attention to build up his business.

If people laid their cards on the table, he would answer yes or no on the spot. And if he didn't show an interest, that was the end of it - he would not inform the authorities unless he thought someone's life was in danger by a person being unbalanced or in a position to hurt someone connected to himself. If a friend of his was in danger from the underworld, he would discuss it with Lennie McPherson.

He had to be on the lookout for people asking him to kill someone or do something else really stupid, after they had already approached another person and been refused. If the crime was perpetrated and his name mentioned, enforcement bodies might think he was the culprit who "did the number."

A prime example concerned one of Sydney's most spectacular fires. A property developer asked to see him. He took a trusted agent with him as usual as a witness in case of trickery. Amazingly, the developer said: "I'm down to my last hundred million dollars. This building has got to go."

He asked Tim if he would set fire to it, a major building - to make a red rash of it in colloquial terms. Tim said: "Sorry, that's not my go." Later the building was burned down in a huge blaze that lit up the skyline. The mere fact that he had discussed it with the owner, although rejecting it, could have placed him in jeopardy if his name was ever mentioned.

Word of the "job offer" became known in closed criminal circles and the building was fire-bombed by someone connected with Tim - Mad Dog Jack Cooper. Although he had done some work for Tim, he mostly acted independently and Tim had always had trouble controlling him. Bristow learned that Cooper did it with three others by knocking bricks out every 20 metres or so and lighting a bonfire in the centre. The blaze took off when it drew on oxygen coming through the holes. Insurance was not claimed but the burnt-out building was freed up for redevelopment.

Bristow always feared he would be blamed for the fire mainly because it was known Cooper had been associated with him. But Cooper was never found out for the crime.

On another occasion Tim was surprised to be asked by an immensely wealthy, respected Sydney man, socially prominent and presumably happily married, to kill a beautiful young actress. They had had an affair and she bore his child. Keeping it all hush hush, he had given her a generous settlement but she had it ripped off her by an amorous con man and did an Oliver Twist, threatening to expose him in the media if he didn't pay more. She upset him by lobbing on his doorstep.

He called in Tim. "I want you to get rid of her," he said, leaving Tim in no doubt that he wanted her killed. In the presence of one of his agents, Tim said: "No, we can't do that" and instead, negotiated another money settlement for the actress without charging her any fee.

A policeman approached Tim and asked him to kill his senior officer, a sergeant who was in charge of a northern beaches station, saying he hated him. The sergeant had been an instructor to Tim when he joined the force. He changed colour and almost fainted when Tim told him of the policeman's threat, finding it hard to believe. Later he thanked Tim for alerting him. The policeman was removed from the force on psychiatric grounds.

Tim's most unusual case in this field concerned a woman who came to his home and, in the presence of an agent, said she was so fat that she felt depressed, her self esteem was low, she couldn't lose weight and wanted to kill herself. She had gone to church and confessed to a priest who told her it was a sin to kill herself and if she did so, she would not go to heaven. She said to Tim: "I don't want to finish up in purgatory, so that's why I've come to you, to get someone to kill me. I have the money. How much will it cost to have someone shoot me?"

Tim tried not to laugh because she was serious. He talked to her sympathetically, had the cops pick her up and helped them arrange psychiatric treatment.

Bristow couldn't save one of his agents from serious injury one night in dramatic circumstances over the fire-bombing of John Singleton's Rolls Royce. Singo was heavily involved in politics at the time, stirring up strong anti-Labor feelings with his ads for the 1974 NSW election. He put Whitlam supporters offside too with his TV ads of a woman supposedly called Leila Eedla who, with a strong European accent, described what Communism had done to her native Estonia, warning this could happen in Australia if people voted for the Labor Party. Tim and Tropical John were given the job of minding her.

Singleton stirred up so much resentment that someone approached Bristow to blow up Singo's car as a warning to him. Bristow, already associated with Singo, naturally would have nothing to do with it and directed all the agents working for him not to touch the job if approached. But one of them, Graham Stolz, took it up at once as a secret solo moonlighting job.

Singleton and some friends had gone to Berowra Waters just north of Sydney for the weekend and he left his Rolls at the ferry point there. In the early hours Stolz set fire to it with petrol but the flames blew back on him and set him alight.

Singo then hired Tim as one of his protectors. Bristow knew the perpetrator who organised it but never gave him up. But six years later while chatting to a police friend, a superintendent attached to Police Internal Affairs, he couldn't help mentioning his former agent who did the fire bombing. As a result Tim was interrogated by Det-Sgt Jack Whelan and obliged to sign a record of interview. Whelan even had the agent's correct name, but a check of Bristow's statement later showed he refused to give him up or co-operate with the police.

Tim figured in another incident associated with Singo at the time of Muhammad Ali's visit to Sydney in 1979. Two of his associates, Tropical John and Iron Bar Freddy, were minding the boxing champ and Tim appeared on Singleton's interview show on Channel 10 with Ali's second, a burly Afro-American boxer named Burundi Brown. Brown, who had been drinking, became offensive on the show and carried on after it. Tim took him on and although hurting his back in the punchup while falling on a chair, knocked out Brown and put him in a hire car back to his hotel.

One of the enduring legends of the Sydney underworld over the years has been stories that some missing criminals have been dropped off at sea. One man known to Tim reputedly wrapped bodies in chicken wire before entombing them in the deep. Although the stories have been exaggerated, some underworld figures met their waterloo that way.

Tim thought he would capitalise on this grim piece of Sydney folklore by naming his boat *The See you Off Club*, having those words duly painted on the side. He often joked that some of those who went out to sea with him off the northern beaches never returned. The Channel 9 news team did a sardonic parody on Tim and his colourfully-named craft.

He liked nothing better than to take people out in his boat. One prominent eastern suburbs socialite wet herself with fright as he bumped along Pittwater and out past Barrenjoey north of Palm Beach at his normal full speed. He repeated the tale of her embarrassment with gusto. Drinkers at the Newport Arms used to say that a day out with Tim on his boat was usually followed by the need to leave town next day because of his boisterous spirits and craze for speed.

Several times on television he talked ambiguously about people joining his "see you off club," leaving it to the imagination that he might have disposed of some in that way. It suited him to let the underworld think he was a gangster and killer. One of his closest agents said: "It was all bullshit. He had to survive in a treacherous business and he did that sort of thing to create an aura of mystery and to add to his tough-guy image."

Although the name of his speed boat *The See You Off Club* was a spoof on underworld goings-on, it turned out not to be so one day in the early 1980s after a number of underworld slayings. Among the colourful characters he sometimes took for a run in his boat was Lennie McPherson, who specially asked him one day to take him for an outing.

They moved out past Barrenjoey to sea, McPherson saying he wanted to go a fair way out. Another boat trailed them and he asked Tim to stay within range of it. At that stage he didn't explain what it was about but Tim's mind was already ticking over. When several miles off the coast McPherson said: "This should do. I want to scuttle the other boat."

But they had to wait two or three hours until a couple of Navy vessels exercising in the area steamed out of sight. Then Lennie asked Tim to motor over to the other boat while the man at the wheel scuttled it. Before he did so, McPherson gave Tim the only details necessary to justify this furtive exercise: "There are two bodies on board."

No names, no packdrill. In his usual clever style, McPherson gave little away. He trusted Tim to a certain extent but knew he was a talker and was taking no risks. He regarded Tim as a frustrated cop, referring to him in a half-humorous, half-sarcastic way as "the detective."

When the other boatman called out okay Tim brought *The See You Off Club* alongside, he clambered aboard and together they all watched as the other boat with its *corpus delicti* cargo slowly filled with water and sank.

Tim told me that story when he was lucid and serious and McPherson was still alive, and I had no reason to doubt it. He estimated that to his knowledge McPherson was responsible for 20 killings, people who were a threat to him, trying to take over his protection rackets or who were a menace to everybody and out of control through either drugs or alcohol. Some of those killings, he believed, were with the approval of certain police.

Another criminal identity whom Bristow took out in his boat was Christopher Dale Flannery, a hit man and gun for hire with the insalubrious name of Rent-a-Kill. Who watched who on those jolly little outings? The association was strange, in view of the fact that they met because Flannery had a $50,000 contract to collect on Bristow's life.

Flannery came from Melbourne after a serious criminal career of several murder charges and quickly entered the Sydney underworld, standing over people and demanding money from casinos. He was generally accepted to be the hit man who shot an undercover drug cop, Mick Drury, through his kitchen window in Sydney. Luckily Drury survived. McPherson and the colourful, well-informed cop Roger Rogerson warned Bristow to be careful of him, saying he was dangerous and unpredictable.

Roger, in fact, saved Bristow's life. The detective searched Flannery's house by warrant once and among the things he found was the sketch of a house and its environs. It showed details such as a tennis court, where a Mercedes drove in and parked, where to hide and showing an escape route. Rogerson had been to Tim's house only once before inquiring on a murder investigation but being an astute cop, thought he half-recognised it. Rogerson showed the sketch to Det-Sgt Nelson Chad who knew the house and sure enough, it was Tim's. They called and showed him the sketch. Tim thanked them and took extra precautions.

Then a police friend told Tim of the Flannery contract on his life. Bristow was due to call on a city businessman from whom he had earlier unsuccessfully tried to retrieve a large sum of money for a client. At the last minute he received a tip from a detective that Flannery was waiting for him in the office of the businessman who had offered the contract, and that Flannery would kill him if given the chance.

I knew that to be true because Bristow rang me at the time at *The Sun-Herald* and asked me to accompany him to the office. I was pinned to the news editor's desk at the time anyway, but the invitation didn't hold a lot of appeal and I declined. Tim quickly arranged for an armed agent to go with him and they called at the office. Flannery was there, a gun clearly showing under his coat. He said: "I'm looking after this man. Back off."

They talked and Bristow told Flannery that Lennie McPherson was a mate of his and had his interests at heart. Flannery understood the implied threat and decided to be friendly. It was typical of Bristow's modus operandi to turn a negative into a positive and to neutralise an enemy. He became friendly with Flannery, a surprisingly personable fellow for a cold killer, meeting him around the town, at the races - and taking him for a couple of spins in *The See You Off Club*. Tim met his wife Kath and kids.

He even joined forces with Flannery on a few jobs. A solicitor with an office in Macquarie Street described to me how he had shaken in his boots when Tim came in by arrangement to discuss collecting $300,000 from one of his clients, who was present. In came Tim, all polite and friendly, accompanied by Flannery and another heavyweight, who at one stage opened his coat to casually display a weapon. A compromised figure was eventually negotiated.

Flannery, whom Tim called Rent-a-Dill, made so many people nervous that he was last seen alive on 9 May 1985. As Tim told the Coroner: "He developed into a robot and couldn't be told." Tim also told the inquest how Roger Rogerson had saved his life and a Sydney paper published the story. Roger was amused to receive about 20 calls from people who asked: "Why did you save that bastard Bristow's life?"

Flannery's wife told the inquest her husband had disappeared after leaving to attend a meeting with George Freeman, for whom he was a gunman protector. Freeman was another criminal who caused some people to permanently join the see you off club, including casino worker John Marcus Muller whom Freeman blamed for bushwhacking him as he arrived home one night. Freeman was shot in the face with a .22 calibre bullet after Muller warned him to stop having an affair with an attractive woman relative of his. Everyone knew Freeman arranged the hit but nobody would give any evidence.

Michael John Sayers, a drug dealer and SP bookmaker who financed the Fine Cotton ring-in scam for con man John Gillespie, was executed at around the same time that Flannery went "missing." Investigators say that Sayers, like most others who joined the club, "couldn't count" in their financial dealings.

Tim began building up a strong reputation in the 1980s by helping developers with their problems, including overcoming industrial stoppages which would have otherwise bogged down in the courts. Among those he represented were Warren Anderson's New World Properties, also

Multiplex and Lend Lease, to name only a few. Anderson was the most interesting client, a self-made man from Perth who did many big projects in Sydney in the 1980s such as Coles supermarkets. A semi-reclusive figure who enjoyed an ostentatious lifestyle, he owned *Boomerang*, Sydney's famous art deco mansion at Elizabeth Bay, and spent a fortune on buying and renovating heritage properties.

Anderson's gun collection of about 600 pieces was valued at millions of dollars, including pistols Napoleon gave to Josephine, rare Colts, an original Gatling gun and General Custer's sword. He paid $2 million for a first edition of John James Audubon's book, *Birds of America*.

Yet for all Bristow's success in obtaining major benefits for developers, he was paid peanuts. He used his contacts to get building applications through that were worth tens of millions of dollars, receiving little in return. A friend of Tim's, Gary Maddox of Sydney, said of him: "If Tim could have managed his aggression and skills in a more beneficial way, he would have been an extremely wealthy man. In my mind, I don't think he asked for what was rightly his in respect of the financial world.

"I think that in reality his personal levels of esteem were low. He preferred to live his success in glory terms, rather than financial profit. He liked recognition and acknowledgment but unfortunately at the end of the day, didn't command the respect he should have had for his achievements."

Tim might well have sold himself cheaply for the results he obtained, but a variety of work continued to pour in. While in London in early 1983 working for Warren Anderson, Tim somehow got himself involved in the mystery of the champion racehorse, Shergar. One of the great racehorses of the 20th century, winning six of the eight classic European races by astonishing margins, Shergar was kidnapped from the Aga Khan's Ballymany Stud in Ireland. The thieves demanded a ransom of two million pounds.

The Aga Khan's syndicate stalled, believing every top racehorse in the world could be snatched if they paid. The syndicate heard nothing more from the kidnappers after four days. Tim had contacts in London who put him on the job. He made some inquiries but decided the trail was cold and the horse was dead anyway and he returned home. No trace has ever been found of Shergar.

Not long after that Tim was responsible for solving Australia's biggest counterfeiting crime, a fact confirmed by Det-Sgt Nelson Chad, then head of the CIB Fraud Squad. Without Tim's detection work and court evidence, the counterfeiters would probably have got away with it.

Fake 100 denomination Deutschmarks were circulating, so good they could not be detected in Australia. The scam was creating a storm in banking circles. It wasn't until the Reserve Bank or other banks here sent them to Germany that they were spotted and German banks refused to acknowledge them.

Complaints were flooding in and Federal police, who then did not have power to prosecute people involved in currency production, had to hand over inquiries for Operation Drake to the NSW Fraud Squad. Each 100 D-note was worth about $A47. Det-Sgt Chad, a cop who actively cracked down on crims, knew Bristow as a good police informant in exposing crime. Tim had helped the Fraud Squad on many safe-blowing jobs, especially in post offices, and had received rewards for his information.

Chad heard that Bristow had some knowledge of the counterfeiting operation and thought that with his contacts he might be able to help. They met at Collaroy surf club on the northern beaches and Bristow confirmed he knew of the gang's operations and offered to help. A few days later Chad received a call from Tim telling him he'd left a parcel addressed to him at Dee Why police station.

The parcel contained a typewritten note with five names and two 100 D-marks, one forged, one genuine. From that Chad and his team inquired and found that the fake notes were being made at Brookvale on the northern beaches where a printer had the most sophisticated photostat machine in Australia. They obtained search warrants and in dawn raids arrested five men, seizing the printing machine, printing blocks and other material, including counterfeit notes in the men's possession.

The gang had taken a suitcase of the notes to Singapore and cleaned up there. The amount ripped off by the gang could not be certified but Chad described it as a multi-million dollar operation. The forgers planned to get the phoney money to South America and South-East Asia and once there pass it through money changers.

They were charged and sent to trial. The Crown had to link up the continuity of evidence between genuine notes used for printing and the counterfeit notes, and needed Bristow to give evidence. Chad was reluctant to put him in the witness box because he was an informant. But when asked, Tim didn't hesitate.

At the trial in the District Court, the Crown was relying on him to swing the case for them. He entered the court in his dark pinstriped suit, homburg in hand, was sworn in, gave his name and when asked his occupation, said in a loud voice: "Retired gangster." They rocked with laughter, even the judge cracked up. But Tim won the day for the Crown. The printer, Ian Victor Gilleland, 45, got five years and the others were jailed too.

With undisguised irony Tim often told the tale of how the German Consul-General invited him to his office to thank him for solving a knotty problem and gave him a cup of tea and a book in German - which he couldn't read.

Then he was off to the UK for a one-day job. A professional man engaged him to rescue his wife who had taken off on a ship with her Canadian Prince Charming. But on the voyage he turned into a monster, taking her money, assaulting her and throwing her travel documents overboard. When the ship docked in London, Tim was there to meet him on board, back handing him a few times before turning him over to New Scotland Yard. The woman returned to her husband.

But Tim stayed on a bit longer after contacting an old friend who was an executive on Rupert Murdoch's *News of the World*. It was early days on the great Wapping newspaper strike and he asked Tim to lend a hand in trying to suppress the printing unions who were just beginning to resist Murdoch's efforts to transfer his four big papers from Fleet Street to Wapping in the docklands, where he'd been secretly setting up a huge printing press.

The mass cavalry charges of police on the striking newspaper protesters had not yet started but pickets were setting the pattern. Tim linked up with several Australian shoplifters whom he'd known at the Royal Oak Hotel in Sydney's Double Bay and they went and talked to union officials. But he could see the strike was going to be long and hard and besides, his heart was with the strikers. He had a look around, not at the architecture or the great churches like the Abbey but the nightclubs and Penthouse bunny clubs.

Just as well he enjoyed a bit of light relief because at home the worst and most demoralising crisis of his life awaited him.

20

THE CASE OF THE GROUSE GRASS

IT sounded like the squeak of the garage door being lifted up. Sue Ellis stirred slightly. Perhaps it was just the wind outside. She went back to sleep.

Sue and Tim were sleeping a little late on this Monday morning, 18 February 1985, arriving home about 3 a.m. after attending a birthday party across town at Strathfield. There was no mistaking the sounds that woke Sue next. Firm tapping against the bedroom window on the wide balcony of their palatial home. Looking out, she saw George Hunter. She drowsily slipped on a gown and opened the front door on the balcony. Hunter, a senior detective sergeant from Chatswood on the North Shore, wanted to see Tim whom he knew well. It was just after 6 a.m.

"Oh George," she said, "We're still asleep. Could you come back later?" He said aggressively: "No. I want to see him now."

She woke Tim and he and George went downstairs. She knew Tim would not be at his best if this were some official matter. When in his pyjamas he was always a pussycat, inclined to be soft and pliant. He was a different man when dressed. In a snazzy suit, shoes polished to a mirror finish and with the homburg in place, Tim was switched on, sharp, aggressive, ready to take on the world.

As she made a cup of tea she could hear the conversation floating up the spiral staircase. Hunter had put a block of Indian hemp in, ironically, the grass catcher of their lawnmower in the garage. She heard Tim say: "You know, George, I don't want any part of this. I'm not interested." Then they moved into the large room next to the garage and she couldn't hear what they were saying any more.

That would be part of Sue's evidence in the nightmare that followed. Before it ended, reputations would be shattered and lives ruined in a welter of lies, deceit, suspicion, allegations and threats, including death threats, attempted coverups, with the culture of police loyalties tested and broken under unbearable pressure as numerous detectives were accused of dealing in drugs worth nearly $750,000. Some people would go to jail.

One of those would be Tim Bristow himself, pleading guilty in remarkable circumstances to a charge of conspiring with police to supply Indian hemp - a crime that he despised and had fought against through his adult life, one he could not come to terms with emotionally and from which he would never recover, either within himself or by reputation.

The incredible spectacle would emerge from court evidence that Bristow, the tough guy, the hard man, had feared for his life, expressing his shame and weakness for allowing himself to be stood over by police threats.

Initially about a dozen police were under suspicion but ultimately two detectives would be jailed, one of them acquitted on appeal, another freed after trial. Two others had charges withdrawn before trial because the allegations were not proved beyond reasonable doubt.

One of those jailed was George Hunter, 59, a detective on the Peninsula for 20 years whom friends testified in court to be a "loyal, honest and generous man," a former Manly football hero and coach of the Manly Sea Eagles in a Rugby League grand final. He was one of the best knockabout street policemen and detectives in the game, with courage to deal with hard criminals. Det-Sgt Hunter was not the academic type who concentrated on his exams to gain promotion. He had only a few years to go and looked like retiring as a second-class sergeant. Colleagues said he was a lot better than that.

The tragedy was that, like Tim, he was no drug dealer, nor were any of the other cops accused. The Chatswood debacle was one of those spur of the moment acts that arose from temptation being suddenly put in their way by drugs, the new crime phenomenon. Drugs had changed the whole fabric of Australian society, including policing. No longer was there honour even among thieves after drugs came on the scene. Ordinary gangsters didn't enjoy the same "respect" any more as crime developed more into a greedy global affair with the drugs scourge.

Drugs put huge temptations in front of policemen that didn't exist in earlier days. Common hoods were running around making unbelievable amounts of money. When drugs or drug money were recovered, it was contraband which legally didn't belong to anyone and was confiscated to be destroyed or to go into consolidated revenue. That is still the case. The reality emerged that when underpaid police were confronted with such a cache, it was a big temptation.

That was some of the general background and philosophy to the drug scam in which anti-drug activist Bristow became embroiled.

The basic allegations presented to the various hearings in local courts before they all went to trial was fairly simple. In early February 1985 an Artarmon women, Miss Anne Pederson, rented her garage to a man known only as Paul who failed to complete the rental document. Soon after, on 17 February, she and two friends forced open the door and found suspicious material.

Uniformed police from Chatswood attended and called Chatswood detectives to the scene. They identified eight large cartons of compressed Indian hemp which were moved to Chatswood police station, each carton requiring two men to carry it. The drugs, said to be in 144 blocks, weren't entered in the exhibit book at that stage or secured in the exhibit room, but placed in the interview room. By next morning they had been moved into the main detectives' office, but by 3 p.m. that day only 95 of the 144 blocks were entered in the exhibit book and secured in the exhibit room.

Early that same morning Det-Sgt Hunter called on Bristow at his home and put a sample block in his lawnmower grass catcher, asking him to sell it. About 11 a.m. Bristow rang a Peninsula surfboard manufacturer named Geoffrey Warren Gibson who came to his home. Bristow gave him the sample and told him there were 90 kilograms of the drug available for sale, saying they wanted $3,000 a block.

Bristow received a phone call from Hunter and that evening went to Hunter's home at French's Forest with a view to getting some of the Indian hemp packets. Hunter wasn't home and Bristow and Gibson went to Chatswood police station where Bristow was told Hunter was at the Willoughby Legion Club.

He went there and saw a number of detectives including Hunter, bought a round of drinks, helped a lady in the carpark get into her car after she locked the keys inside, and went to Chatswood police station, parking his Mercedes underneath. There he saw two detectives whom he named as Detective Wolfgang Schinnerl and Det-Sgt John Cosgrove, toss down from a lighted upstairs window 47 blocks of Indian hemp which Hunter caught in a towel and loaded into Bristow's car.

Bristow with Gibson then drove to Narrabeen where Gibson transferred the drugs to his vehicle and went to his own home where he secreted them in his premises. At 7 p.m. the following day, Tuesday 19 February, Gibson was arrested at his home and 47 marijuana blocks in compressed form were located. As a result of information Gibson supplied, Bristow was interviewed and later charged with supplying the drugs to Gibson.

Those were the bare bones outlined by Mr G. Blewitt for the Public Prosecutions Office in Newtown Local Court before Magistrate Mr B.J. Hayes, when Bristow and the detectives, Hunter, Schinnerl and Gibson, first appeared on a charge of conspiring to supply Indian hemp.

Behind that sparse legal scaffolding lay a story of intrigue, confusion, panic and trauma as the participants manoeuvred in the desperate situation to avoid exposure. The attempted coverup was already moving, again according to Mr Blewitt at that first hearing. He said that on Wednesday, the day after Gibson was arrested, Hunter approached Detective Ryan at Chatswood and indicated that he wanted him to say he saw Bristow at the club and had wanted to see him about a problem.

Later that evening while Ryan was showering at his home, Det-Sgt Cosgrove called and while he was under the shower said: "You have got to say you didn't see Bristow the other night, there's big problems." Cosgrove was excited and agitated. About two hours later, at 12.30 a.m., Hunter telephoned Ryan and asked: "Did you get the message?"

Mr Blewitt said that either on the following Thursday or Friday, Hunter contacted Detective Damp at Chatswood and said: "The other night you didn't see Big Tim. Right? You got a call to go to the Legions club. You drove there, you didn't see Big Tim. You've got to be strong on that now son, do you understand that?"

On Tuesday 26 February the following week, police from the Internal Security Unit began inquiries at Chatswood and after they left, Hunter approached Detective Damp and indicated there were big problems. But he said: "They've got nothing on us, can't you see they haven't got a brief? All you've got to do is say you didn't see Big Tim. No-one saw you. It's easy mate. I'm getting good inside information from a superintendent mate, they've got nothing."

Detective Damp asked how much of the grass had been snipped off and Hunter replied: "Mate, only a small amount." Then Det-Sgt Hunter went on to say: "Can't you see they're going to put me in jail? You're going against your workmates - you can't do it."

"What about Gibson?" asked Damp. Hunter said: "Well, if he talks, they'll get to him. He might get a bullet." Damp said: "What about if we talk?" Hunter said: "It might be the same."

Next day the internal security police interviewed Hunter, Schinnerl and other police including Ryan and Damp but before they did, Ryan told Schinnerl he couldn't do what they asked. Schinnerl said: "If you don't stick by us, we'll all go down" and Hunter said: "Be strong - it's our word against Gibson's."

Mr Blewitt submitted to the magistrate that the allegations were serious and because of the threats that had been made, the prosecution feared the witnesses were in some danger.

At that hearing Bristow's counsel, Mr Peter Givorshner, raised some of the pressure problems Tim was having from the police. "It defies imagination," he said, "as to why the police have found it necessary to go to his home in the early hours of this morning, rearrest him and bring him before this court when he is due to appear at Manly Court on the 3rd of April (1985), for the same charge."

He said Tim had lived in the same house for 28 years, had worked for large newspaper companies at times, had presented himself at Manly police station to be arrested and charged, had not been charged with any attempt to pervert the course of justice and was not connected with any of the allegations that had been raised in court.

Magistrate Hayes agreed, saying the facts put Bristow out of the scene where the threat of a bullet was alleged to have been made and allowed him bail of $20,000 without security, but he had to surrender his passport.

All those charged in the local courts asserted their innocence and reserved their defence.

After it blew up with the arrest of Gibson, Tim had found himself in a terrible position. He loathed drugs but found himself caught up in a situation at the behest of Chatswood detectives. In reality he just drove the cannabis around for the detectives to give it to a dealer who, on his evidence, they nominated. Tim had it in his possession for a limited time and - again on the evidence - had no financial interest in it.

But that was enough. The defence of duress applied only if the threat was immediate. For that defence to work, he needed a gun at his head.

Bristow had another immediate problem. Right at that time he was facing a charge in Manly Court of alleged assault and malicious damage to a door. It followed an incident shortly before on 4 February when three men broke down the door of Balgowlah man Joseph Shineberg's unit, accompanied by his wife, and seized his four-year-old son for the wife in a custody dispute. Police had declined to take action for lack of evidence and Mr Shineberg took out a private summons against Bristow.

Although he denied assaulting the person in any way, Tim was concerned because of his previous conviction for assault and in his confused state of mind, with the case coming on quickly, he did not want to upset anyone in authority, whether a Chatswood detective or not. He wanted their help, not their hostility.

He was receiving threats and the Manly assault case was one of the things being held over him, with claims that the charge could be strengthened by police. He was told he'd be "letting the boys down" if he didn't support them. It was also alleged to him that his best mate, a senior police official, was involved in the drugs scam - a falsehood, as it turned out, aimed at committing him to support the scheme.

Sue Ellis said privately of the situation: "Tim was beside himself, sick with worry. They were putting unbelievable pressure on him. I said to him if you get involved in this, that's it. He said to me I just don't know what to do, I'm between a rock and a hard place. My mate is involved and I've got this case pending..."

On the Wednesday morning, two days after the grass catcher incident, Manly detectives raided Bristow's home on a warrant after taking a statement from Gibson. They searched his home, took possession of his car for forensic tests and took him and Sue to the station for questioning. Tim simply denied everything. His then solicitor, Mr Jeffrey Ibbotson, was present but had to leave before Bristow finished and signed his statement.

Sue was sitting in a separate side room at Manly station for most of that day and finally needed to go to the toilet. A young detective had to get permission for her to do so. When she came out she found about five detectives in a huddle and heard the senior one say: "We'll just nab Bristow on this. We'll get him for the lot."

He knew she must have heard him and demanded angrily. "What are you doing?" The young detective escorting her said: "Oh, she's just been to the toilet." The senior cop would later be one of those from Manly in serious trouble from Justice Wood's royal commission into police corruption.

A streetwise person, Sue had her suspicions confirmed by overhearing that remark. She could see how sticky it was becoming with police about to cover up for police and she refused to give any information in her statement. When they were allowed to go she was anxious to tell Tim what she'd heard but when they got in his car, still white inside and out from dusting powder used by the cops, he said "don't talk in the car," in case a bug had been planted.

On arriving home they stood out on the lawn as she told him: "Don't trust any of them. They're going to lumber you with it all. You're going to be the scapegoat here."

Bursting with anger, self-recrimination and frustration, Tim felt he had to do something in spite of the threats. He arranged a secret rendezvous at Mona Vale with Superintendent Ernie Shepard of the police internal security unit and told him of the police involvement. "I don't know who to trust or which way to turn," Tim said. One of the good guys, Ernie promised to look into it.

By now Bristow knew how it had all come unstuck. The two men whom he had taken on the Balgowlah child custody raid were Gibson and his associate, Glen Thornton. Both had done debt-collecting work together for him. On 18 February, when Sgt Hunter brought the sample to his house and asked him to sell it, Bristow met Thornton in a coffee lounge late that night. As they played backgammon, he told him all about it in confidence. Gibson came in and said he had put the drugs away.

Next day Thornton went to drug police and dobbed Tim in and also Gibson. Tim understood he was paid $10,000 for the information. That's how the police knew to move on Gibson so quickly. Tim could not believe the perfidy of Thornton in turning informer because he had helped him out several times by giving him money so he could pay his rent.

On Friday 1 March, just two weeks after Hunter's fateful early morning visit to Bristow, Manly detectives contacted the solicitor now acting for Bristow, Richard Allsop, and told him to bring Tim in because they wanted to charge him - on that day. Allsop was suspicious. He knew Tim was due to appear in Manly Court on the following Monday 4 March to answer the assault charge and didn't want him facing the prospect of being in custody over the weekend without being able to apply for bail. So he gave an undertaking that his client would present himself on Monday morning to be charged.

When told they wanted to charge him that day, Tim could see the picture more clearly. He believed he was now caught between the good cops and the bad cops. The cops from the internal security unit were wanting to interview him to investigate the drug scam and nail the crooks, and the others wanted to whack him before the good guys got to him.

He said to Sue: "If I'm charged today, I probably won't be able to get bail and will be in the Manly cells over the weekend. When I face the assault charge on Monday, I'll be brought into court from the cells. I'll be part of the police system and made to look guilty straight away. I'm going to make myself scarce so they can't find me over the weekend."

Within the Bristow family, the shame of his situation caused much distress. Max said to him: "I'm sorry, you've got yourself into this and I don't want my family involved."

Tim called on a young friend who was glad to help. He went with his friend in his small car, crouching awkwardly in the back whenever they saw a police car, to pick up some clothes he had stashed near his home and to pick up his car which was being repaired. He then left his car overnight with an old girlfriend at Mosman and slept the night in his young friend's bed. He was gone by dawn, to another friend on the Central Coast.

The young friend said of that incident: "He was distraught. I'd grown up hearing what a legend this man was and then I see him scared."

Saturday's *Telegraph* carried a story saying a private investigator whom Drug Squad police wanted to arrest in connection with a marijuana case had gone into hiding and they were searching for him. The cops were stage managing the story and leaking it. They then turned up at his house early on Saturday morning, only to find the bird had flown. A neighbour told Sue, who had left at 6.30 to teach tennis, that they charged in like storm troopers.

Bristow turned up at Manly by appointment on Monday to be charged with the drug offence and obtained bail. Brother Max was there to support him after all. In the assault case, Magistrate Helen Larcombe dismissed the information against Bristow when Joseph Shineberg withdrew his civil summons. But it would not be the last of it.

The drug charges proceeded through the local courts. On 15 November 1985 at 302 Castlereagh Street in the city, Magistrate Mr C. Gilmore committed for trial Bristow, Det-Sgts Hunter and Cosgrove and Detective Schinnerl on the charge of conspiring to supply Indian hemp. He said he was satisfied there had been an agreement between them and Gibson to supply and distribute it.

Gibson had been granted immunity from prosecution to give evidence, but Magistrate Gilmore was obviously not impressed with him as a witness. The magistrate said if the Crown relied only on Gibson's evidence "I realise he emerges in these proceedings as a somewhat unsavoury character by his own admissions as to his willingness to become involved in the drug scene." He also said it was inconsistent that Gibson had tried to protect Bristow on one hand and at the same time tip a bucket on him.

At another hearing Magistrate David Hyde dismissed charges to pervert the course of justice against two other detectives, Donald Murray and Kevin Bradley.

Tim also sought immunity and signed a long statement for Det-Inspector Strong and Det-Sgt Moeller at the internal police security unit. When he went there he bumped into Det-Sgt Bill Duff, a friend of Sgt Hunter, and felt sure that news of his presence there would get back to Hunter. But after some apprehension, he went ahead with his statement anyway. The Attorney-General's Department refused his immunity request.

He then took stock of all the evidence and his chances at trial, discussing it with his solicitor and friend Mark Johnson, and with Jack Hiatt, QC, an experienced former prosecutor and a senior barrister who had handled many big cases. They considered the evidence against him to be strong with difficulties in the way of proving his innocence, although he was a reluctant participant who was frightened of the police officers and had felt he had no other alternative at the time. Also, his lawyers said duress would not succeed as a defence because the threats had not been immediate. It was suggested he would get a far lighter sentence if he pleaded guilty.

Tim decided he would plead guilty and stand up and be counted by giving evidence against the police. Suddenly all the fears, doubts and confusion that had made his life a misery were gone. Bristow's mind was clear and he was in control of himself again.

Bristow's signed statement to Inspector Strong, tendered in evidence at his trial, revealed that he had employed Gibson and Thornton to escort and protect a courier in a cocaine deal at Port Stephens in a drug operation known as the Amsterdam connection, and had informed the police of that situation in order to catch the drug dealer. He expected Gibson and Thornton to be under surveillance but the police did nothing. His action had caused friction with Gibson and Thornton.

He said Gibson was the assailant in the Shineberg assault case "if any assault took place." Annoyed that police had done nothing about the cocaine matter, he had mentioned all this to Sgt Hunter a week before Hunter put the marijuana in his grass catcher.

Bristow said that when Hunter came to his home and left the sample, Hunter said: "This is special marijuana. See what you can do with it." Bristow had said he had no use for it and Hunter replied: "What about your mate, tied up with the assault?" Later at Chatswood station, Hunter had said to him: "I have a heap of drugs, the grouse stuff." Bristow again protested that he didn't want to be involved and Hunter said: "Don't worry, everything is sweet. This is a chance of a lifetime."

Bristow also said in his statement: "I was concerned and frightened. George Hunter has a gun, he is a policeman and his connections are very strong with the underworld."

On the Tuesday night when he phoned Hunter to tell him he thought Gibson had been arrested, Hunter told him not to admit having been at the Legion Club or Chatswood police station. Bristow had gone along with that when the police called to question him next morning, although he said he didn't trust the police and realised that whichever way he went, he was checkmated. He said he advised Gibson to pay the police the extra money they wanted when they asked for $4,000 a packet and not to let them down "because they will blow your head off."

On the way to his trial and sentencing in the District Court (criminal jurisdiction) at the end of Macquarie Street on Thursday, 28 August 1986, Tim walked from Mr Hiatt's chambers with him and his solicitor, Mark Johnson. Every few metres as he made his usual VIP progress around the courts, someone said, "G'day Tim" and wished him well, including QCs, politicians and retired judges.

One barrister called out: "How're you going, Tim?" and he said loudly with a laugh: "I'm going up the river." He could see the irony of it all. He pleaded guilty before Judge Smyth. Mr Saunders QC with Mr Newport appeared as the Crown prosecutor, and Mr Hiatt QC with Mr Givorshner for "the prisoner," as they quaintly say in the courts.

Det-Sgt Heinz Juergen Moeller outlined the facts, naming the police and the allegations against them, saying there would now be further committal proceedings against the detectives due to a statement from Bristow, who would give evidence against them at those hearings and at the trials.

Moeller agreed with Mr Hiatt that pressure from Det-Sgt Hunter on somebody to commit a crime would be pretty heavy pressure.

Q: As a matter of your opinion, and sometimes justified by events, some quite senior police officers do act in a criminal fashion, do they not?

A: Yes.

Q: Sgt Hunter is one such?

A: Yes.

Moeller said he'd heard that as a result of Bristow making his statement on 1 August causing new charges against the police, there had been a threat to his life.

His Honour then asked Mr Hiatt about the assault charge against Bristow "in which Sgt Hunter said he might be able to bring some evidence to the disadvantage of Bristow." The judge was told a private summons was withdrawn, then the police had instituted fresh proceedings after having been satisfied earlier they did not have evidence against Bristow.

Sue Ellis gave character evidence. In essence, she said she had been with Tim a long time, he was a good man and she loved him. Stephen Charles Bristow, Tim's son, said he was attending Kings School when his father was jailed for assault, but he had a good relationship with him and recalled that Tim had helped many young people with drug problems in the area where he grew up.

John Dowd, MP for Lane Cove and Shadow Attorney-General for the NSW State Opposition who would later become a judge of the Supreme Court, said he was volunteering to give evidence and did not wish to claim parliamentary privilege to avoid answering questions. He said he'd known Timothy Bristow for about sixteen years and Bristow had often given him information on criminal matters without restriction on how he could use that information. Mr Dowd said he was very conscious of Bristow's public reputation.

Asked his view on Bristow's attitude to society, Mr Dowd said: "Well, in the time he has come to me at my request or volunteering, he has tried to assist me since I have become visible in the organised crime area, to do the job I have to do. He has demonstrated to me over that period of time a respect for the society he works in.

"He has gone to some trouble to obtain information for me, knowing it will be used to assist criminal investigations. I have believed him to very much respect the society he works in until I heard of this matter."

Mr Dowd said he immediately assumed it was a "put up job" because of his previous attitude to drugs until Bristow told him about it himself. Bristow, he said, had a rather convoluted way of speaking but he had seen his statement on the matter and subject to convolutions, his verbal explanation to him was consistent with his statement.

Mr Dowd said he could accept that Bristow "would do this out of fear of going to jail for some reason, or of the people involved, knowing what I know about them." He didn't question Bristow's statement that he had done it without financial reward.

Det-Supt Ernest Septimus Shepard, of the police internal security unit, said Bristow had been actively assisting police since March and he'd spoken to him numerous times to assist him in taking action against police whom he felt were involved in corruption or misconduct.

He'd spoken to Bristow twice at Narrabeen on the matter now before the court. Asked if he remembered what was said when Bristow came to the driver's side of his car at Narrabeen, Shepard replied:

"Yes. We had been discussing this particular matter and persons involved and he indicated to me that he was in fear of his life from persons connected with those who are involved in this particular matter. His final words to me before he departed were 'do you think they will kill me?' And as he said it, I could see fear in his face as he left."

Q: From your knowledge of the people involved, did you think it was a reasonable fear to entertain in the circumstances?

A: Yes.

Q: Do you have some concern for the safety of the prisoner in Long Bay Jail?

A: Yes.

Dr Stella Dalton was prepared to give evidence on his behalf but in an unfortunate oversight Tim did not approach her. She knew Tim's anti-drug attitude and work better than anyone.

Before passing sentence, Mr Justice Smyth pointed out the seriousness of the crime which carried a maximum sentence of 15 years. The evidence against Bristow was that the police concerned chose him to ferry the drugs out of the police station and to arrange for their sale.

"It is said by you and on your behalf," said the judge, "That you were at all times reluctant to assist George Hunter and the police to carry out this criminal activity. But that you were prevailed upon by threats which you treated seriously. It is also said on your behalf that you did not receive any money from your part and you deliberately decided you would not share in the proceeds. There is some conflict between your position and the statement of Mr Gibson, the ultimate wholesaler of the substance."

[Gibson had alleged in his version of events before Magistrate Mr Gilmore that when Bristow told him that the police wanted $4,000 a block he suggested Gibson sell them for $4,200 and they go halves in the profit].

The judge said to Bristow: "In support of your contention, it is argued that your whole history is consistent with your attitude to drugs, that is, you have always been anti-drug involvement. In my view, you should be given the benefit of any doubt in that regard, and I accept for the purpose of sentencing you that you decided not to participate in any profits from this operation."

His Honour took into account Mr Dowd's evidence of Bristow's assistance, that he had not participated in the profits, that when his request for an indemnity was refused - although Gibson was given indemnity - he still assisted the law enforcement agencies and still intended to give evidence on these offences at personal risk to himself. He said he did not find it difficult to accept that Bristow's life was in danger due to his stance.

However, he felt there was no alternative but to impose a custodial sentence. He accepted that in Bristow's case he showed contrition. "Rightly or wrongly," said the judge, "I take the view that you are thoroughly ashamed of the part you took in it, and probably you are equally ashamed of what you would no doubt consider as your own cowardice in being stood over by a senior police officer. Recognition must be given to that fact."

Judge Smyth said that without the compensating factors mentioned, he would normally be giving Bristow a head sentence of eight years with five years non-parole. But he sentenced him to five years with two years non-parole, stipulating he was to obtain all earned and unearned remissions.

Tim Bristow, the man who had sent numerous crims and cons to jail over the years, was placed in a paddy wagon with some of the day's worst desperadoes rejected by the courts and taken to "The Puzzle."

But in a pre-recorded interview, he still had something to say on Channel Nine's national *Willesee* programme that night, telling Peter Wilkinson he was pleading guilty not because he was guilty but to avoid a possible 20-year sentence if the jury found him guilty.

Wilkinson asked him as Sydney's toughest private eye: "Have you ever knocked anyone off?" Bristow said: "I've never knocked anyone off in my life. I've belted quite a few in self defence and for other reasons."

Wilkinson: "Quite a few knee caps?" Bristow: "No, it's never been my game. That's a fallacy."

Then he took a parting shot at the cops: "They'll have to kill me to shut me up now."

21

BERRIMA - TIM'S BIG HOUSE

FOR Bristow, surviving in one of Her Majesty's confinement establishments was a question of setting standards for himself.

But as he found out, it was difficult to avoid trouble even in the low security Berrima Training Centre. He knew from previous experience that many people in the slammer were unpredictable. He didn't know what they were thinking or how they might react, their ideas of right and wrong were different, some were tricksters or mentally peculiar, others spent their time scheming on "jobs" they intended carrying out when released, and when not doing that they preyed on others inside.

Andrew Leary, a barrister friend, remarked to Lennie McPherson, a client of his, that he was concerned for Tim's welfare. "Don't worry about him," said McPherson, "He'll be all right. He's the toughest man I've ever met." Coming from Lennie, that was a big rap.

Tim merely imposed his own normal standards on himself, to stay alert and keep active, with one difficult addition for so gregarious a character - to keep to himself as much as possible without appearing unfriendly. He listened to what others had to say, even if he thought some were mad, while trying to overcome his own gloomy thoughts, feeling degraded as he did to be branded a drug dealer.

He was transferred to Berrima in the Southern Highlands after a short stint in Long Bay. The bracing air and picturesque country setting brought back memories of happier days when his parents had a holiday home in the nearby lovely town of Bowral where many wealthy Sydney retail and wool folk had weekend retreats.

Berrima Jail's claim to fame was that Captain Starlight the bushranger had once been a guest there. Now its guests were largely ex policemen and surprisingly for a low security place, quite a few murderers. Tim immediately made a good impression on the superintendent, Mr Burge, who put him in charge of the workforce. He worked like a beaver to set an example and to keep himself fit and active.

But in spite of minding his own business, problems were thrust on him. He outlined the problems in a signed statement, punishable if untrue, to Mr M. Carter, the senior assistant superintendent, to protect himself in case of future violence. As events would unfold, it was a wise move.

In his statement of 29 November 1986, he referred to difficulties with a prisoner named Bill Booth, a boxer with whom he'd had a fight in Long Bay in 1975. He said Booth had pulled a knife on him in Berrima and threatened him by saying: "I'll shiv you, you old dog." Bristow did not retaliate. Another time Booth had threatened him with shears, saying: "I'll bloody well shiv you." Again, Bristow moved away without reacting.

He said Booth had also incited another prisoner named Christopher Lorenzo to continually try to provoke him by calling him a dog, meaning informer - the lowest form of prison life.

He said in his statement that prisoners told him Lorenzo had knives and that Lorenzo and Booth were going to get him. Allegations were also made about a prisoner there named George Crawford who was said to be paranoid about

Bristow. According to Tim, Crawford was friendly with members of the Toe Cutter Gang, a group of Sydney criminals in the '70s who specialised in snipping off the toes of victims with bolt cutters to encourage them to hand over the proceeds of robberies.

The threatened violence finally erupted. Bristow was in the shower one day when he was alerted by a warning shout from another inmate, Jack Cooper, in the next shower. Lorenzo and another prisoner came at Bristow with knives and he felt sure they would have got him if he hadn't reacted so quickly. With a little help from Cooper, Bristow defended himself and belted them both, using his special Newport Arms grip to bang Lorenzo's head into the wall.

The would-be killers were transferred to Goulburn Jail. For saving his life, Bristow would stick by Cooper, a small-time but violent criminal from Queensland who traded on the reputation of being a killer. One of Bristow's assailants, Christopher Anthony Lorenzo, would be convicted in 1993 for the brutal murder of an orthodontist's wife, Mrs Marguerite Edwards, who was bashed and strangled in her Woollahra home.

Unable to accept the stigma of drug pusher without some retort, he busied himself when not working in the gardens or rebuilding the tennis courts, to seek release on licence in return for helping the police department with information on criminal activities. His solicitors applied to the Release on Licence Board and sought support from the Police Commissioner.

But although various investigators came and interviewed him and were glad to accept his help, the authorities would not release him on licence. After all, his evidence was threatening to send several cops to jail. And he had pleaded guilty to a serious crime, even if a victim of circumstances.

He found it difficult to accept his position as hopeless. He wrote to the Ombudsman and the Attorney-General Terry Sheahan. Tim was singing like a canary, or offering to. He knew he was putting his life at further risk but couldn't help himself. He still felt so incensed, frustrated and shamed at the drug conviction he believed he had nothing to lose.

Bristow gave a blast to the cops in Glebe Court in the first hearing of the new charges against them of conspiring to pervert the course of justice, based on his decision to give evidence against them. But just before he did that, Sue Ellis told Magistrate David Hyde of an incident concerning Det-Sgt Hunter.

She said in evidence that Sgt Hunter in 1980 had asked Bristow to "load up" an ex-agent of his with drugs but he refused. Next day Bristow was arrested in connection with an assault charge. Hunter had returned with a young policeman and when she heard Tim say he was not pleased, Hunter said: "That's what happens when you don't do what you're told."

Asked why she remembered it, she said: "It was a representative of the law enforcing body, coming to your home and making threats."

Tim had already made an official complaint in writing from Berrima to the Ombudsman about the same incident. He said a former agent of his, Graham Stolz, had complained to Keith Paull of the police Internal Affairs Bureau about having to pay protection money to police over a bordello Stolz operated at Brookvale. Stolz was also "dobbing in" police generally.

He said George Hunter came to his house and said he was embarrassed by the complaint because he had to fix it and he wanted Bristow to load Stolz up with drugs to stop him. Bristow said he wouldn't do that to anybody. He alleged Hunter came to him again and asked him to do something else to Stolz. Bristow then complained about it to Internal Affairs. He was then threatened with a charge of being an accessory to an assault at Balmoral.

He said two North Sydney detectives then came to his home "and charged me falsely with the Balmoral assault to shut me up and for which I later paid $500 to get out of. I was falsely imprisoned at North Sydney police station until 4 p.m. that day."

Bristow said he went to Parliament House and complained to Cliff Mallam, the member for Campbelltown. Mallam phoned the Police Commissioner Jim Lees who ordered that it be investigated. Tim received a letter saying it was being looked into, then a senior officer saw him and suggested it wasn't worth going on with the Hunter complaint.

"They put the charge on me for bargaining, that's how it works," said Bristow. "The prosecutor offered no evidence against me on the assault charge...I agreed to hold no animosity on the false charge."

He also broadly outlined these allegations in Glebe Local Court after volunteering to give evidence against the police.

In his Glebe Court outburst after Sue's evidence, Bristow told Magistrate David Hyde: "I would rather die than be a drug dealer, and if it meant going to jail to get these guys (the cops), then I would go to jail." He said he was prepared to give evidence to get the police because "I despise them all."

The cops got square with him a month later by pushing the alleged Manly assault. They had decided not to act on the complaint for lack of evidence in 1985 and then Mr Shineberg withdrew his own summons. But when it became clear Tim intended giving evidence against the Chatswood detectives, police reactivated the case in early 1986, charging him by summons with malicious damage and assault causing actual bodily harm. And they made it stick, wanting to make him look bad when the police trials came up.

Armed police brought him from Berrima for the assault hearing in November 1968 in farcical conditions, with tight security at Manly Court. Police used metal detectors to search all persons entering the courtroom - all for a complaint that was almost two years old.

Mr Shineberg alleged his former wife knocked on the door, which then "exploded" as two "coves" came in and held him while a third - allegedly Bristow - took his son and handed him to Mrs Shineberg. He was then allegedly punched.

Bristow told the court Mrs Shineberg had come to him, said she'd had a serious operation recently and her ex-husband had assaulted her when she tried to get her son back. He denied he went inside the unit, saying he didn't have an inquiry agent's licence and sent two other agents in. He went to the door on hearing a bang and Mrs Shineberg passed the child to him.

His barrister, Mr Givorshner, submitted the case was not proved beyond reasonable doubt as Mr Shineberg did not know who kicked in the door and his identification of Bristow was only "fleeting." But Magistrate Mrs Larcombe, who had originally thrown out the case, found him guilty and gave him another 12 months, to be served concurrently with his present drug sentence. Bristow later appealed.

Then Kevin Murray, QC, got in on the act while defending four of the detectives in Paddington Local Court on charges relating to the Indian hemp. He and Tim were enemies, Tim having upset some of his clients earlier with his inquiries. Also, as counsel for Louis Vaja, Murray had made the false allegation in court that Tim had hit Vaja from behind with an iron bar - a claim proved so wide of the mark on the evidence that Murray must have tossed it in deliberately, knowing it was false. Now, Murray put the boot into him in Paddington Court.

"The man is a proven if not convicted criminal," he said. "He is of notorious infamy on the Peninsula. He is a compulsive psychopathic liar... the prosecution must be embarrassed to rely on his testimony." The *Manly Daily's* front page headline of that smear was "Bristow branded as liar - defence attacks 'thug' testimony."

In one hearing, while cross-examining Sue Ellis and attacking Tim's credit over his German Shepherd dogs, Murray said to her: "I also believe you have a vicious cat." A vicious cat! Sue's poor old friendly puss would only attack strangers by licking them to death.

And again, when two of the detectives were committed for trial in the Castlereagh Street Local Court, Murray had another go, saying Bristow's evidence should be disregarded because he was "completely and utterly undesirable." But Magistrate Hyde said he felt he should not disregard Bristow's evidence, even if it had been put to him that he was a name dropper who sought the company of police officers.

As if that wasn't enough pressure to fell a Mallee bull, more was to come. Early on the morning of Monday 6 April 1987 a warder at Berrima went to Bristow's cell and told him to get dressed - he was going to the Coroner's Court in Sydney for the resumed inquest into the death of a judge's wife, Mrs Pearl Watson. Armed police from Sydney were there to escort him.

He couldn't believe the precautions. He was placed in a big black maria with two armed cops in the back and two in the front, with two cars as backup. He felt like Al Capone under siege by the Untouchables. Arriving at the court in Glebe, he was put in a padded cell after being allowed to make one telephone call. He rang Sue and explained his situation. Reliable Sue came with barrister Peter Givorshner to represent him.

The Coroner, Kevin Waller, was inquiring into the death of Mrs Pearl Watson, wife of Parramatta Family Court Judge Ray Watson. She had died from shocking injuries after a home-made bomb exploded when she opened her front door at Greenwich on the lower North Shore at 8.15 a.m. on 4 July 1984. Another Sydney Family Court judge, Judge Richard Gee, was injured when a bomb exploded at his home in Belrose a few months previously.

The Court was told by John William Carroll, who ran an explosives business and formerly a bordello at Gosford, that a local woman had told him she knew the identity of the bombers. She allegedly told him that Tim Bristow and two other private investigators, Graham Stolz and Reg Shatford, had carried out the bombings. It was alleged that Bristow was "the brains" behind the bombing, that Stolz made the bomb and Shatford placed it at the Watson residence.

Carroll denied suggestions from counsel for the three men that he had fabricated the story in order to claim a $500,000 reward offered for information leading to the prosecution of the bombers.

Mrs Carol Vitnell, then of Copacabana on the Central Coast, denied in court that she'd made the allegations about the three investigators. She said she knew the three men but knew nothing of their alleged involvement.

Tim felt vulnerable. He believed a plot had been hatched to take advantage of his present situation in order to claim the $500,000 reward to solve the murder, and that some police might be involved. If charged, he feared he would probably be convicted. He didn't know where the next salvo was coming from and accepted his lawyer's advice that he should remain silent.

In what was an anti-climax in a case where witnesses gave widely conflicting evidence, the usually talkative Bristow refused to answer questions on the bombings asked by Priscilla Fleming, QC, counsel assisting the Coroner, on the ground that they might incriminate him in some offence. However, he said he was not involved in the blasts. Stolz and Shatford also both denied the allegations, Stolz saying Bristow "would not have the brains" to do the bombings. Bristow had worked with both men but no longer had good relations with them.

The Coroner, "with a sense of disappointment and frustration," returned an open finding. He doubted the evidence of John William Carroll and named a number of suspects, including Reg Shatford, recommending that the police cancel the pistol and inquiry agent's licences of Graham Stolz.

Bristow believed the person who killed Pearl Watson was associated with a gas-loaded bazooka gun that was being used in Sydney crime activities, but to name that person would have brought a whole range of allegations and threats, causing him further problems. He felt sure the person was also connected with the killing of Judge David Opas of the Family Court who was shot at the front door of his Sydney home in 1980.

Tim also learned later from a Homicide detective friend that after the bombing allegations surfaced against him, CIB police had been planning to throw the book at him by charging him with a number of other unsolved murders. Tim claimed it was 14, but that was obviously an exaggeration by him to highlight the situation and add to his notoriety. However, the more likely situation was that they were looking at 14 murders to see which ones could be applied to him. In any event, the prospect of being "loaded up" with even one murder while he was restricted in prison was a terrifying experience.

The District Court trial against three Chatswood detectives relating to the drugs conspiracy began in August 1987 and lasted a gruelling eight weeks. Det-Sgts George Hunter and John Cosgrove and Det Wolfgang Schinnerl pleaded not guilty to charges of conspiring to supply Indian hemp and conspiring to pervert the course of justice.

Sue Ellis told the court: "You may claim Tim to be a lot of things which he is not, but one thing he definitely isn't, is a drug dealer." She also said there had been much "disinformation, lies and half-truths" published about Bristow and "horrific things" had been attributed to him.

Bristow was the chief Crown witness. He alleged that when Hunter loaded 98 kilograms of marijuana from the police station into his car Hunter said it was "a chance of a lifetime" and "you're mad not to be in it." Bristow said he told Hunter at that time: "I want nothing out of this, but I want to get off the assault charge at Manly." He also told the court he was no drug dealer, was strongly against drugs and had been "weak to get involved."

The long trial took its toll, particularly on the jurors who deliberated for five days to reach a decision. When the foreman read out their verdicts, he was visibly upset. Around him all seven women jurors and two of the five male jurors wept openly. Suddenly the pent-up emotions and anxiety of the past eight weeks had been released. But George Hunter, who had his 59th birthday three days earlier, the former rugby league captain and coach so highly praised by his character witnesses, showed no emotion standing in the dock as he was declared guilty on both counts.

Cheers went up from the packed public gallery as Cosgrove, 44, was acquitted on the supply charge. That quickly changed to a collective wail of grief from his family and friends as he was found guilty of the second charge of perverting the course of justice.

"Oh he can't be," cried his elderly mother and "that was so wrong" sobbed his teenage daughter. His two teenage sons threw their arms around him in the dock, sobbing. Distraught family members clung to each other for support as their husband and father was led away to the cells.

A jubilant Schinnerl, 37, punched the air with a clenched fist and a loud cry of "yo" as he was acquitted of both charges, bolting from the dock to join his emotional wife Debbie outside the court.

Detective Inspector Heinz Moeller, who did the investigations, found it difficult to speak after the verdict, telling the court Cosgrove and Hunter were no longer entitled to police superannuation. Kevin Murray, a tough campaigner, told Judge Shillington the past eight weeks had been the most debilitating of his legal career. "It is difficult to exaggerate the effect of such a trial on a person," the barrister said.

The judge sentenced Cosgrove and Hunter to prison. Cosgrove later appealed and was acquitted and Hunter remained in custody until his release on 1 August 1991. He ended up in Berrima - after Bristow had served his time.

The rest of Tim's time in the pokey was uneventful, except for visits by National Crime Authority people and US officials wanting to talk to him about the Nugan Hand Bank, and reporters interviewing him.

One of his fellow inmates was Rex Jackson, the tough but amiable former NSW Minister for Corrective Services who was imprisoned for letting prisoners out early for cash to fuel his gambling habit. Tim introduced him to Jack Cooper who taught him to make clocks, which he sold.

In a legal sense, Rex was unlucky to be caught - Federal police trapped him only by default by tapping someone else's phone and his name popped up with strange references to "tickets." Jackson complained to Premier Wran that he believed someone was tapping his phone but too late, the report of his activities was already on the Premier's desk.

Rex told friends on his release from Berrima that Bristow was the strongest man he'd ever known. While rejuvenating the tennis courts Tim always filled his wheelbarrow to overflowing but one day it got away from him and he plunged six or eight metres over a cliff, injuring himself with bruises and cuts. He refused hospital treatment in case he didn't get back to Berrima and later as a result had to have all his teeth removed.

Sometimes he went to a hall near Bradman Oval in Bowral to play table tennis. For light relief one day he grabbed a red-bellied black snake he found in the bush, put it in a bag and released it on the prison lawn, laughing as prisoners ran and shut themselves in their cells.

He also enjoyed unofficial "conjugal rights" with a girlfriend named Jana who visited on weekdays. They went into the bush behind the tennis courts.

Many old friends visited like football officials Ken Arthurson and Gordon Willoughby, Sue and Di Parkinson at weekends. Lennie McPherson visited four times and Roy Thurgar, another man of the criminal *milieu*, also came.

But many people, for whom he'd done the most favours, shunned him. That would not change following his early release after 18 months for good behaviour.

22

THE ADJUDICATOR

THE first thing Sue insisted on when Tim came home was to have a high security fence installed right around their extensive property with an electronic gate. Tim agreed. "That's to keep the coppers out," he told everyone.

Among the first telephone callers was a woman identifying herself as one of the jurors who convicted the police. She just wanted to welcome him home, wish him and Sue well and say she thought it was wrong he'd been jailed when he had no intention of dealing in drugs.

He sought to pick up where he left off, but things weren't the same any more. Many former associates dodged him or were uncomfortable in his presence because of the drug taint. The genuine ones didn't change but mostly the friends and clients who went missing were those he'd helped the most. Some would probably have been in the cooler themselves without his help.

To some people, his conviction didn't sit with his reputation as an anti-drug crusader. Was Tim really the unsung hero who liked helping people so much, or was he just a guy who did some bad things along with the good? There was no clear answer to that conundrum. Except that there were extenuating circumstances and it was fair to say his luck in associating with corrupt cops had finally run out.

The stigma made him more conscious of wanting to be accepted and although he'd always been prepared to do a good turn rather than a bad one, he now went out of his way to help others - and not for money.

Sue knew that under that volcanic exterior and tough talk, he was soft with a kind heart. She saw that as one of his most likeable qualities. But she also saw it as a drawback because some people used him and took advantage of his generous spirit. Provided they had not done him wrong, he would give them a go despite their reputations, and would even give them a second chance. His love of drama and thriving on it didn't alter the fact he was basically a good fellow. It annoyed her that he couldn't or wouldn't see that people were taking advantage of him.

Sue gave an interview to a magazine which described how she'd dutifully stood by "the man described as an underworld figure, conman, hitman and standover merchant who will stop at nothing to get results." The story said they lived in a fortress-like home with high electronic gates and guard dogs roaming the grounds, that Sue was worried because she'd heard threats made against him.

"Life is more stressful than ever," she was quoted as saying. "We are harassed a lot by police raids and allegations against Tim of murder, machine-guns and corruption. But I've stuck by him because I love him. If he were a drug dealer or murderer like people say he is, I wouldn't be here."

Tim too said a few words in his defence. "I've done some things I'm not proud of," he said with masterly understatement, "but I've always acted as a service to the community. I've saved more lives than anyone, acting as a mediator between people hell-bent on murder."

Sue rounded it off: "I really wish he'd give it all up. I think he's compensating for things he did in the past. But he's 60 now and he can't keep punching everyone out. I'd give anything for some peace."

Peace was the last thing they'd get. Tim's phone began ringing constantly as his reputation became even more lurid due to his second jail term. And instead of going quietly, he would be more of a law unto himself than before. He'd met every challenge without backing down, many times in defiance of the law, not as a criminal challenge but a challenge of men - men who went to him and asked him to do certain things and he dealt with them in his own way.

His situation now was a bit like the old wild west, where Clint Eastwood cleaned up the evil doers and put away the Colts for a while, only to find the varmints on his doorstep again, forcing him to strap on the 45s once more. Reinvigorated, he'd take 'em on again.

People in renewed numbers sought Bristow's services and business boomed. Some thought he could do almost anything and the requests put to him were ridiculous in their expectation. But in most cases he felt he should try. He attracted criminals just out of jail or about to be released who wrote to him seeking work. These crazies boasted about their criminal skills, how they could kill...

Criminals misinterpreted him like everyone else who judged him on reputation alone. Crims set out to rob or stand over somebody for their own benefit, but Bristow was different in that people came to him for help and advice and if he was satisfied there was a fair dinkum need, he'd say "all right, I'll fix it." He genuinely didn't like to see anyone suffering.

Although he now set out to help more people to atone for his drug shame, his experience in jail made him harder in other ways. In the drug fiasco he had assumed he was operating on a trusting man-to-man basis, but when it blew up the others dropped him in the soup. It made him more pragmatic and cynical, more forceful and determined to take up the cudgels against people of power and also, hopefully, to prove he wasn't a crook.

When a woman from Kalgoorlie in Western Australia came to him as a last resort, he accepted the challenge to penetrate tight security and cause an insurance writ concerning a fire which destroyed her hotel to be served on FAI chief Rodney Adler on the last day of the writ's currency. Others had tried for four years and failed. Bristow engaged a young process server who made his way around Adler's secretary who lectured him on the importance of good manners, found his way into Adler's office and served the document on him.

Adler took the young man to court, seeking aggravated and exemplary damages for trespass, stress and for the inconvenience he suffered by having a document served on him. He sought compensation of $8,000 plus FAI's legal costs, claiming the process server was "standing over" him and "made me feel uncomfortable," although he agreed the young man did not abuse him, raise his voice or threaten him physically. However, the magistrate, Mr Pierce, pointed out that Adler may be trying "to use a sledge hammer to crush an ant" because the process server was only 19 at the time in 1994, that exemplary damages would crush him financially when he was only doing his job with a writ that was "in its last gasp."

The process server apologised in the Downing Street Local Court for his bold act in barging into Adler's inner sanctum but was ordered to pay $500 for trespassing, $4,000 for FAI's costs plus his own legal costs. Later the process server might well have pondered on whether thousands of lamenting investors in insurance giant HIH felt "uncomfortable" when Rodney Adler was accused of deceit, lies and greed at the Royal Commission inquiring into the $5.3 billion collapse of HIH to which Adler had sold FAI at an inflated price.

Many thought Bristow was mad for fearlessly taking on such corporate giants. At Palm Beach one of Sydney's richest men accosted him and said: "I wish you'd piss off Bristow and stop upsetting my friends." Tim retorted: "Perhaps you would like to pay their debts." Apparently it was OK to pursue the little people, but not the wealthy.

Tim looked upon those criticising him as stooges who, unlike himself, were not prepared to stand on their own two feet. Tim had a saying which he pointed out to his operatives: "Real men never die with a bitter taste in their mouths. They finish the job by closing the doors they open. Get the job done, get it done."

He courted trouble from cops and enforcement bodies by turning up at official inquiries and royal commissions, offering information, giving evidence, sometimes laughing and joking at the facade of it all. He was asked to leave one inquiry because a witness felt "uncomfortable" with his presence in the public gallery.

One or two friends advised him that he was being used by the media and cops who came to him for information, suggesting he would not receive any favours in return if he asked. But he ignored that. His lack of discretion at times added to his bad reputation, but he considered that a plus because it brought him more clients.

He'd reached the stage where he didn't really care what they said about him as long as they talked about him. The raunchy *Ralph* magazine took the piss out of him in an appalling article which surely was not meant to be taken seriously, making him out to be worse than Jack the Ripper.

It said things like he'd knocked out so many teeth he expected to be made president of the Dentists' Association. Max's wife Ann was so embarrassed she went around her local newsagents hiding the magazine behind others on display, hoping customers wouldn't see it.

But Tim wasn't as silly as some thought. The world had changed. Just as the Mafia had changed to a corporate image, and Las Vegas had been transformed from a sawdust hangout for mobsters to a corporate tourist town, the Sydney scene was different too. The old-style criminals were no longer visible, the underworld less accessible and more regionalised, the movers and shakers were now from Asia, competing with other ethnic gangs. It was a more dangerous and unpredictable world.

Tim had now distanced himself from the action and had lieutenants to do his bidding. He accepted the jobs and still called the shots, training his men and sending them out as foot soldiers. He wasn't money hungry, regarding it more as a bounty.

One of his main lieutenants was a small chap he called The Gnome, who said Tim made him what he was. "I feel so proud to work for him and I owe this man so much," said The Gnome in explaining their symbiotic relationship, attached as they were to each other for mutual benefit.

The Gnome was as small and insignificant as Tim was big and commanding. He'd sit there quietly saying nothing while Tim thumped the table at a meeting pulling someone into line, but when unleashed he had all the menace of Tim. A good threatener, was how Tim laughingly described him.

The Gnome said of Tim: "His compassion is beyond measure. That's what it means for a man like me to walk with him because I'm a cripple and a midget compared to him. And to send me out to front for him, that's greatness. That is Tim Bristow. I couldn't join the Army in America because of my disabilities. I was born with one shoulder down and I try to balance myself by keeping my hands in my pockets.

"I came here from Ireland and never sought a pension or went on the dole. I just worked and Tim saw that. He got me and developed me. He's done that to many people. Criminals don't do that. We live in a shithouse world. There are too many people in authority under false pretences and they gang up on the good people of this world.

"They gang up on the heroes who die because of these arses, who don't stand up and be counted, who don't take chances. Tim Bristow is one of the heroes, a true blue Australian. He moulded me into a strong individual who believes in himself. He made me so happy and proud of myself.

"He also put me on the threshold of risk and danger but I placed myself in his hands because I knew he would look after me. I've seen what he could do. When he said you're right, you were bloody well right. That's a man. He never wavered. Never."

But in his new approach Tim created problems for himself in one sense by not being ruthless. He gave clients too much help, too much information and they went away and didn't employ him again. They either thought they could do it themselves or they said they were a friend of Tim Bristow and ruthlessly and blatantly used his name, even threatening people to get results.

When he did a job he explained everything to a client, even about his opponent's motives and character, talking for hours, things that would help the client. Was it ego? No, Tim knew what he was doing, educating the fellow so he wouldn't be robbed again.

The Gnome, who because of the reality of life needed the money, tried to persuade Tim to give out less information so they would get paid, but he took no notice. "He did it with everybody in a roundabout way," said The Gnome, "and it's the goodness I liked about him."

Another reason why some people didn't use Tim's services again involved a human nature problem. Once Tim and his boys had moved a mountain for someone, they knew the client's situation intimately and the client feared it might be used to Tim's advantage for blackmail. The client then avoided Tim and often bagged him - due to the criminality inside the client, not Tim - and it upset Tim when that person dodged him socially.

Others were parasites who came to Tim deliberately to make the connection and get his advice so they could go away and use the name and reputation of a man who, unlike themselves, could get things done. They had no intention of paying, and didn't. They were thieves. But if they came back he'd help them again. These were some of the people who said Tim was a criminal and no good. They made themselves sound important.

Some clients, who had not done everything in their power to obtain the money owing to them, would simply go away and do it themselves when the solution was explained to them. They didn't think it could be so easy. But they too had a touch of larceny in them and didn't pay.

For one reason or another, many clients were at Tim's feet one moment and his throat the next. He had to constantly deal with treachery, including from his own workers. Usually he didn't know until he received a phone call saying someone had been threatened using his name. Moonlighting was a problem by some of his operatives taking on jobs that he'd refused, or double crossing a client. He had a strict rule that no woman should ever be hurt or assaulted. He still belted anyone who stepped out of line.

Some of the enforcers he employed didn't know when to stop and he had to impose strict conditions through his lieutenants. They were regimented and the weak or undisciplined ones fell by the wayside. It had to be that way - he had no badge and was paid only on 100 per cent results. When his men walked the streets with him, he knew they were like him. That's why he was a force.

One criminal just out of jail came to Tim's house to start work. "No smoking in my house," Tim told him as they sat around in a group. The fellow, big and strong, went 'ahead and lit up. Tim jumped him and knocked him out.

A man with a fuel business at Alexandria was having problems with burglaries and called Tim in. He gave a man not long out of jail a chance by putting him into the business as an undercover worker. Then the place was robbed again and Tim knew instinctively his man was working in with the security guards. He took him to a house, belted him and handed him over to the cops.

Bristow had merciless moonlighting problems with Jack Cooper, the man also known as Mad Dog Williams who saved his life in Berrima and whom he employed to help him sort out problems in the building industry. To discipline Cooper he also punched him for smoking in his house, humiliating him another time by counting out money for him on the table, then taking some back. Cooper copped it without a word.

Mad Dog worried him by dealing in guns, bringing in machine guns and AK47 assault rifles from New Guinea and selling them in Sydney. He drove Tim up the wall by bringing the guns to Tim's house once or twice. Tim found him difficult to control. He had to stop him on jobs from carrying a tomahawk in one of his socks for fear of what he might do. Mad Dog wore a metal glove made in jail and if rubbed the wrong way, it would tear off a person's skin. Tim was always curbing him and on one occasion had to deal out summary justice for a serious breach of instructions.

It happened in the days when the Penthouse bordello was in George Street, where Tim got to know the proprietor, Michael Kazacos, by rescuing a young girl from there and sending her back to her parents in New Zealand. The pimp controlling her came to Tim's house to object and shaped up wanting to fight. Tim flattened him without even leaving his chair. Treated as a celebrity at the Penthouse, Tim used it as an office to meet his clients, calling it the "boardroom."

He didn't sample the wares although he often had a free sauna and massage there. His photo hanging inside plus his "Newport Legal Services" sign outside stopped crims from robbing the place. Tim always laughed at the printed message inside the door as clients left: "Thanks for coming."

[Kazacos, a depressive who said Tim was more of a father to him than his own father, later shot himself dead after moving the *Penthouse* to new downstairs premises in Pitt Street, scene of the old *Latin Quarter* where Ducky O'Connor met his demise. The new owners didn't want to continue using Tim's services and removed his Newport Legal Services sign and his picture from inside. In the first six months they were robbed several times by Triad gangs without even wearing masks, waving machine guns about - indicating the respect criminals had shown for Bristow].

Kazacos liked guns and kept shotguns, rifles and pistols on the top floor. If Tim wanted to he could borrow one. Tim didn't carry a gun, The Gnome was scared of them but Jack Cooper always wanted one. So this day The Gnome had to collect $100,000 owed by a businessman at Circular Quay and Jack said: "We'd better take some guns. This guy knows a lot of funny people and he'll put the heavies on to us."

So The Gnome packed two rods with instructions from Tim not to give one to Jack. But he didn't have to show them to get the money. Arriving back at the Penthouse by car, Cooper asked to see the guns to check if they were loaded, telling The Gnome to "run upstairs mate while I park the car." First thing Tim asked him was: "Have you returned the guns?"

He exploded in anger when told what had happened, threatening to knock The Gnome out. "Please, please Tim, he's parking the car," he pleaded. They waited four hours. Cooper didn't show. That was Friday. On the Sunday Tim was waiting at the Penthouse with The Gnome when Cooper returned. Without a word he knocked Cooper cold. When he came to, Tim questioned him. He'd done a robbery over the weekend.

Cooper was found shot dead in his van at Sydney airport in 1991. Tim felt sure McPherson organised it because Cooper was out of control and trying to take over some of McPherson's territory. Bristow had pleaded with McPherson to save his life but Mr Big wouldn't listen.

Bristow felt he had to employ such desperate, violent people to give himself an image of toughness and to prevent other criminals and hired gunmen from coming at him in retaliation for his work as a debt collector.

But trouble just seemed to follow Tim as surely as night followed day.

One day at Brookvale on the northern beaches he noticed police crouched behind vehicles outside a house and realised it was a siege. A powder monkey, or licensed explosives expert, was holed up and threatening police. Bristow knew the man, Wayne Bruderer. He walked up as large as life and told Bruderer he would shove his gun up his arse if he didn't come out. Bruderer gave himself up.

Bruderer was later jailed in 1990 on several counts including threatening to blow up Dee Why police station and Manly Hospital, after being diagnosed by a psychiatrist as paranoid and having a "personality disorder of some magnitude." Police were terrified of him and when they moved him from Manly police cells to the court, they asked Bristow to come and get him out of the cells. He later died in Long Bay, reportedly by suicide.

A few months later the barbarians were at Bristow's gates just before 7 a.m. and he knew they hadn't come for an early mug of tea. But he had to let the eight cops in because they had a warrant to search his house. What's more, they were from his old grouse grass graveyard of Chatswood station. "A bit of a coincidence," said Tim cynically, knowing he was due to appear before the Building Royal Commission in three weeks time.

They had two signed records of interview alleging he had a hidden AK47 automatic rifle which had been used in a murder. They couldn't find the rifle after a systematic search but aha! They located in a cupboard downstairs an old antique gun with parts missing, a family heirloom, that hadn't been used since about the Boer War. They charged him with possessing an unlicensed firearm, but he was later acquitted.

The real reason for their visit emerged when they made a close inspection of his concrete tennis court and surrounds. The detectives wanted to have it dug up to search for bodies that Tim had allegedly buried there. He and Sue Ellis, for whom Tim built the court, were extremely indignant. He went to the press and ridiculed that one.

Then when the cops allowed him to see the records of interview at Manly Courthouse later, it all became clear. The fellow making the allegations had worked for Tim as one of a team. But his special criminality was blackmail. He was moonlighting by going back to Tim's clients and saying he wasn't being paid enough money, demanding more. Tim found out and belted him in the time-honoured fashion before sacking him, hence the fellow's mischievous complaint.

Next allegation, where was Tim on 10 January 1989 when Assistant Federal Police Commissioner Col Winchester was murdered in Canberra? Someone had claimed that Tim was "the trigger man who blew Wincheser away." Two Federal cops, Brendan McDevitt and Michael Tuckerman put it to him, recording his denial on video camera.

The next drama in Tim Bristow's life was the Royal Commission by Roger Gyles, QC, into the NSW building industry. And it was a beauty, a breath of fresh air in usually stodgy public inquiries. Most people tell lies in the witness box. It happens every day in every court in the world. Tim got up and told it as it was. The inquiry would have been a fizzer without him. It was hilarious stuff, overshadowing the reality.

Tim described in detail how scared workers returned to the job on building sites after he had "a little chat" to them. As a motivational speaker he would have left broadcaster Alan Jones for dead!

Not only was Tim the star witness, dropping a few buckets here and there, but he went to the commission investigators beforehand and made lengthy statements in writing, setting out how companies like Civil and Civic had called him in to prevent stoppages and what he did and said to union officials and delegates to "shorten them up." And the commission paid him expenses for his troubles.

He should have been acclaimed a hero for stopping the rorts such as bomb hoaxes and deliberate damage to completed work, especially with the slow economy at the time, but instead he came out of it with several others as "a person appearing or reputed to earn a significant part of his livelihood from criminal activities."

His signed statement of 14 January 1991 was a gem. He said people came to him for advice because of his bad reputation. He did it for money except under the old chums' act. An old school mate, a senior executive of Civil and Civic, had employed him to fix the troubles on their sites. Tim said he took three carloads of blokes to the George and Bathurst Street site to talk to objectors there and he put his friend Jack Cooper in as a worker at Campbelltown, having him voted in as the union delegate.

Tim explained how he went there to "shorten up" the troublemakers, taking his good friend Len McPherson. They donned hard hats and went up on the scaffolding. There the main troublemaker yelled: "Are you the new sub-contractors coming on site?" Tim said no, they were different contractors and asked: "Are you the Irishman causing the trouble?" The union man said he was no Irishman but a "Scotchman."

Tim said: "Well, you'll probably know my friend, he's a Scotsman too. His name is Len McPherson." The fellow nearly fell off the trestle.

Tim arranged for "bad luck organisers" to visit the troublemaker at his home and he paid him $3,000 from his own pocket to take a holiday and leave the site, making him aware he could have bad luck if he stayed. He also put Jack Cooper in as a worker on the St Vincent's Hospital site where they were nine months behind because of 90 stop-work meetings in a year, mainly through bomb hoaxes. That solved problems there. He had two union delegates deported who were illegal immigrants.

Tim's evidence made daily headlines. Asked why he had put Cooper to work on the sites he replied: "There was no good putting a wimp, dwarf or cripple there. I wanted someone who had authority." If men he put on the sites wanted to do something drastic like threatening someone, they had to chat to him first.

Mr Abbas Abrood, project manager of an Artarmon construction site being hit by continuing industrial action, said Bristow called the workers into a tin shed where he addressed them, telling of a troublesome Darling Harbour project worker who had the misfortune of falling from the first or second storey of a building. He denied hearing Bristow suggest a gun had been shown to the man, who chose to jump. Bristow's talk he said was "conciliatory" and he was shocked and pleased to see them return to work.

Another witness from that site, delegate Frank Biscan, said Bristow told a group of bricklayers: "Sometimes when I arrive on site, accidents do occur." He claimed Bristow did say a worker jumped after he showed him a gun but on this occasion he ended his chat with a rallying call of "how about you all get back to work and give it a big effort?"

There was more of the same, including Tim once paying $70,000 to a BWIU organiser for developer Gary Dent to get the Redfern Mall project moving. Large cash sums for other bribes had been made available from a bank. Also, when meeting union blokes in a pub once, he took along a team of heavies, one of whom was "an exterminator but a nice fellow."

Just as well they didn't ask Tim about his bribing of Macquarie Street politicians. In his expansive mood he would have been able to tell them plenty about the cash bribes he delivered to certain politicians in Macquarie Street on behalf of some Sydney developers.

Tim also forgot to mention one amusing little scene. About a dozen workers from the Trades Hall were on their way to a city site for a protest meeting when they spotted Big Tim and Big Lennie standing on the corner of George and Bathurst Streets, observing them. They dispersed, deciding it was healthier to go to the pub.

Tim's starring role in helping the economy through the "bile and guile" principle was shaded briefly by a command performance from Mr Big himself. He savaged Tim's reputation, calling him a "bludger" for exploiting his association with Lennie.

McPherson brought guffaws by imitating "Timmy" Bristow's fruity voice and haughty manner when describing how Bristow had taken him on to building sites. And, heaven forbid, Lennie was appalled to find out later that Bristow had used his presence to intimidate people on the sites.

After Bristow had taken him to one site and introduced him. Lennie thought "hallo, he's at it again." They had an amiable chat to the bricklayers "and those poor buggers left the job the next day because they were frightened of me." And to rub salt into the wound, Lennie said Tim in one case had pocketed $9,000 which they were to have shared. "I haven't spoken to the bludger since," he said, with theatrical emphasis.

Great entertainment. But Lennie didn't find it amusing to be charged on two counts of perjury as a result of his evidence to the building commission arising from a visit with Tim to the premises of Knebel Kitchens. He thought he'd save money by not having counsel represent him at the commission, and he also thought he could finesse them there by not even taking the opportunity to decline to answer questions on the ground that he might incriminate himself.

McPherson was sent for trial. Tim was called to give evidence against him for the Crown. It worried Lennie that his counsel, Andrew Leary, may not cross-examine Tim effectively because of the barrister's friendship with Tim. But Leary, a man who had handled 5,000 cases with one of the best strike rates at the Bar, questioned Tim so brilliantly that McPherson was acquitted. Lennie called out "God bless the jury" and Judge Shillington ordered angrily: "Take that man away."

Then came the Royal Commission into police corruption by Mr Justice Wood. Tim revelled in it. Wild horses wouldn't keep him away. He didn't "roll over" like some, but behind the scenes he was fizzing to the investigators about crooked cops. Most of Sydney's crims got a mention generally at the commission, corrupt cops were exposed, one or two suicided, others gasped for air and some of the boys from Manly police station got a drubbing.

It was too much even for Tim's loyal lieutenant, The Gnome. Every time he bumped into someone in the underworld or a heavy at The Cross, they'd say to him: "Are you still working for that ——! That ——! We're going to finish him off."

Said The Gnome: "They all knew Tim was fizzing. He didn't even try to hide it. They all hated him, including some of the cops. Then he expected me to walk into the royal commission and sit with him in the gallery. I feared for my life. I said to Tim I'm going to have to separate from you for a while. So I took a break and left him for my own safety."

The Gnome had the impression that McPherson didn't like Tim much either, but stayed on side because of a sneaking respect for him. Lennie had lost a lot of power as a bird dog for certain cops as the old brigade retired. He knew Tim still had authority with many honest cops and could get something done, and he didn't want to put that power to the test.

The headlines and his devil-may-care attitude simply boosted Tim's reputation even more and pointed the way to a new career path. Suddenly he branched out from the image of being a mere enforcer and became The Adjudicator. Warring parties, who looked like spilling blood, asked him to sit in on discussions and settle their disputes.

He was like a judge, sitting there in the middle and listening to their arguments. Only he didn't refer to law books. It was the law of men and common sense, backed by an implied threat that transgressors who did not comply with his justice or abide by agreements reached would be dealt with in a way they would understand. With muscle.

Parties asked him to preside but often he called them together on a client's behalf. The Gnome returned and played an important role. One day I inadvertently sat in on one of these adjudicating sessions and the subtlety of it all was a bit beyond my understanding at first. I was getting a lift into town with Tim and on the way he said: "I've just got to stop off at an office in North Sydney for a while. You might as well come in." No other explanation. Tim was always stopping off somewhere.

We went into a big office which I assumed belonged to The Gnome. He was seated at one corner of a long table. At the other end sat a big fat bloke, Italian, and down one side were three others, all of Italianate appearance. Sitting opposite them, against the wall, was a friend of Tim's whom I'd met, a veteran of two Vietnam war tours.

Tim sat me well out of the way down one end of the room. I wondered why but said nothing. He apologised for his lateness and shook hands with the four Italians. Taking off his homburg he placed it on the table and sat at the end of the table next to The Gnome, opposite the fat guy and around the corner from the other three. Then he began talking, friendly, politely, not loudly but firmly.

As he did so, I noticed the Vietnam man open a leather case and take out a big silver pistol. It looked big enough to blow a hole in the wall. He toyed with it, polishing it with a chamois, casually, but it was always pointed generally in the direction of the Italians.

Tim talked on in a fatherly way, saying, "Well, you really do owe this money, fifty grand, and I think you should pay it." The three in the other group laughed contemptuously. The main spokesman said forcefully: "We owe —— nothing." Clearly they had come to the meeting with no intention of paying the debt which Tim was trying to collect. They were confident, intending to show their authority verbally and with muscle and would not back down.

Bristow asked a few questions to pin down the debt. One or two names came out including race fixer and drug trafficker Aussie Bob Trimboli, and comments indicated that these guys came from Griffith. Suddenly The Gnome leaned forward, thumped the table and yelled a string of expletives: "You owe the ——money and you'll —— pay!"

Tim quietened him, saying: "You just sit there and keep quiet. I'll do the talking." But The Gnome was like a savage dog straining at the leash. A minute or two later he thumped the table again and yelled: "You have to ——pay up!" I could see what they were up to now. Playing good guys, bad guys. Tim was the conciliator, the reasonable man and The Gnome was the hard man, the threatener. It was a skilful performance, obviously they were well practised at it.

Throughout all this, the fat guy at the end sat motionless and expressionless, his coat open, hands by his side. I glanced across at the Vietnam man. He was holding up a bullet to the light, still polishing his pistol, watching, seated where he had a clear line of fire to the Italians.

The tension increased. I gathered from the conversation these were Trimboli's men who were growing grass instead of grapes and had dudded an Australian in a deal by giving him a bad product. He'd handed it back but they would not refund the money. I knew how Tim hated seeing Anglo-Saxon Australians robbed by Italians or any other ethnic group. It was the principle that mattered, not the nature of the debt.

One of the Italians made a veiled threat. The Gnome came in at once: "We'll meet fire with fire and you will be — —," creating the illusion he and Tim had an army behind them. It reached a climax. If a deal was not done here, it would be too late. Tim and The Gnome gave the clear impression they were not leaving without a deal. The defeat of the Italians had begun gradually with The Gnome's abrupt steeliness in thumping the table and their fear had set in when they finally got the message that Tim's side was not backing down.

Tim recognised that moment. I saw him bump The Gnome's foot under the table to say nothing more. Then the Italians said all right, they'd pay. It was a perfect case of obtaining justice by implied force, subtle in its own way but definite.

I drove into the city with Tim where he had a shoeshine before meeting other clients waiting at his favourite haunt, the Hilton Hotel. It was just another job. It wasn't until later that The Gnome told me the fat guy had the guns. The Vietnam man was instructed to shoot him if he went for them. Those fellows had been involved in drug murders.

It was almost impossible to beat a man like Bristow who went to a confrontation like that with the belief that he was going to win. All the other tough men The Gnome knew would not confront the enemy like him. They'd try some trickery, use an intermediary or set a trap. McPherson or George Freeman would never have exposed themselves like that, sitting down with killers to obtain a resolution.

He was like a fortress within himself who objected to the slightest interference with his person or clothing. If anyone touched Tim's polished shoes, he'd jolt them in the ribs for attacking his personality. He thumped an agent for accidentally sitting on his hat in Eliza's restaurant one day. If anyone spilled cigarette ash on his tennis court, he'd upbraid them.

Crims who ran around putting guns to people's heads to collect debts but still did not get paid, wondered how Bristow managed to collect without doing the same. The jobs he still had to do would show why.

23

THE PSYCHOLOGY OF FEAR

MANY of Bristow's clients came from friends of friends who went to school with him, people with money and connections from the top echelons of society. But a lot of debt work came from the streets.

Even criminals brandishing guns who would think little about shooting anyone standing in their way, wanted to engage Tim when failing to collect a debt on commission, asking: "How do you do it?"

They simply could not bridge the gap between the criminality of the gun and violent things they wanted to do to people, with the psychology needed for success. Tim taught his chief lieutenants never to make direct threats. The fear of what *might* happen was far worse.

If they said I'll shoot you if you don't pay, the person could imagine that and deal with it, possibly calling their bluff and suggesting they both go to the police station right away. But leaving them with the cold doubt of what might actually happen tended to break them.

The Gnome was a master of the technique. And it was so unexpected from a person of such insignificant physique that it came as a shock. He always said he was working for Tim Bristow and the illusion of that violent reputation was usually an immediate clincher.

The fear would start working on their imagination. Would Bristow call at their house? Trying to cope with the nagging doubt was usually far more potent than having someone crudely hold a gun to their head. When The Gnome was finished with them and walked away, most people were psychologically beaten. The only exceptions were people who genuinely didn't have the money, in which case they just left it be, or hard tough types who had the muscle to resist. Then the situation had to be assessed.

Their method had many variations. A businessman in Park Street owed a friend of Tim's $25,000. The Gnome and a "heavy" went to see him using Tim's name, but he told a story of woe about losing money overseas, etc. When The Gnome reported back, Tim said no, he had the money and could pay. He gave The Gnome a short-nosed six shooter in a brown paper bag with instructions on what to do.

He went back, had a talk to him during which he said: "Mate, you've got to find the money." As he got up to go, he said: "I've got a message for you from Tim. If you don't have the money, go to the bank and get it," and he left the brown paper bag on the desk. The fellow opened the bag where it lay, looked inside and said nothing. The Gnome said: "I'll be back at three o'clock tomorrow." When he returned the money was on the table. The gun had not been moved from the exact position where he'd placed it about 24 hours earlier. It was just a piece of psychology that worked.

One resounding tribute to Tim's ability in this tricky area was the day he got money out of Sydney property developer Big Jim Byrnes who, as Paul Barry pointed out in the magazine *The Good Weekend*, took a poor view of offensive people trying to recover money. Unpleasant suggestions were usually made to them. But when Tim and The Gnome called, Big Jim couldn't have been more obliging, offering to pay up and even buying them a cup of coffee.

For many who went to Bristow for help, it was a long journey. They believed in the legal system, the police, and they'd been let down, ripped off, not knowing where to turn and, having made the decision to see a man of his reputation, they procrastinated. It was difficult to unburden personal problems in front of him, something akin to going before a priest. But it gave them hope and a chance to get their spirits back.

Victims of the system, they harboured feelings of injustice in their hearts and some hated society. Tim enjoyed giving people like that a feeling that they could come back to life again. All were frustrated, some had taken it out on their families and wanted to commit suicide or see someone shot. He hardly ever knocked back those jobs, finding a way to avoid calamity or violence and getting the right authorities to help where possible.

They could not find justice any other way, not from the police or the courts. After barristers and solicitors were finished with them, they were usually destitute. Then they would ring Tim - and it happened often.

Barristers and solicitors who thought Tim and his boys to be scumbags had usually got all their clients' money before passing them on. However, some genuinely felt compassion for their clients and advised them to go to Tim because he was the only one who could get the job done. In all such cases, Tim knew there was little money to be made on the deal.

In one instance where a client was owed $60,000 by a printer, his solicitor posted a bill for $60,000. Tim's boys got the money but it only paid the client's legal costs.

Some people in business are so clever and rapacious they leave their victims destitute, unable to afford legal fees or to make their debtors bankrupt, being too busy trying to make a living. Those were among the people Tim helped, but he didn't go looking for them.

The Bristow psychology formula was used in many personal situations where, due to embarrassment or lack of official action, no other solution could be found. Bristow's boys even enforced their own apprehended violence orders where the cops failed. In one case a Portuguese family was being terrorised by a Portuguese man due to an old regional feud - they had brought their prejudices to Australia. He was wrecking their gardens at night, throwing stones at them and making serious threats. A lawyer they employed could do nothing.

He had broken the AVO four times and regarded it as a joke due to a general lack of respect for the law. Finally, after two years, he was due in court. The Gnome and two big lads went to the court and looked for him based on a description, loudly questioning likely fellows and saying they worked for Tim Bristow. He didn't front when his name was called.

They then went to his home and enforced "Bristow's AVO" by kicking in the door and telling his family: "One more ——phone call, just one and you've got a problem." The message came back to Tim by phone: "Please, finish, finish." That was the end of it.

Tim asked a lieutenant to visit a woman in the suburbs to see what she wanted. A mother of pretty blonde twins about eleven years old, she wept as she told her story. The girls were latchkey children who let themselves in each afternoon while both parents worked to pay off their mortgage.

A male neighbour bathed and dressed them and looked after them until the parents came home. But he was a pervert playing with their private parts and the girls, who didn't know right from wrong, were very fond of him. The parents felt they'd lost control of them.

"We need help," said the mother. "My husband is so embarrassed he can't talk about it. We've been to the police several times for two years but they keep saying there's been no violence, they haven't been raped and we can't do anything."

That was before the subject of paedophilia became a public topic and domestic violence, too, was still being swept under the carpet in Australia. The lieutenant spoke to the children to make sure, as always, that action was justified. The parents were too strapped financially to pay Tim for his services but he told his man: "Get it done. Give this pervert the message and if he doesn't accept it, touch him up."

They knocked on his door but he had a chain on it and after peeping out, he slammed it shut. They broke it down, told him what it was about, said they were working for Tim Bristow, then one of them punched him on the jaw and they went back to Tim's house.

The cops rang almost at once. His men listened while Tim spoke: "What happened? They broke his jaw? I'm sorry to hear that. But I don't know anything abut it. As you know a lot of people use my name..." He told his operators to go home and keep their heads low. They knew he would never give them up.

The cops interrogated Tim a week later. They knew he was involved and wanted to charge someone. He weathered the storm and said he would expose their inactivity: "Do you want to wait until this fellow rapes them and ruins their lives?" he reasoned. The mother rang three months later wanting to meet Tim but he sent his man. She bought him a cup of coffee and said she and her husband were so happy, the perv had sold up and gone and the girls were happy.

A similar situation arose soon after on the North Shore. Tim said to the Gnome: "Go and see this woman. Her husband's a businessman and runs a big operation. They had a Christmas party and there are supposed to be a few problems. See what she wants."

She explained what had happened at the party at their home a week before for about 60 staff - a case of manager fingers boss's daughter. Every time her 17-year-old daughter went into the laundry area to get someone a drink, one of the managers followed her in, closed the door, thrust a hand up her dress and fingered her. The mother complained to her husband but he was too pissed to bother about it.

The mother said: "I can't sleep, my daughter is crying all the time and it's destroying our lives. My husband won't do anything about it and someone said Tim can help us." The Gnome believed her but spoke to the girl to make sure she was an innocent kid. He was satisfied the mother was acting out of a belief in proper standards, which were going down the gurgler in our modern society.

He reported back to Tim who asked: "What do you want to do?" He said: "An old Irish punishment." About a week later a headline appeared in one of the morning papers: "Naked man found tied to tree." A jogger found him about 6.30 a.m. in a north shore bushland area with ants crawling all over him. Honey had been spread on his body and he'd been there all night.

The Gnome with two helpers had picked up the offender, taken him for a ride and done the deed. He then said to him: "Mate, you can't do what you did. If it had been one of my daughters, you'd be in serious trouble."

Six weeks later The Gnome saw the mother again in a meeting with her husband to arrange payment. She said:

"Thank you." The husband didn't say anything. In all these cases, women were stronger than men.

The case of the gawked-at gigolo was among their most effective. An attorney, a QC, approached Tim to do a job for his former wife, while he stayed in the background. He'd left his wife for a younger woman, she'd taken it badly and needed psychiatric help. But she was left with plenty of money.

The lady, although of mature years, was still pretty and, trying to get her life together again, attended a lonely hearts party at the Mosman rowing club. There she met a man who charmed her and the romantic chap took her under the club and seduced her like a teenager. She fell in love with him. As it turned out he was a gigolo, naturally interested in her money, sending her for a new hairstyle "to make you look more beautiful."

She kept taking large sums of money out over the next few months and the bank manager became suspicious and rang her son. He went to see his mother and found her living with this chap. He told his father, the attorney. They knew from the bank that $180,000 had been withdrawn.

The attorney could do nothing. Under the terms of his divorce he could not make contact with his ex-wife. She controlled her own bank account and was within her rights. But he wanted to see the money returned. Legal action was out of the question. The attorney's demeanour was down. He went to Tim as a last resort.

Tim briefed The Gnome, who usually did the planning for these operations with his boys at Ivan's *Cafe XX11* in Pyrmont. But first, to check on the facts, he had a discreet chat to the lady who had been alerted by her son. "I'd never felt so good in all my life," she said. Then he arranged for her to go to dinner with the gigolo at a Crows Nest restaurant which had a carpark underneath.

When the couple sat down, The Gnome tapped him on the shoulder and said politely: "Could I have a word with you for a minute. This is a very private matter. Would you mind stepping outside?" He did so and The Gnome led him to the carpark where his three big boys emerged.

The Gnome said: "I work for Tim Bristow. We know what you're doing. You're a ——gigolo. You've extorted $180,000 from this woman." Then he broke him by humiliation. "I don't know how you guys do these things," he said. "I want to see your dick."

The boys took off all his clothes. Then The Gnome started laughing while gawking at his member. The boys, big hulking fellows, started laughing too, their shoulders heaving as they stared at him. "Jesus," said The Gnome, "Look at his small dick! He's got a sweet tongue all right and can wheedle money out of this woman, but he hasn't even got a decent dick."

After more laughing, he gave the gigolo the message: "From now on, don't let me come looking for you. You do as you're told. When I call you, you turn up. Make arrangements now to repay the money and don't go near this woman again."

The Gnome intended taking his clothes and leaving him there naked but he begged to be given them back. They were returned after he made arrangements to repay. He wasn't roughed up or hurt. He had taken the money under false pretences, claiming he was a developer putting up buildings but instead he was flying to the Hobart casino, dressing up as a dandy and gambling it. He repaid it in eight months. That was a classic case of succeeding through psychology and meaning business where the law was futile.

The case of the Gentleman Judge highlighted the personal problems gays had with one another, with Bristow called in to act discreetly. The proprietor of a male bordello in Bourke Street, East Sydney, told Tim on the phone a gentleman client of his, a judge of the Supreme Court, had a problem. He sent in The Gnome who interviewed His Honour not in his chambers, but in the bordello.

He met him in the Conservative Room designed for barristers. The judge sat in his underwear on a king-sized four-poster bed with a drape over the top, one foot resting casually on a case of Moet and Chandon. Two boys - young boys - in light underwear were serving him champagne.

"Would you like a glass of champagne?" asked His Honour. "Yes thank you," replied The Gnome and he sat beside him on the bed. The judge explained his problem. He had a lover, another judge, and he wanted to "disengage from this relationship." Going a bit further, he said: "I would like him to be removed from my company. I'm having a good time here with my friends," indicating the boys, both blond with short-cropped hair. They looked to be 15 or 16.

All this was new and strange to The Gnome, a straight guy who just had tunnel vision in following Tim's instructions and getting the job done. He'd never heard of the word paedophilia at that stage. He discussed the job with Tim who explained that "poofters didn't really disengage" from their partners when they tried to do it themselves, because they knew too much about each other and clung on tenaciously.

How to do it then? The Gnome set out to destroy the other judge's dignity within himself, not letting anyone overhear. He took him by surprise, approaching him in the lobby of the Hilton Hotel while the boys remained to one side. "Excuse me," he said to the judge of the District

Court, "but your friend Judge (mentioning the name) has asked me to have a word with you.

"I work for Tim Bristow." He saw the judge blanch at the name. Next he referred obliquely to his bisexuality by saying: "How can you raise a family and live this life you're living? If you don't keep away from the judge, we will see you again and next time, Tim will be with me."

He then turned and walked away from the judge. That's how The Gnome did it, by surprising the person, shocking him, penetrating his mind, ripping it apart and walking away - not like a criminal rushing in and demanding of his victim "give me the money." Several years later the judge bumped into Bristow in the city, shook hands, simply wished him well and kept going, obviously appreciating the discretion that had been used.

Just as discreet but not so subtle was the case where Bristow was asked by a well-known Sydney personality to warn off his boyfriend, a solicitor and businessman. The relationship of some years was much more intense and required stronger words than in the case of the District Court Judge, as formulated by Tim. He pressed The Gnome into service once more.

He approached the solicitor unexpectedly and gave him the message, but he showed fight, forcing The Gnome to say: "We see and meet people as we find them. On this level I'm speaking to you as a man and a gentleman. But if you want to travel down the rungs of this ladder to the gutter, we'll meet you there as well. Now, where do we stand?"

The two former lovers then met, talked and rearranged their business dealings. Tim received a call from the solicitor who said bitchily: "It's quite all right, I don't wish to see (mentioning his name) any more. He's a paedophile, he has little boys running around and I can't handle that."

Neither subtle nor discreet was the Bristow raid on a male bordello near Police HQ which we'll call *Larry's Lads*. The two partners had fallen out, and the main one wanted the other out. But first he wanted the money he claimed his partner owed to him, about $40,000. The main partner, a former police prosecutor, engaged Tim to sort it out as he saw fit.

Tim sent The Gnome in to investigate the circumstances. He observed that the main partner had a prominent Sydney solicitor as his boyfriend. But he was jealous because the solicitor was bringing in youths including young university students and defiling them - they weren't gays, just innocent youngsters.

The Gnome was disgusted to learn that the solicitor was also taking them home for the weekend on the pretext of helping them with their studies and drugging them, spiking their drinks, in order to have sex. He believed the man was a paedophile.

To complicate the situation, the second partner was bringing in transvestites from Thailand for the bordello. The Gnome was intrigued to see them dressed up looking like any attractive woman. The main partner told him: "You could take one to bed thinking they're a woman and finish up with a coconut tree."

The bordello had seven rooms, all exotically furnished, a conservative room, the baby room where they had a bed like a cradle with a "baby" in it, the blue room, a pink room and one presented like a barrister's chambers with polished wood and law books at the back, French doors leading into it and a bed in the middle.

There were touches of artistic crap like butterflies dangling off the walls and in one white room with blue stripes around the top were large jars containing peacock feathers, used to tickle 'em up the back passage. Society figures, the rich and judicial people went there.

The Gnome was thrown off balance by this unconventional behaviour but Tim told him not to worry about it all. It was in the blood, he explained, a rush that could not be controlled, like Judge David Yeldham of the Supreme Court soliciting men and boys in public toilets, protected by police because he was "on side," but who later suicided. Tim told him the gays hung on to their relationships by digging into one another's private lives. He knew them to be vicious and jealous, asking him to do violent things to former lovers, but he always avoided it.

Tim decided the only way to handle the problem at *Larry's Lads* was to put on a raid and take direct, positive action - no horsing around. He suddenly arrived there one afternoon with a big Maori guy, two other tough hombres and The Gnome. All the queer goings-on ceased abruptly when they rushed in, kicked in the doors on the lower floor and ripped the phones out. Two of the enforcers dashed upstairs shouting "get downstairs everyone," pulled the phones out there and herded them all into an open kitchen area.

A big man, a boyfriend of one of the bordello's partners, began to complain. Tim barked "sit down" and pushed him into a chair. Most were naked, trying to cover themselves by crossing arms and legs. Several Chinese patrons screamed, other Chinese were going "ooh ooh ooh" in a kind of whimpering sound. The rest were speechless. All looked terrified.

Tim's voice boomed "shut up." Silence fell. Then he made a speech directed at the second partner, whom he knew would be present. "You pay the money you owe or you lose your interest in the brothel, " he said.

It brought to a head an unhappy situation between two gay businessmen who were incapable of negotiating their differences on their own. Arrangements were made for a financial settlement and the main partner took over. It showed just what lengths Tim was prepared to go to resolve a dispute, by dragging naked people out of bedrooms and lining them up.

The most tragic and bizarre story Tim ever dealt with concerned a hermaphrodite and it always bugged him to think that he failed in his mission.

The person, born on the Central Coast of New South Wales, tried to hold his secret to live as a normal human being, but it was impossible. Doctors had photographed him and somehow the pictures found their way into a Sydney magazine, sold for money. He was hounded in stranger-than-fiction articles.

Confused and depressed, he left home and took an assumed name, but still the magazine pursued him. He saw several solicitors and tried to fight back, but they would not take up his case. He had no money. Eventually he found his way to Tim, as many desperate souls did, and with his sympathy for the underdog, he agreed to help at once. Then he was hit by a car and spent several months in hospital.

The sad episodes of this man's life took an even worse turn when a hospital worker raped him just to have the grotesque experience of his abnormality. Tim put the trustworthy Gnome on the job, but before he threw himself into the task he insisted on examining the man's physical condition for proof. They arranged for barrister Andrew Leary to represent him with a view to suing the magazine which had dogged him so cruelly.

The Gnome, who always had a driver, had the hermaphrodite in his car taking him to see Andrew Leary for a conference in his Martin Place chambers. Coming off the Harbour Bridge, the driver missed a left turn into the city and went further on through to Chinatown.

Suddenly the man, thinking he was being double crossed, broke out in beads of sweat and cried, "Oh no, not another photo shoot." He jumped out of the car at a set of traffic lights and disappeared into the Haymarket crowd. He could not be located and never made contact again.

The jobs continued to roll in for Tim and his boys...while befriending Sydney multi-millionaire socialite Adam Butler who later suicided owing to drug problems, Tim found a second suspect in the backpacker murders case who probably should have been charged, but police had already solved the case to their satisfaction with the conviction of Ivan Milat and it didn't go any further...he tracked a Chinese man who fled Sydney and recovered most of the $750,000 he'd plundered - by locating him in China!...he also solved two big diamond heists.

In the first diamond robbery, jewels worth $2 million were snatched in the eastern suburbs. Tim was called in, not the police, and solved it in a matter of days because of his tremendous knowledge of the criminal, underworld and gay scenes. He suspected two gays, confronted them with his boys, and they handed the jewels back at once. The owner didn't want any publicity and nobody was charged.

The second one wasn't so simple. A bank executive had jewellery worth about $500,000 stolen from his home and the cops couldn't solve it. But Tim found that a Melbourne gang was responsible and arranged for the jewellery to be bought back for about a third of the price. That's the only way the jewels could be recovered.

The gang continued to do jewel busts in Sydney homes using inside knowledge which Tim believed came either from banks or security people. They introduced a new twist to an old racket - the thieves were paid at a discount price by the victims, who after getting the jewellery back then "double dipped" by collecting the full insurance for loss of the jewellery.

Then there were the intriguing Bond documents. Alan Bond, 1983 America's Cup hero and poor immigrant boy personifying the Aussie dream of battler made good, was under severe pressure when he hired Bristow in 1994 to remove a swag of documents relating to his company affairs.

After posting Australia's biggest company loss of $8.23 billion for Bond Corporation in 1989, Bond was declared bankrupt in April 1992 and was jailed for two and a half years in May 1992 over the missing millions from the Rothwells bank collapse in Perth. In one deal his family company made $16 million tax free from a $1 million investment. But he was released from jail on appeal in August 1992.

In May 1994 Bond was being interrogated in the Federal Court in Sydney over the foreign whereabouts of his fortune through a maze of overseas company deals. He swore on the Bible: "I have no hidden money overseas, I have no hidden money anywhere." His bankruptcy trustee was trying to land him for any undisclosed assets and the Federal Police were trying to follow the money trail overseas.

But behind the scenes and hidden from the authorities, Bond was trying to kick start in Sydney again through a silent partner called Whaka Kele, a New Zealander. Bond had invested $5 million through Kele in a series of deals. (Bond would not be released from bankruptcy until February 1995 when creditors accepted $3.25 million in settlement).

Kele had spent $2 million of Bond's money as a front in establishing 10 companies which Bond intended picking up on when he came out of bankruptcy. The businesses weren't going well and Bond wanted to get back from Kele the $3 million still swinging. That's when he called in Tim Bristow to recover the money. Tim and a lieutenant had two meetings with Bond and a solicitor in mid 1994. One of the first tasks was to retrieve $130,000 which Kele had passed to a business associate at North Sydney.

It must have been embarrassing for Bond to engage Bristow. They had met some time before, but not in the best circumstances. Bond had upset one of the directors in *Pips* nightclub and Tim was called to throw him out. In his usual unvarnished way, Tim said: "If you don't get out, I'll knock you out." Bondy finished his champagne and left.

But that was a minor matter in the new scheme of things. Knowing that the authorities were out to clobber him, Bond then asked Bristow to remove some documents from Kele's office in the city and store them in a secret location. He was paid up front for the job by the bankrupt celebrity entrepreneur.

Kele's office was in Pitt Street near Hunter Street, above an ANZ bank. Stored there was a pile of documents on Bond's unofficial company deals through Kele - hot property and vital evidence that could be used against him if the cops got hold of them. Tim was just told to clean out the office and store the contents in a certain place, but he knew the documents weren't about Goldilocks and the Three Bears.

Without any warning to Whaka Kele, Bristow and The Gnome with several assistants dressed in white coats like official removalists arrived at the office early one morning after parking two trucks below in Pitt Street. As they went to enter the office they were stopped by two cops. One was NSW crime buster Supt Bob Inkster. He told Bristow: "We don't want you, but we want you to step aside. We want free access to the office for a few hours and then you can do what you have to." Behind them were several cops also dressed in white coats who now had *their* trucks parked outside.

As they came in, a man in the office picked up his brief case and walked out. Not knowing who he was, the cops made no attempt to stop him. It was Whaka Kele. The contents of his brief case might have been highly interesting.

Bristow had no choice but to agree or face arrest. Tim and his lieutenant were shocked to be sprung like that. They hadn't talked about it except in a veiled way on the phone. They worked out that the cops must have tapped their phones, otherwise they could not have moved so quickly on the day.

After three hours the cops called Bristow on his mobile and let him in. It transpired that they took all the documents they needed to incriminate Bond, relating to 10 of his companies. Feedback from Federal Police later indicated that the documents and others they led to were vital in convicting Bond in February 1997 for defrauding Bell Resources of $1.2 billion. He went in for four years (on top of three for fraud over the painting La Promenade) but finished up serving less than four years.

After spending $750,000 and seven years on the hunt, Federal police simply gave up trying to find Bond's missing millions overseas. But the Whaka Kele documents showed the tycoon had $1.5 million in a New Zealand bank and properties in Australia, including on the Gold Coast. Those assets were frozen.

Bristow's action to remove the documents had forced the hand of Federal and State cops. If they had waited any longer, those and other documents might have disappeared, so indirectly Tim did them a favour. They did a series of raids in Sydney and Perth a week after seizing the Whaka Kele documents.

Several years after Bristow's removalist role, the cops gave him back some of the documents after finishing with them. One gave a fascinating insight into the pressure Bond must have been under just before calling Bristow in - even to making a desperate murder threat against Kele.

The document related to a telephone message from Bond taken by Diana Bliss, then acting as secretary/receptionist to Whaka Kele. She wrote it out on a blue message pad and presumably handed it to Kele. The time was 2 p.m. on 3 May 1994.

The message (repeating what Bond had said to Diana Bliss on the telephone about her and Kele), was headed "to Whaka from Alan Bond." The details said: "If the money doesn't arrive, both you and him will get shot. He will be at Macaveles (sic)."

The "you" referred to Diana and the "him" to Kele. The "Macaveles" of course was the top restaurant, Machiavelli's. The money reference was part of the $5 million Bond had invested through Kele. That document helped nail Bond on his Australian operations, showing he had invested money not disclosed in his bankruptcy hearing.

Neither Diana nor Kele were "shot" by Bond. Far from it with Diana, whom he later married, but Kele went missing after the raid on his office and hasn't been seen since. He was last heard of in Ireland.

The drama of Bond's documents was just another example of Bristow turning up where the big stories broke.

24

THE CHANGING SOCIETY

TIM Bristow had spent his life dealing with angry men, punishing those who acted outside the law, sorting out the thieves who enjoyed a life of comfort after robbing others.

Many of his cases went along the same lines: Cheat takes money, goes bankrupt or liquidates business but still drives fancy car and lives in big fortified house. Victim spends thousands on lawyers but law can't help.

He might have broken the rules here and there and used a bit of biffo, but it was the only means of getting some justice into the situation. He believed it was better to fight dirty and win than just fight and lose. He steered away from courts. Nobody won in a court case. If your opponent lost, he'd appeal and double the ante.

His old school mates still related to him, despite his reputation. And the reason they fell all over him when meeting, why he was in disrepute while they were the cream of society as judges, barristers and successful businessmen, is that Tim was out there taking society's blows.

He'd lived on a knife edge with no respite, nuts ringing him at all hours with their problems. But debtors still ran out the back door when he turned up. Friends or associates who bumped into him in town were still greeted with his familiar phrase: "I'm still annoying people" followed by the rumbling laugh.

He still commanded respect, still confronted danger and threats. After collecting $40,000 for a client from a city builder, he was threatened by two hit men, one a gunman called Bert who had made his name as a trigger man for underworld organiser George Freeman, then deceased. "You can't do this," he told Bristow. Tim replied: "Do the best you can."

The killer said: "Walk around The Cross and see what happens." Tim and a couple of his boys did so after giving him notice of their intentions, talking to people, making sure they were noticed. Nothing happened. He would not back down or show any mercy to anyone who challenged him.

Bristow continued to pull off some slick detective work, as in the case of Philip Bell, the lifetime sex offender who scandalised Sydney by preying on children at his Whale Beach home and Darling Point unit. Smartly dressed and rich, with film stars, artists and television personalities as his neighbours, Bell enjoyed a flamboyant lifestyle without raising the eyebrows of the Palm Beach social set.

Bristow knew Bell was a homosexual, but not a paedophile. He had occasion to speak sharply to him once for blocking a friend of his from membership of Palm Beach Surf Club because he was a Jew. He believed Bell had pull as a relative of a respected judge who would not have condoned his actions for a minute. When the truth began to out on Filthy Phil and he fled Australia, Bristow gave the cops the tip he was in South Africa where they arrested him. Bell was jailed for 14 years in 1999 for 70 sex offences on boys as young as 12.

Tim continued to frequent the Hilton Hotel at lunchtime each day, having a shoe-shine, holding court with some of his operatives while he discussed business with varied clients. But the world had changed, Sydney had changed and the way private eyes did their work had changed. He didn't like what he saw, especially the way his country was going.

Clients were less inclined to pay, yet they expected more from him. They imposed on his good heart to avoid payment, especially if friendship was involved. An old football colleague of Tim's, in a big way as a developer and associated with the richest people in Sydney, was owed $11 million over a development and could not get paid. Tim and his boys leaned on the debtor, a developer, and gained a result. But Tim didn't get paid his percentage. His boys couldn't do anything about it unless Tim initiated it because the client was his friend. Tim just said: "Oh, let it go."

That wasn't the only incident where big money was allowed to slip away after much effort had been exerted. Tim and his team collected $300,000 for a husband and wife who paid them $20,000 and owed them another $20,000. When the husband came to settle at Tim's house, he brought his wife and kids and she wept copiously, saying they couldn't afford it because the money had gone into their business. The Gnome, who was waiting to pay the boys, drew Tim to one side and asked him what he thought. "Let her go, forget it," he said.

One of Tim's lieutenants was approached by three barristers offering $100,000 to get pictures of a leading politician in a compromising position with his boyfriend. They knew when and where the lovers met. They would pay half the money in two days time, the rest on completion. Two days later they met again and had a big envelope containing a dossier and $50,000. But he knocked it back. Tim wouldn't touch it.

The close relative of a rabbi and a criminal friend were running a gold and diamond smuggling racket with rich Jews in Israel, and in the process they embezzled huge amounts of money in Sydney and Melbourne. Tens of millions of dollars were said to be involved. Even criminals in Long Bay were ripped off and they put out a contract on the rabbi's young relative. Tim was brought into it by the rabbi to save the young man's life, which he did, warning off the criminals. But then it turned into a nightmare with the young Jew using Tim's name all around the place to threaten people. It went on for months, taking Tim's time night and day. And he wasn't paid one cent of the money promised for his troubles.

The Bristow of old would never have put up with that. He'd have eaten them. But now it was Tim trying to make amends for his past deeds. Tim was mellowing and slowing. He was not yet yesterday's man but the cushion covers in his lounge room gave a clue: They featured the faces of the past, Humphrey Bogart and Judy Garland. He was clinging to old principles and memories of the glory days.

Standards and values that he had observed all his life were changing as the past crumbled around him. Many old friends and contacts had retired or passed on. Even Big Lennie was gone. The clever criminal who stayed on top of the Sydney underworld for almost forty years by covering his tracks and pretending publicly he was just a big ignoramus, died of a heart attack on 28 August 1996 while using the phone in Cessnock Jail, where he was serving time for assault. He left an estate estimated at $10 million.

He also left behind his views on various colourful characters, recorded on tape by a journalist to be used after his death and published by the *Sydney Morning Herald* under the journalist's *nom de plume* of Ned Lydon. This is what Big Lennie had to say about Big Tim:

"Do you know how many times I've met Bristow face-to-face? About 10 times. [Yet] I f—ing practically live with him, according to *him*. He seems to have his head into an awful lot of bulls—, doesn't he? I've got nothing against Timmy. He's a danger to me, but what can you do? He's a f—in' loudmouth. Talks a lot of bulls—. I've saved his neck a few times, and he f—in' knows it, too, the silly-looking' c —."

A showman to the end. And demonstrating a bit of feeling against Tim, which he never did while alive, except in jest. But Tim certainly made great play of his friendship with "my big mate Lennie," which probably irritated the big fella. However, they met more than 10 times. In the end Lennie, like Tim, was overtaken by technology. He was caught for assault by talking too much on the phone. He had six lines, using three in and three out. When someone rang in, he'd ring back on another line. But the cops had all six bugged.

The style of true private eyes had changed due to the advance in technology. It was now more specialised, focusing on industrial espionage and knowledge of the law in certain areas like copyright infringement and trademarks.

In the new computer world the successful PI had to know how to get into someone's hard drive, or to specialise in some criminal aspect like arson, and be able to write sophisticated reports suitable for court evidence. A few cowboys were still running around but the day of the old movie-style gumshoe like Tim who fronted up using street nous, shoe leather and personal contacts to find things out, were just about over.

Yet, there was still a need for someone like Bristow to deal with the charlatans who could not be curbed by lawyers or policemen, bound as they are by rules and regulations. His special skills would always be needed due to the darker side of life being stronger than the good.

Tim and The Gnome and his other operatives refined their methods to meet the new requirements in complicated cases, bringing in experts like multi-talented Frank Wheeler - Wheeler the Dealer - to assist after identifying a debt beyond all doubt. His specialty was negotiation and data acquisition, such as sniffing out bank account detai internationally.

Born in Texas, he is a remarkable adventurer who went to university in California, taught outboard, marine and motor cycle technology to prison inmates, flew planes for NASA and the American Government in Mexico and Central America for 13 years, survived a crash landing in the Guatemalan jungle, was the first man to ride a motor bike around Australia for a bet in 1972, built the world's first solar-powered boat to go in the ocean, created boat endurance records on the Hawkesbury River and on Sydney Harbour, drove a power boat to New Guinea and back, and so forth.

He came from a privileged background. His great great grandfather, William Wheeler, was vice-president of the United States from 1877-81 and a New York attorney, said in encyclopaedias to be an honest one. "If he was, he's the only one I've known about," said Frank, who dislikes attorneys. One in Sydney charged a client of his $107,000 trying to recover a $15,000 debt.

"I'm the main negotiator," he said, "I'm a licensed commercial agent but I help people make decisions that are good for them, to save them time and money. I factor deals and help them organise payments. I'm the straight man, the day crew. If I fail, others come in." The "others" included a big lad who is a dentist by profession, helping out in areas of persuasion because he believed in what they were doing.

Wheeler, a huge man in stature, went to Tim after a lady doctor friend of his had $8 million ripped off her in a property deal. They all clicked and he started working for Tim's team. The stories he and The Gnome alone could tell men robbing people without the ordinary person defence against them, would fill two books.

elieved that unless a debt was $300,000, it wasn't g any legal steps for because it could cost attorneys and two or three years before you could get to court. And even if handed a judgment, it was often just an unenforceable piece of paper saying you were owed the money, being a civil and not a criminal matter.

One of their more recent case histories concerned an inbound tourist operator who had all his clients pay up front for vacations in Australia, building up goodwill by paying all his bills on time. Then at the height of the tourist season he closed down his $2 company, left airlines, hotels and bus operators hanging, pocketed $2.4 million and vamoosed. Even when going into hospital he used a false name, but Frank Wheeler tracked him and served a subpoena because he had property in other names.

A con man in Queensland ran around with $200,000 in a suitcase targeting people on inside information who had received superannuation payouts. He knocked on their doors saying he could get 20 percent interest on short-term loans by investing in mobile telephones. He kept bringing back their returns early on small amounts until he got a big investment from them, then disappeared with the cash. One victim had been a Fraud Squad detective for 25 years. "It's incredible, but it happens," said Frank. "It's a tricky world but I actually do care about helping people who are caught."

Tim and his boys saw Australian law as being so weak as to breed criminals, allowing them to rob people and get away with it, then go on doing it. Australia was a young country and the laws needed to be tightened to meet changing values. As standards changed, many of the old loyalties had gone, people were less honest today perhaps because of technology and globalisation making the world seem a smaller place, and money had become all important.

Once there could be a revolution in Afghanistan and people read a few pars about it in the papers. Now they saw it in their homes every day with actual pictures, people using guns, killing, looting, protesting. The continuing reality of it all tended to break down people's discipline and erode our natural, orderly way of life.

Now violent young punks were running around the streets of Sydney, Melbourne and Brisbane with no respect for the law or the police. In Kings Cross, ethnic gangs were feuding to take over the place. If it wasn't the Chinese or Koreans, it was the Vietnamese or Yugoslavs, the Lebanese or some other Middle Eastern group.

No matter what the do-gooders, academics or windbag politicians said, Tim knew from experience what had contributed to the problem. The young Lebanese and Vietnamese migrants who had come here had known nothing but civil war, and their attitudes to the law were reflected even in some of those born here. They saw us as a soft touch, ripe to be ripped off and many had brought their religious and ethnic prejudices with them too.

Tim related to all the older migrant groups who had made their homes in Australia and he'd seen and appreciated how they had settled into the Australian way of life, integrating and adding their own touches to the mix. But he didn't think much of the new breed from Asia and the Middle East, at least those who were attracted to crime.

He went on TV in a discussion on his way of life and said: "I'm a Christian and I'm proud of it." It was a strange comment for a man who showed little outward interest in religion after being christened a Catholic, but it indicated his attitudes and personal values.

Tim did not like to see the traditional Australian way of life changing due to pressure from minority migrant groups wanting to impose their standards, religions and ways of life. He felt that Moslems, for instance, didn't want to become Australians but wanted to change Australians into their ways

- some had even advocated their own State in Australia based on Islamic laws. From his travels abroad he didn't know any place where Moslems and Christians lived in harmony and he didn't want to see Australia go that way in future.

He believed not enough was being done to encourage migrants to become Australians, blaming the policy of multiculturalism which caused division, and also weak short-sighted politicians for not showing more leadership in preserving things essentially Australian. Australia was the only country in the world where everyone was more or less equal, where a bum could have a drink with a millionaire. But politicians were letting traditional Australian values be diluted by not standing up and having the guts to maintain Australian culture.

On the subject of crime, Tim had firm views after a lifetime of dealing with it. He believed there had been an attempted cover-up of ethnic crime, of the Lebanese or Middle Eastern gang rapes, home invasions and protection rackets on restaurants and other businesses by Middle Eastern and Asian gangs. More young women had been raped by the ethnic gangs than had been revealed, but no action was taken. He deplored the weak, puerile attitude of politicians in not defending the rights of Australians to speak out about ethnic crime without being branded racists.

Tim's man The Gnome experienced the new atmosphere of violence in business when his son was almost kicked and beaten to death while helping a client legitimately pick up some jewellery from a shop in a Sydney inner western suburbs shopping mall.

His son, a licensed mercantile agent, went with an Indonesian importer to legally repossess part of $40,000 worth of jewellery which had been handed to a jewellery shop run by Lebanese Arabs for sale on consignment. Two cheques had bounced, some money was paid but the agreement was broken and they were entitled to pick up what was unsold. The Gnome went with them for support.

They presented their papers and politely asked for the unsold jewels. Instead they were set upon by four Arabs, knocked down and kicked. The Gnome lay down and covered his son's head with his body to stop him being kicked to death. Security guards sitting nearby did nothing. When the son produced a camera and took a photo of their assailants for evidence, they smashed the camera and laid into them again.

The cops were called but refused to charge anyone. When The Gnome protested, they threatened to charge him with creating a public nuisance if he didn't leave, warning him not to come back. Both he and his son needed hospital treatment for multiple injuries including broken ribs and his son needed treatment by a neurologist.

But before walking away The Gnome said to the cop in charge: "You're fucking scared of these Arabs, you fucking wimp. And you've got a badge and a gun. You Australians have lost your balls."

He said later he had felt real fear for the first time. "What's happening to this country?" he asked. "They all said it wouldn't happen here, but it is. There's something terribly wrong going on when this sort of thing can take place in a perfectly legal situation and the authorities do nothing. This is real life! Wake up Australia."

Tim Bristow now took a different view to when he was in the police force and first saw corruption at work. Having seen it all, he now realised there was always going to be some corruption in the force, some "bile and guile" as tough cop Rocky Walden had told him all those years ago.

"It would be nice to think that everyone in the community was decent and honest, but it's never going to happen," Tim said to a friend who raised the topic. "Same in the police force. It's unrealistic to expect it, especially as they have to deal with the worst types of people every day.

"Sure, some cops were crooked and did business with criminals in my time. There were some vicious, dangerous criminals but there were also tough cops to deal with them. The system worked. People felt safe, not like today when young punks, ethnic and Anglo-Saxon, are running around with guns and knives, bashing people and threatening to take over the streets. Today they fear nothing. In my time, they feared the coppers. They must fear the police again before we can have effective law and order."

The trouble today, according to Tim, was that the cops had gone soft and were too academic in their approach. With hardly any experience out on the streets, they studied to get a certificate of criminology and suddenly they displayed "fruit salads" on their shoulders, shiny epaulets proclaiming their expertise. Yet they wouldn't know how to wield a baton.

Community policing had stuffed the system. The English idea of roaming around and being nice to shopkeepers, waving to them, should work in theory but it didn't in communities where drugs had infiltrated everywhere. Fancy sending cops out on pushbikes to curtail crime, said Tim. No wonder people had to put iron bars on their windows.

Tim didn't blame the cops. He felt for them in their difficult job. They needed support to get back on track and restore some respect to the law.

He blamed the politicians who were all talk, who didn't support the police but used them as an excuse when something went wrong. The judges and magistrates didn't support the cops either, but change had to come initially from the weak-kneed politicians who had the power. They interfered too often in the running of the force without backing them. The police culture of looking after their own was formed because they didn't get the necessary community support.

He believed NSW Premier Bob Carr and all his Ministers were weak and soft on crime. They made the right sounds, especially at election time, but that was all. Cabramatta was an example of their kid gloves approach and cover up of crime problems.

In Tim's opinion, judges and magistrates took the wrong view when someone was arrested and charged with, say burglary. It was unlikely to have been his first offence, although that may not be proved, but he was always treated leniently as a first offender and usually let off as a result. He also believed juries should be told a person's criminal background.

The politicians, judges and magistrates were not strong enough on crime and violence and this had affected the way the police went about their jobs. How could they be tough on crime when they were always looking over their shoulders with so many bodies ready to pounce on them like the Privacy Commission, Police Integrity Commission, ICAC and various do-gooding community groups? As a result, cops were just going through the motions. Who would want to be a cop?

In the wake of this namby-pamby approach the ranks of good detectives had been decimated by disbanding specialised groups such as the Armed Holdup Squad, the Motor Squad, Breaking Squad, because someone had found a bit of corruption. How could genuine knowledge be built up?

Tim believed there was justification for the *Consorting Act* to be brought back, and for police to have paid informants again. Once, when a serious crime or robbery occurred, cops did the rounds of their informants and often it led to arrests. That didn't happen any more. Some cop in a crime intelligence agency working nine to five like a bank clerk did it sitting at a computer. There was no information feedback from the streets any more.

Tim also believed something like the old 21 Division should be revived as a flying squad to deal with trouble makers. Hoodlums and vandals felt they had nothing to fear and as a result had no respect for the law or fear of cops. To them, freedom meant freedom to do what they wanted.

The Carr Government's disastrous public relations import Peter Ryan, when Police Commissioner, even threw out the Special Branch and destroyed all its security records - when terrorism was becoming an issue. What a farce. Meanwhile, violent protesters paraded the streets, burning flags, damaging property and assaulting police and getting away with it.

Even the name "police force" had been changed to "police service" by out-of-touch politicians. What a joke, what a surrender to the criminal class. Tim believed that until we had a fair dinkum politician with the courage and insight of someone like former New York Mayor Rudolph Giuliani and his Police Commissioner William Bratton, to get stuck into crime with a "zero tolerance" policy, the thugs, bashers, murderers, thieves and other serious law breakers would go on increasing and adding to the community's detriment. In New York, crime had dropped dramatically.

Bristow knew the clock could not be turned back. But things had gone too far, the pendulum had swing too much in favour of the new class of criminal and wrong doer. The cops needed more support to do their job in the public interest. If they didn't get it, the quality of life would deteriorate.

25

Last of a Legend

TIM'S life was marked by stress, pressure, lack of sleep and an enormous output of energy.

Gradually the strains began to affect his health. He kept it within himself, never complaining but went into town less often than before from about the year 2000, choosing to work the phones from home, punting on the horses more than before.

He developed diabetes, which troubled him for several years. He also began to suffer from Parkinson's disease, which gave him tremors in the hands like Muhammad Ali. Tim also had a heart complaint for several years and occasionally had to go into hospital to have shock treatment for it, checking himself out at the first opportunity.

At one stage he had a big toe amputated because of the diabetes and kept it in a bottle, showing it to people and joking about it. When the doctors in Sydney Hospital told him they would have to amputate one of his feet, he just got up and walked out, saying "no thanks."

Emotional stress seemed to be associated with his general condition, especially the diabetes. His friend Di Parkinson, who made a study of things metaphysical, said that one day she saw Tim's aura against the light. It was navy blue and she thought that couldn't be right because blue was the love colour, and that was only part of Tim's nature.

Then she saw it split into two blues, one a sky blue, indicating to her that he was two people as she knew him to be in his life, a good and bad character. According to Di she then saw a red slash come down through the aura field which she took to be the anger and rage within him. I didn't quite know what to make of all that, but it was in this period when Tim's health was beginning to fail that I learned something that had puzzled all of us who knew him over the years.

Tim had always jumped from one subject to another. He would talk about one topic and while you were still thinking about that, he would be on to something else. Many people unkindly said they thought his brain was scrambled from boxing or being beaten about the head in fist fights. He was also disorganised and late for appointments.

The way he went about taking Bilgola Boy to the Melbourne Cup at the last minute was ludicrous, giving the horse no chance. That was fairly typical of Tim, doing his own thing, making his own rules. But it would be wrong to say he was always disorganised because the amount of detailed work he covered successfully over the years was enormous, and his memory was always impressive.

Yet, the disorganisation was a recurring theme. When he was racing his first horse at Gosford one day, he picked up Dr Stella Dalton at Parramatta and took her to his home on the northern beaches, intending to go to Gosford by speed boat via Pittwater. At a time when he should already have left, he began meticulously cleaning his English Church's-brand shoes. When he got there, the race was over.

Tim had been like that from a child - easily distracted, but also with bursts of temper, forgetful in daily activities and time schedules, easily bored, beginning a task and not completing it and sometimes difficult to self-motivate.

Unknown to us at the time Tim was suffering from attention deficit disorder (ADD), also called attention deficit hyperactivity disorder (ADHD). He had the main characteristics of hyperactivity, impulsiveness, emotional turmoil and - to those who knew him intimately - low self esteem, while appearing greatly confident to others.

Twenty-odd years ago, nobody had heard of ADHD. Now it is the most common behavioural disorder of American children and is probably over diagnosed. The disorder had a past. Back in 1902 British doctors thought that kind of behaviour in children was due to a subtle brain injury and in the 1940s and '50s children with those symptoms were supposed to have minimal brain damage. But by the mid-1970s doctors were treating it with amphetamines such as Ritalin and then it gained its present name.

If Tim had been diagnosed as having ADHD and treated with drugs, he might have been a completely different person. His mother would not have wanted to admit there was anything wrong with her "beautiful boy," but Tim had most of the ADHD symptoms which made him a difficult and puzzling character to understand. It also stopped him reaching his potential. Yet nobody realised his problem until it was far too late.

It no doubt explained his erratic behaviour over the years, the sudden inexplicable actions for no apparent reason, like throwing a bucket of water over his second wife, Glenda.

One of the other sad features of Tim's last few years was his reduced libido. Two things that mattered to him were his good looks and his potency, and both deserted him, although when dressed he still looked an imposing figure. Tim's attempts to overcome that droopy look created some of the funniest scenes imaginable and the best of Bristow humour.

First he went to a doctor at Double Bay to have penile injections to cause an erection, assuring friends that they used a very fine needle and it was less painful than a flu shot. Then he said the doctors gave him a contraption that looked like a big plastic tube which he demonstrated to two women at his home one day.

"I'll show you what it can do," said Tim. He placed it over his pride and joy and began pumping it up. The droop disappeared all right, but he couldn't get it off and had to walk around the house like that for some time. The ladies just fell about laughing, supporting each other to avoid falling over with mirth.

Viagra would have been easier but it wasn't available then. Tim then took to giving himself needles and the inevitable happened - in order to put extra throb in the nob he overdosed and suffered from an extreme case of what doctors call priapism - an erection that won't go down.

He had to go to Mona Vale Hospital and was there for two days with a permanent erection. You never saw so many nurses in attendance. They came from all over the hospital to look, patients too, and in between wincing with pain, Tim discussed it with them, laughing loudly and cracking jokes with all sorts of double meanings.

The doctors had to operate on him to solve the problem and while the nurses were in stitches, he had stitches of a different kind. He probably needed the boost because he still had at least one lady on the side, although the roles were reversed - she was stalking *him*.

In his quieter moments when looking back on the chaos of his life, Tim confessed to friends that he wished he had taken his father's advice and become a barrister. He knew now the help he could have been to people through the law. But having the required discipline might have been a problem. Tim would have been offering to meet the judges outside!

He also wished he had taken the opportunity to play the piano. In his memory he could hear his grandmother's classical pieces and his father playing *Clair de Lune*.

Towards the end Tim was often confused by medication and the progressive effects of his Parkinson's disorder. To avoid being seen in a weakened state, he didn't go into the city in the last year or so of his life. Yet later, the *Daily Telegraph* would claim that in this period Tim was meeting criminals in the city to plan a contract killing in a Haymarket pub. Just another wayward snippet to add to the legend. But as Chief Inspector Brett Cooper of City Central police pointed out when asked, the report based on anonymous information was wrong, should not have been in the paper and he placed no weight on it at all.

By contrast with his normal state towards the end, when I wanted to double check some final details of Tim's life with him on Thursday 13 February 2003, his mind was clear and sharp like the Bristow of old. He laughed and joked a lot as we talked on the phone several times, being alternately amusing, cynical, worldly. In previous weeks we had talked daily about his life, comparing, confronting, testing each other's patience. Bristow could be exasperating, speaking in a convoluted way before coming to the point.

Luckily I had finished all my research into Bristow's life, extending over many years. At 9.30 on that Thursday night of 13 February, while tapping away well into chapter six of this biography, I received a fateful call from his loyal and loving partner of 27 years.

Tim was dead.

Through tears, Sue Ellis described how she had arrived home from teaching tennis at 9.10 to find him sprawled on the front balcony, still slightly warm. She had spoken to him on the phone less than an hour before. Mail was scattered around him. He had obviously walked down the path that night to the letter box. As it would turn out in recapitulating the events, he had done so to farewell a lady friend, whom he said "excited and incited him." He lived another life right up to the time he died.

When Sue found him, he was lying face down, his faithful dog beside him. Crying with shock and frustration, she somehow mustered the strength to turn him over and was horrified to see the blood drain from his face. Desperately she felt for a pulse, but could find none. She rang 000 emergency and a doctor instructed her in applying mouth to mouth resuscitation. A neighbour who heard her cries came to assist and he too applied mouth to mouth. Then the ambulancemen arrived and worked on him with their instruments. But it was to no avail.

Unable to write another line after receiving the call, I went to the house at once to help Sue in any way I could. I'd known him for almost 40 years and in all that time he had never uttered an angry or unkind word to me apart from our first abrasive meeting in the *Daily Telegraph* news room.

It was an eerie feeling to see the big man lying prone and lifeless. Even in death he looked huge. Reflecting on his unusual energised life, I found it hard to accept that finally he was gone. But the remarkable thing about him was that he had survived so long. If most ordinary men had taken the risks he had, faced the same dangers, annoyed as many people and made as many enemies as Bristow had in the course of their daily lives, they would probably have died an early death - knocked off by enemies directly or taken out by hired hit men. That he had lived so long in a violent world was a remarkable feat.

I was the fifth writer to attempt his Damon Runyonesque life story. The first was Paul Brickhill, author of best sellers *The Dam Busters, Reach for the Sky* and *The Great Escape*. He died before finishing it. Two journalists and an author each worked separately at it but wilted under the challenge.

I wondered how to handle this now. Tim had been a friend, a mate. Obviously if he were still alive, I would have felt duty bound out of loyalty to treat certain areas of his life with delicacy. Even if I tried as always to be objective, some of that cautious thinking was likely to creep into one's work, if only subconsciously. To do otherwise would have marked me as a ruthless, callous person, taking advantage of his friend's trust.

But now the legendary larger-than-life private eye was dead. His feelings could no longer be hurt. I had no restrictions, no moral chains to prevent me from dealing in the unvarnished facts as I knew them. His secrets would not die with him as many would hope, even if some of the names would have to be left out for legal reasons. As I stood before his inert body, I determined to finish the story on the basis of respect for Tim Bristow, with nothing but the truth.

Tim had died with dignity. He no doubt would have lived longer if he had taken his medication on time and listened to his doctors. Sue had had a continuous battle with him over the timing of his medication and insulin shots. Then again, he would have been minus one foot if he'd taken notice of some doctors. Getting around with the aid of a stick didn't appeal to Tim. He went out while still looking strong to the outside world.

Two young female constables were at the scene, Sharon Smithers and Dionne Smith, of Dee Why Station. Then came a police inspector. They took no chances, calling in the Crime Squad an hour or so later to check for foul play. Bristow was that kind of man, big, controversial, a giant in the murky cloak and dagger world he inhabited. But it was a heart attack.

Di Parkinson was there to support her friend Sue. They both gave him an emotional farewell there on the balcony in the clear night air under the stars. Di said, as if he were still alive: "You can't go out, Tim, without being properly dressed." She splashed his favourite after shave on his face and combed his hair. Then they knelt, kissed him and said a prayer for his salvation.

Tim's funeral at St Thomas's Anglican Church, North Sydney, was packed. Many of the 300 mourners wept. The newspapers gave him plenty of copy along lines of the colourful character who liked to be known as a gangster but didn't quite make it. Some of his boys were dressed entirely in black. His Gordon rugby jumper and trademark homburg rested on the casket.

Sue wore his mother's diamond-encrusted sapphire engagement ring for the first time. Stella Dalton was there with her and Tim's daughter, Isis, the bachelor of science graduate and pentathlon athlete who had just missed out on the 2000 Olympics. Stephen, too, tall, suntanned and handsome, surprised at the strong feelings he now had for his late father. And a lady in a motorised wheel chair whom Tim helped somewhere along the line.

The minister, Reverend Simon Manchester, said Tim was a big man who helped a lot of people but was no saint. Ann Bristow paid a tribute, so did an emotional Max, describing Tim as "very Sydney" and ending with a quote from a a popular Hollies rock song: "He ain't heavy, he's my brother."

I spoke too, bringing a chorus of "hear! hears!" from the congregation when I said that those who bagged Bristow were usually the ones who'd never met him.

Everyone flocked to the Gordon Rugby Club for the wake where many a tale was spun. The crowd laughed as impromptu speakers regaled them with impersonations, revisiting some of Tim's outlandish exploits. The general talk though was that he did a lot of good for a lot of people.

The last word belonged to The Gnome. Leaping on stage, he summed up Tim Bristow's tumultuous life:

"We fought and won many battles together, and in those we lost we bit the bullet. The Grim Reaper arrived and we fought him too. But last Thursday evening I heard the referee say it's round 159, and Tim's out!"